who begat michael who begat melville who
In who begat bessie smith   assc
at morpheus who begat fo   ega
mo who begat whitman who begat   ene
ng chinese funerals escorted by black aerop
leather skies beaming soft unbroken rays o
ainters mourning dead pictures of lost faced
cessful suicides in emptied bays of frantic
to glass faced swamps filled with superstitiou
mental statues of sculptured bone lyin
lks bending under constant shuffling of har
dropped from pocked eyesacks of ancient se
f hard breasted adding machine girls in store
d coffee talking of last night's copulations
nd itinerant umbrella peddlers lost in rainles
buttock and crooked neck ballet dancers sec
secret blankets of brilliant dust blindly flyir
d limping vehicles filled with shaggy mouth
nan dog with stilettos of fear and dreams c
s money shoes money muscles money houses
ney pointed shoes money hats money brains
o pimp patterns of money success grasped
editorial writers false teeth credit dentists
chested bus drivers eye shadow salesgirls all

em brothers so they could play with those de
l of that mental wine used on sad holy day
ghosts hanging around on the corner waitir
hide in their shoes anxious to throw peach
for the guys to know that it is time for th
for all the hard work they are doing to the c
the dust to run up those old white steps in t
the roof where mag has her goat milking aw
he television aerial spitting those electric
keep those blue cars rolling along that musc
time to eat second hand lobsters from the po
al church near the middle of the street jus
by raindrop pressures on the headbone most
ntion of radio got that italian fellow in troul
city about politics and the negro vote stickir
mped out the window and broke the legs of
at of mag's lying there waiting for some
m a prescription for rock and roll rolling ove
ashing the reality wall man anti-man agai
illed skin hunched lanterns cold owl shive
waiting death you are now a minor vice yo
ver cold death you are not death yet warmer
an to you a minor vice life do not leave u
lo we know we live or have lived living am

Praise for Bob Kaufman

"With this magnetic new unveiling, Bob Kaufman trenchantly sunders endemic retrocausal error and neglect that has casted his fate into a secondary enclave of lesser mastery. To set the story straight it was his spirit that helped sire the Ginsberg that we know and not vice versa. It was he who magically hoisted the invisible umbrella under which Kerouac and others such as Corso were enabled to protractedly flourish. Arrested 39 times for poetic brilliance via bravura he was the absolute contrary of the sterile academic scrounging for golden verbal eggs. Never concerned with immediate notoriety he passed across unerring emptiness as a poetic lahar sweeping in all directions at once. He volcanically en-veined the Beats as a mirage enveloped Surrealist; not as a formal poet, but one, like Rimbaud, who embodied butane. Following the scent of his butane on one anonymous North Beach afternoon led Philip Lamantia to audibly utter to me that Bob Kaufman as per incandescent singularity is 'our poet.'" —**Will Alexander**

"Uplifting the voice of this under-sung literary master to future's light is the mission of the *Collected Poems of Bob Kaufman*. This poet's poet on the cliff edge of no ledge is still continuing to foster new surrealizations. Read this bebopian wordsmith, his pen turned saxophone and ink notes that are black tears." —**Kamau Daáood**

"He was an original voice. No one else talked like him. No one else wrote poetry like him." —**Lawrence Ferlinghetti**

"So much did he embody a French tradition of the poet as outsider, madman, and outcast, that in France, Kaufman was called the Black Rimbaud." —**David Henderson**

"Bob Kaufman's life is written on mirrors in smoke." —**Jack Kerouac**

"In collecting Bob Kaufman's work, the editors have sought to bind earthquakes with book paste. These pages vibrate, a pulse not from way out, but from *way in* this strange, strange country. Wearing the poet's trembling, subterranean eyes, I see the dirt of imperial graves, grocery store corpses, swank gas chambers, and bomb shelters cut an inverted skyline against a too orange American sun. Blinking, I look up and the real sun seems just as radioactive, which is perhaps what leaves me the most shaken. To call these poems 'surreal' seems, now, to muffle Kaufman's prophetic genius. He saw us, our images in pools of blood, milk, and saxophone spittle. Maybe it was ever our shivering made the ripples that distorted the reflections." —**Douglas Kearney**

"[M]orally and poetically, there is Bob Kaufman, pre-eminently." —**Philip Lamantia**

"Kaufman I knew—I spent time with Kaufman. One night, boy, I was at this building that was on First Avenue and First Street. It was a sort of triangular-shaped building and Ginsberg, Peter Orlovsky, LeRoi Jones and Kaufman and myself were in this room. And I just stood there. And there was no question in my mind who the force was in that room. He was like a spirit... He came to the Five Spot one night I was working there, and said, 'You've got to come with me after you finish work.' I said, 'Look, Bob, I started working a quarter after nine, I won't be finished until four o'clock, I can't do this.' So he said, 'Yes you will,' and he came at four o'clock and he took me over to what is now Soho and he read poems to me until about quarter after one the next afternoon. And I remember walking out of that loft completely energized—I hate that word—but completely transformed. He was also, probably, the most extraordinary looking poet of his time. I mean that helped, of course. He was extraordinary. When he was in his last periods and he didn't speak I was in Frisco and I saw him. He just came up to me and he said like this [*makes a beckoning gesture*], and we went and had coffee. And this happened twice. We went into coffee shops. And we just sat there." —**Cecil Taylor**

"Bob Kaufman is one our most vulnerable, mysterious and beautiful of poets, a nomadic maudit, surrealist saint of the streets, votary of silence, the consummate Outrider with trickster imagination and visionary power. What does it take to be such a poet-man, veils/layers of existence laced with hardship, suffering? Not many like this anymore. The Black American Rimbaud, as he was christened in France. His poems make me weep and bow with humility and wonder. I last saw him, shape-shifting shaman on Ken Kesey's stage in Oregon, swirling in a torque of rage, enlightenment, and prescience. Pure product of America's madness: fury and tenderness. The writing is complex and lays its soul baring down on jazz inflected syllables and riffs for all to read and tremble within. No serious canon is complete without this insistent rhythm, poetic acuity, and a body's last resort to sing." —**Anne Waldman**

"*Collected Poems of Bob Kaufman* should finally liberate the kaleidoscopic surrealism of this San Franciscan, and in many respects, secular Franciscan, poet from the shadows of Allen Ginsberg and the other Beats. While poems like 'Night Sung Sailor's Prayer' and 'Believe, Believe' presage both the linguistic flights of Will Alexander and the affirmative exuberance of Ross Gay, the bulk of the book hearkens back to familiar figures like Blake, Apollinaire, and Artaud. In the end, of course, Bob Kaufman is Bob Kaufman, and as this collection confirms, the poems tend to extremes, lurching between the sweeping force of a tornado (e.g., 'The American Sun' and 'The Ancient Rain') and the precision of a stiletto (e.g., "Demolition" and 'I Am a Camera'). Kaufman's libertarian tendencies (see, for example, 'Abomunist Manifesto') made him a largely apolitical, if compassionate poet, but what comes through above all else is a human being beset by the furies and desires he/she unleashed. *Collected Poems of Bob Kaufman* is a memoriam of unmitigated joy and abysmal despair." —**Tyrone Williams**

COLLECTED POEMS OF BOB KAUFMAN

Edited by Neeli Cherkovski,
Raymond Foye, and Tate Swindell
Foreword by devorah major

City Lights Books | San Francisco

City Lights would like to thank Coffee House Press, New Directions, Chris Felver, Rachel Ladeby, Joaquin Nagle, Ira Nowinski, Vince Silvaer, Dean Smith, Casey Stoll, and Malcolm Whyte for their assistence in making this book.

Cover and book design by Linda Ronan

Library of Congress Cataloging-in-Publication Data
on file

City Lights Books are published at the City Lights Bookstore
261 Columbus Avenue, San Francisco, CA 94133
www.citylights.com

CONTENTS

Editorial Note

This volume contains the three books Bob Kaufman published in his lifetime: *Solitudes Crowed with Loneliness* (New Directions, 1965), edited by Eileen Kaufman, *Golden Sardine* (City Lights, 1967), edited by Claude Pélieu and Mary Beach, and *The Ancient Rain: Poems 1956–1978* (New Directions, 1981), edited by Raymond Foye. We have left these books intact, although we have occasionally chosen a different printing of a given poem or, in rare instances, referred to recordings of the poet for his own preferred version. In a few instances, the same poem appears in multiple books and we have let these repetitions stand. *Solitudes Crowded with Loneliness* collects the two broadsides published by City Lights in 1959, *Second April* and *Abomunist Manifesto*, while a third, uncollected broadside, *Does the Secret Mind Whisper?* (City Lights, 1960), appears as its own section.[1]

The section titled "Uncollected Works" contains many poems from small magazines and public or private collections, diligently unearthed by Tate Swindell, who also compiled the valuable biographical chronology containing much new information. Seven of these uncollected poems as well as "Does the Secret Mind Whisper?" appeared in *Cranial Guitar: Selected Poems* (Coffee House Press, 1996), edited by Gerald Nicosia. Although Kaufman assumed a vow of silence in late 1963, and did not resume writing and public readings until 1973, Eileen Kaufman continued to send out poems to anthologies and little magazines, trying to earn small sums to support herself and their son Parker, and this is why certain poems in the "Uncollected Works" section bear dates from this time.

This collection concludes with nine remarkable poems (beginning with "A Buddhist Experience") written at the very end of Kaufman's life, addressing mortality and his Buddhist faith. These poems originally appeared in two numbers of the *Haight Ashbury Literary Journal* (edited by Darrell Gauff, Joanne Hotchkiss, Noni Howard, John Meehan, and Alice Rogoff), and the anthology *Beatitude: Golden Anniversary 1959–2009* (edited by Neeli Cherkovski and Latif Harris). These nine poems were drawn from a larger composition book that Kaufman kept in the final year or two of his life. After he died in 1986, the notebook passed into the possession of his companion Lynne Wildey, and after her death several years later it disappeared and is presumed lost, thus adding one final unfortunate chapter in a life that had far too many.

As writer and editor, Neeli Cherkovski has supported and honored Bob Kaufman's work for over forty years and, perhaps more importantly, gave Bob a place to live when he was homeless, proving the exception to "all those people who gave me thick books to read when what I really needed was a warm meal." John Geluardi, like his mother Alix, was and is a lifelong friend to Bob, Eileen, and Parker Kaufman and facilitated the contractual agreements with the estate. The editors would also like to thank Elaine Katzenberger, Garrett Caples, and City Lights Books for their support of this project.

RF

Note
1. The back cover of the City Lights broadside of "Does the Secret Mind Whisper?" includes the following note: "The 'secret mind' whispers and the 'caught flesh' shouts in this opening section of BOB KAUFMAN'S novel-in-progress. This part merely provides the atmosphere in which the 'characters' are to appear—and disappear." That Kaufman initially conceived of this text as part of a larger prose work probably explains why it wasn't collected in *Solitudes Crowded with Loneliness*.

ETERNAL POET
devorah major

Bob Kaufman is a poet; Bob Kaufman is a man steeped in a mythology sprinkled with a few facts. For many he exists as the man who wrote poems on newspaper margins, the man flowing with piled, jazz-infused visions as wife or friend transcribed his surrealistic rants, the man yelling poems at strangers parking their cars on North Beach street corners, the man repeatedly and repeatedly arrested on San Francisco streets, at times after being harshly beaten by the arresting officers, the man who took a vow of silence unbroken for eleven years. For me he began as the father of a long-forgotten toddler playmate. He was my parents' friend who came to house parties and wreaked havoc. He was the author of a yellow-covered little book of poetry that held my father's favorite poem, which he often quoted:

> The first man was an idealist, but he died,
> he couldn't survive the first truth,
> discovering that the whole
> world, all of it, was all his . . .

("Suicide")

He was the one who spoke, at least to my father and me, during his mythological, monkish, self-imposed silence. He was for me always most real on the page; he was for me, and remains for me, alive and vibrant as a poet whose truths continue to shine with a brilliance that even drugs, alcohol, and electroshock torture could not snuff out.

My memories of Bob Kaufman are few and fleeting and always in concert with my father. My father and I were walking towards Broadway. I think we had just left City Lights Bookstore. We were in North Beach to get a gift, birthday I expect, for my mother. As we hit Broadway there was Bob Kaufman leaning against a light pole. My father called out; Bob saw my father and remembered him and the two of them hugged and laughed. It had been years since they had last talked, but the ropes that bound them as Afro-diasporic brothers of fate, as comrades of 1950s North Beach streets, and as part of the small cloister of Black male artists and writers who haunted those alleys and bars, were as strong as ever. Bob asked after my mother, my brother, and then me. My father told him repeatedly that I was standing right there, that I was grown now. Bob chuckled when he finally understood and invited us to his small hotel room.

We walked a couple of blocks to the room, which was dark and sparse, and, sharing the bed while I perched on the one chair, the two of them talked in that shorthand way that only friends understand, a sigh here, a quiet laugh there, and an unspent tear on the other side. I was witness only. My father told Bob that I wrote poetry and was pretty good. Bob, as I remember, took no notice. We left and it seemed there was a certain sadness in my father's goodbye.

A couple of years later I was given a featured reading spot at the long-demolished Coffee Gallery where Bob had often held court. My father, a pipe smoker at that point, had gone outside to fill a bowl and inhale a few lungfuls of aromatic smoke. As he stood in the doorway, Bob walked up. My father asked Bob to come in and hear me read. Bob sipped on the beer my father had bought him and sat through a few of the opening readers until I was called to the stage. I signed the back wall with much humility upon seeing up close all the names of former featured readers etched large and small, printed and cursive, on this monument to North Beach poetics. Then I read my poetry, sincere but raw, infused with the passion of the '70s, with a Black Arts spin and a young romantic love compulsion. Bob drank beer with my parents and waited until I sat back down. He gave me his approval, "Good stuff" or some such phrase, and left the place. I was absolutely buzzing with excitement. Just his presence, his quiet support, was my ticket to continue to ride the wild and sometimes tortuous seas of poetry.

That was the last time I remember seeing Bob in the flesh. But his words, his poems, had been my companion through my lonely and misfitting teens. I had carried *Golden Sardine* and *Solitudes Crowded with Loneliness* from San Francisco to Hong Kong, and then onto Kathmandu, Nepal, Kabul, Afghanistan, and Istanbul, Turkey, only to arrive in Paris, where I spent a couple of weeks working and sleeping at George Whitman's bookstore, Shakespeare and Co. One day, after finishing my couple of hours of chores to pay for my bed for the night, I came downstairs to see a young Parisian reading Bob's *Solitudes Crowded with Loneliness*. I was amazed. "You like Kaufman?" I asked in my limited French, rich with vocabulary and impoverished with grammar. "Yes," he answered in English, "he is the best." He said something about Rimbaud and Baudelaire, and I said, yes, I knew some of their poetry, too. I asked him if he had read *Golden Sardine*. "He has another book?" the young man asked in surprise. "Yes, I have a copy upstairs." He appealed to me to let him read it. "I can't lose it," I told him. "It has carried me over half the world." He promised me that he would not move from that spot. I brought him the book and he sat for the next couple of hours reading it and then returned it to me with effusive thanks. I was intrigued. In Paris Bob Kaufman was literary hero while in America he was mostly unknown, and when remembered, it was mostly mythology and lies. *The Collected Poems of Bob Kaufman* presents the real Bob Kaufman, a man who lived and spoke through his poems.

In April of 1925, as the seventh of thirteen children, Bob Kaufman was born of mixed ancestry, in New Orleans, Louisiana, with an Afro-Caribbean mother from Louisiana and a Jewish father of German and French ancestry, at a time when interracial marriage was illegal. Maybe it was that heritage—hewn in a city that was so racially conflicted and culturally rich, that heritage nurtured in a city where his Martinican grandmother's Vodun, the Catholicism of his mother, and the Judaism of his father—that taught him that the world was a complex place where love and spirit, and faith and reality, held central and often conflicting roles. Bob Kaufman was steeped in diverse traditions before he boarded a Merchant Marine ship as a teenager and spent six years sailing the world, and, in stories he told, survived four shipwrecks while circumnavigating the globe several times, tasting exotic foods, reading a breadth of literature, seeing wide swaths of art, and learning a global history from the underside up.

What is most exciting about this volume of poetry is that it shows that Kaufman cannot be fit into one box. He certainly is a Beat poet, although you will rarely find his name or his seminal role listed in articles and books about the Beats. But then he was not "beat" in the meaning attributed to Jack Kerouac, beat down and beat back, rather he was of the beat and through the beat like the jazz poetry that he performed. He was a Beat poet who in his poem "Oct. 5th, 1963"—which takes the form of a letter to the editors of the *San Francisco Chronicle*—noted that:

> It is not the beat played by who is beating the drum. His is a noisy loud one, the silent beat is beaten by who is not beating on the drum, his silent beat drowns out all the noise, it comes before and after every beat, you hear it in beatween, its sound is

> Bob Kaufman, Poet

He can rightfully be considered a surrealist poet, as the French like to say, the "Black Rimbaud." After all he did "acknowledge the demands of Surrealist realization" ("Sullen Bakeries of Total Recall") and then again what other kind of poet would write, as in "Bagel Shop Jazz":

Shadow people, projected on coffee-shop walls.
Memory formed echoes of a generation past
Beating into now.

Nightfall creatures, eating each other
Over a noisy cup of coffee.

Mulberry-eyed girls in black stockings,
Smelling vaguely of mint jelly and last night's bongo
        drummer . . .

But I think what Kaufman wrote, what Kaufman orated, what he be-bopped out of his brain and soul, was not more than real to him, but simply real. It was what he saw and how he saw it. When he asks, "Would You Wear My Eyes?" he doesn't just ask the question, he dares the reader. Are you willing to see a "face . . . covered with maps of dead nations" ("Would You Wear My Eyes?")? Do you want to discover, like he did in his "Jail Poems," that:

All night the stink of rotting people,
Fumes rising from pyres of live men,
Fill my nose with gassy disgust,
Drown my exposed eyes in tears.

He offers both critiques and applause to artists in a broad range of fields—Dylan Thomas, Baudelaire, Billie Holiday, Bartók, Picasso, Mondrian, Hart Crane, Lorca, Camus, and others—letting us see and know the many wells from which he drank.

For Kaufman there are no lines between poetry that spews from the evening news—the bottomless valley of forgetting from whence he lifts Caryl Chessman, and sings dirges to the children of Hiroshima, and questions Camus in hard, biting questions about the writer's colonial position on Algeria—or poetry that echoes with choruses of music—mostly, but not only, jazz and blues—or poetry that grows from a tree of spirituality rooted in Buddhism but aware of the breadth of Christianity and the depths of traditional African religion.

I remember my father telling me a story about Bob calling him and telling him that he needed to come to North Beach the next day and help build a Buddhist temple. My father tried to tell Bob he had other obligations, but Bob pressed him, and in the end my father found himself with a team Bob had organized helping to build a Buddhist temple in San Francisco. Maybe that effort and his years of silence is why Buddhism is the cloak most people wrap Kaufman in. No doubt he had a Buddhist practice, but there has always been a unity reflecting a breadth of cross-roads to and through faith in his poetical vision. And when he speaks directly to God, not only his humor but also an idea of spirituality that is inclusive of more than Buddhism is intact:

> It's all right fellows, it's just a joke,
> you had me scared for a moment God, i thought you were serious,
> i was beginning to believe that this was really your idea of life,
> i know second fifth, but you made it sound so unbelievable,
> You're the only one in this whole big universal gin mill, believe me god,
> who could get away with it, even that oldest boy of yours
> & yet even he, your own
> fleshlessness & bloodlessness, was helpless when it came to dirty jokes.

("I Wish . . .")

Or in his "Heavy Water Blues" when he notes:

> When reading all those thick books on the life of god,
> it should be noted that they were all written by men.

> It is perfectly all right to cast the first stone,
> if you have some more in your pocket.

From *Golden Sardine* and *Solitudes* through the *Abomunist Manifesto* and its later addendum through *The Ancient Rain*, from gems of previously uncollected poems through *Beatitudes* (a magazine that Kaufman co-founded and edited with Allen Ginsberg, John Kelly, and William Margolis), this volume lets Kaufman reveal his life and legacy, his strengths and weaknesses, even as he surveys America, the planet, and indeed the universe with humor, satire, passion, and a lucidity born of jazz riffs and African rhythms. When all is said and done, Kaufman is a poet of the world; mythologies and histories hold court in his poems.

Bob Kaufman will always be surrounded by myth and mystery. He was in San Francisco first in 1946 as a maritime sailor and returned some years later. But was it with his brother Donald in 1950, as some have said, or with Burroughs and Ginsberg whom he met in New York, as others aver? Thus, if one wants to know Bob Kaufman, it is best to look not in the filigree memories and scraps of official papers that can be offered, but in his poems. His life is laid out there.

> Whether I am a poet or not, I use fifty dollars' worth
> of air every day, cool.
> In order to exist I hide behind stacks of red and blue
> poems

("Afterwards, They Shall Dance")

It is in his poems you find his love for his son Parker, his second wife Eileen, and several other friends and family members who shared his road if only for a season. In his poems you find Kaufman

> Seeing only the holdings
> Inside the walls of me,
> Feeling the roots that bind me,
> To this mere human tree

("Private Sadness")

Kaufman is also unabashedly Black or, in the fading lingo of his times, Negro. He proclaims who he is but seems to also magnify to become more than just his person, as in "Oregon" where he chants:

> You are with me Oregon,
> Day and night, I feel you, Oregon.
> I am Negro, I am Oregon.
> Oregon is me, the planet

Kaufman is indeed a Black Beat and wants this to be remembered, wants his sense of self to be remembered. I don't doubt Kaufman heard people repeatedly say, "I don't see color," which loosely translated means, "I don't see you." Bob Kaufman demands to be not just heard but seen and to have his people seen, as in "Untitled":

THE SUN IS A NEGRO.
THE MOTHER OF THE SUN IS A NEGRO.

One wonders if Kaufman was always a poet. True, he told some that he studied briefly at New York's the New School in the 1940s where he met William Burroughs and Allen Ginsberg, with whom he traveled to San Francisco, but this was likely part of the mythology he created. (Ginsberg, for example, said they met in 1959.) Is it more likely that he became a poet much earlier, while he walked the streets of New Orleans, while he sailed the planet's numbered seas? Although he was dead at the relatively young age of 60 after living nearly half of his life in San Francisco, he left an impressive body of work, albeit small in the number of pages, nearly all of which can be found in this volume. Here one finds the familiar and the more recently unearthed and translated, the deeply personal and the adamantly political, the profoundly spiritual and wryly philosophical, all braided with cosmic and comic realities of our universe. This book is a reflection of Kaufman's genius, a welcome gathering of his songs and chants, a needed compendium of the depth of his heart and the breadth of his knowledge and the humility of his spirit.

When Kaufman speaks in "Dolorous Echo" of holes in skin and hairs on head that won't stay dead ending with "When I die, / I won't stay / Dead," he speaks a truth that we can be grateful for. Alive and in full verse, his poems can be found here revealing his life, his soul, his prayers, and his reflections on our planet and universe in language that reads as vibrantly today as they were when he spat them out, filling the ears of all who would listen.

You can, of course, simply read this book, poem to poem, and become immersed in the rhythms, the emotions, the insights, the songs. But I recommend you put some music in back as you read. Play some Charlie Parker and Thelonious Monk, go find that Billie Holiday, discover or rediscover that Coltrane, find not only some Ray Charles but some gut-bucket blues, and slip in a bit of Bartók to better hear the muses who fed his soul. And then prepare to take a journey that climbs mountains and may dangle you over dangerous cliffs, will lift you upwards towards the stars and drop you back into the brutal reality that is America, before it sets you free in the wondrous possibilities that inhabit our universe.

The Facts: NMUer Robert Kaufman, in charge of the Union's sound truck campaign to bring the story of seamen's wages to the people, takes a turn at the mike on 14th Street, one of the truck's many stopping points.

(PILOT Photo)

SIU Members Support NMU's Wage Drive

SIU rank and filers are voting with their feet—on NMU picket lines—against the double-talking, do-nothing wage policies of their secretary and misleader, Harry Lundeberg

Bob Kaufman, National Maritime
Union activist, New York City. *The
Pilot*, July 20, 1945. COURTESY
STANFORD UNIVERSITY

Bob Kaufman confronts police
at Co-Existence Bagel Shop,
Grant Avenue, San Francisco,
1959. PHOTO BY JERRY STOLL. BY
PERMISSION OF CASEY STOLL AND
THE ESTATE OF JERRY STOLL.

Bill Margolis, Eileen and Bob
Kaufman, printing *Beatitude* #1.
The Bread and Wine Mission,
Grant Avenue, S.F. 1959. PHOTO
BY FORTUNATO CLEMENTI

Joan Savo, Bob Kaufman, 1960.
Oil on board, 29 x 14 inches.
COLLECTION RAYMOND FOYE,
PHOTO BY RON HORMER

Bob, Parker, and Eileen Kaufman,
c. 1962, New York City.
PHOTOGRAPHER UNKNOWN.

Bob Kaufman, Grant Avenue, S.F.
1974. PHOTO BY MARY ANNE
KRAMER, SAN FRANCISCO
HISTORY CENTER, SAN
FRANCISCO PUBLIC LIBRARY

Bob Kaufman and Allen Ginsberg,
Savoy Tivoli Cafe, S.F. 1977.
PHOTO BY IRA NOWINSKI

Bob Kaufman, Coffee Gallery, Grant Avenue, S.F., 1978. PHOTO BY IRA NOWINSKI

I AM A CAMERA

THE POET NAILED ON
THE HARD BONE OF THIS
WORLD,
HIS SOUL DEDICATED TO SILENCE

IS A FISH WITH FROGS EYES

THE BLOOD OF OF A POET FLOWS
OUT WITH HIS POEMS, BACK
TO THE PYRAMID OF BONES
FROM WHICH HE IS THRUST
HIS DEATH IS A SAVING GRACE
CREATION IS PERFECT.

BOB KAUFMAN.

Manuscript for "I Am a Camera," *The Ancient Rain*, 1981.

Bob Kaufman Reading, Spaghetti Factory, North Beach, S.F., 1981: Poets Ira Cohen (seated), Neeli Cherkovski (kneeling). PHOTO BY IRA NOWINSKI

Reading Second April, 28 Harwood Alley, S.F., 1983. PHOTO BY RAYMOND FOYE

Bob Kaufman and Gregory Corso, Grant Avenue, S.F. 1982. PHOTO BY CHRIS FELVER

Bob Kaufman, 1982. PHOTO BY CHRIS FELVER

BOB KAUFMAN CHRONOLOGY

1925
April 18: Born Robert Gernel Kaufman, son of Joseph Emmet and Lillian Rose Kaufman, at 1565 North Miro Street in New Orleans, LA. Bob is the seventh of thirteen children. **August 21:** Baptized at the local Corpus Christi Catholic Church at 2022 St. Bernard Avenue.

ca. 1930
Attends Valena C. Jones Elementary School located at 1901 North Galvez Street.

1938
January 19: Joins the Boy Scouts as part of Troop No. 144 of the St. John the Divine Division Boy Scouts. **May 30:** Father dies around the time Bob graduates from Albert Wicker Middle School, located at 2011 Bienville Street.

ca. 1940
Home address listed as 1660 North Tonti Street, New Orleans.

1942
Late Spring: Graduates from McDonough #35 High School, located at 655 South Rampart Street, which was the first high school for African Americans in Louisiana. **June 18:** Issued a Certificate of Service as a messman in New Orleans. **June 24:** Ships out from Galveston, TX, on the *Winfield Scott*, as a utility. **September 10:** Discharged in New York City. **Late September:** Travels back to New Orleans. **October 29:** Arrives in New York City on the USAT *Yarmouth*.

ca. 1943
Joins the National Maritime Union—affiliated with the Congress of Industrial Organizations—and begins working his way up the ranks.

1943
Early 1943: Ships out from New York City on the *Henry Gibbins*. **April 29:** Arrives in New York City on the *Henry Gibbins*. **May 15:** Ships out on the *Henry Gibbins* from Brooklyn, NY; it's unclear when he arrives back. **September 27:** Ships out from New York on the *George B. Selden* as a messman.

1944

January 7: Discharged in New York City. **February 10:** Ships out on the *James B. Eads,* as a utility, from Philadelphia. **May 13:** Discharged in Calcutta, India. **June 22:** Ships out from Calcutta, on the *Harold L. Winslow,* as a messman. **August 28:** Discharged in New York City. **October 26:** Marries Ida Inez Berrocal. **November 11:** Ships out from Baltimore, on the *Henry N. Sibley,* as a messman.

1945

January 25: Discharged in New York City. Uses 1070 Fox Street, Bronx, New York City, as his address. **March 10:** Issued duplicate Permanent Certificate of Identification and Certificate of Service, as the originals were mutilated, and endorsed as a second cook and baker. **March 23:** Ships out from New York City, on the *Hendrik W. van Loon,* as a utility. **June 13:** Discharged in New York City. **July:** Appointed Chairman of the Rank and File National Maritime Union (NMU) Strike Mobilization Committee; attends meeting in Washington, D.C. with NY Congressional Representative Vito Marcantonio. **August 11:** Ships out from New York City, on the *George Davis,* as storekeeper. **September 29:** Daughter Antoinette Victoria Marie Kaufman is born. **October 22:** Discharged in New York City. **November 14:** Ships out from New York City, on the C.C. N.Y. *Victory,* as chief pantryman. **December 10:** Discharged in Boston.

1946

March 18–April 19: FBI file claims Kaufman attends NMU Maritime Training School in New York City, identifying NMU as a Communist Party organization. **June 24:** Ships out from New York City, on the *Hood Victory,* as chief pantryman. **July 24:** Discharged in New York City. **August 1:** Ships out from New York City, on the *Hood Victory,* as chief pantryman. **August 20:** Discharged in San Francisco. **September:** Claims to have been sent to San Francisco to organize NMU workers for a strike. **October 30:** Ships out from San Francisco, on the *Roanoke,* as a messman. **November 11:** Discharged in Los Angeles.

1947

January 7: Ships out from New York City, on the *Santa Isabel,* as a messman. **February 24:** Discharged in New York City. **February 26:** Ships out from New York City, on the *Santa Isabel,* as messman. **April 7:** Discharged in New York City. **April 25:** Publishes two letters in *The Pilot* (NMU's newspaper), one denouncing "the present hysterical campaign against the Communist Party" by the House Committee on Un-American

Activities and one making proposals for an upcoming NMU contract; also reported in the same issue as giving a talk onboard the *Santa Isabel* about the menace of Franco's Spain. **May 22:** Ships out from New York City, on the *Santa Isabel*, as officers' messman. **June 30:** Discharged in New York City. **July 1:** Ships out from New York City, on the *Santa Isabel*, as officers' messman. **August 11:** Discharged in New York City. **October 11:** Scheduled to ship out from New York City, on the *River Raisin*, as a utility, but is listed as "Failed to Join." **October 15:** Ships out from New York City, on the *Cristobal-Lounge*, as steward. **October 29:** Discharged in New York City. **November 5:** Ships out from New York City, on the *Mormacowl*.

1948
January 8: Discharged in Baltimore. **March 13:** Ships out from Baltimore, on the *Mormacport*, as general utility. **March 22:** Discharged in New York City. **March 23:** Ships out from New York City, on the *Mormacport*, as general utility. **June 7:** Discharged in New York City on his final voyage.

1949
Uses 935 Longwood Avenue, Bronx, New York City, as his address. FBI file reports his presence at NMU's Waterfront Section Headquarters; presumably being disciplined for activities unbecoming his union position. **May 5:** FBI file indicates an agent visited 935 Longwood Avenue and spoke with Ida Berrocal, who said that they had been separated for a year and that she hadn't seen him.

1950
July 16: Upon visit from FBI, his mother states that she has not seen Bob in three years. Presumably the FBI has lost track of Kaufman after he is blackballed by the NMU and stops sailing. Rumored to be living at 53 East 11th Street, New York City.

1951
July 24: Declared a poor security risk by the U.S. Coast Guard and his application to renew his mariner's card is denied. Expelled from NMU for "degeneracy" or admitting to drug use. Rumored to be living at 242 West 10th Street, New York City. Moves to San Antonio, TX, with younger brother Donald. They work for a family friend who has a nightclub.

1952
Whereabouts unknown.

1953
March 24: Mother dies of cancer. Travels to San Francisco with brother Donald. Donald recalls seeing Bob jump on the table of Vesuvio Cafe, a bar in North Beach, and reciting poetry as the crowd swelled.

1954
April 5: Squats at the Wharf Theatre in Monterey, CA. **November 4:** Divorces Ida Berrocal.

1955
January 24: Employed at The SF Mart Club, a supper club, located at 1355 Market Street. Uses the address 525 Baker Street. **March:** Employed at Asilomar YWCA Camp, located at 800 Asilomar Blvd., Pacific Grove, CA. **October:** Receives traffic ticket in Los Angeles.

1956
March: Employed at the Beverly Hilton Hotel as a caterer. Uses the address 1810 North Serrano Avenue. **May:** Quits job and travels up the coast. Abandons car in Big Sur and resides in Monterey.

1957
Relocates to San Francisco.

1958
February 1: Reads at Coffee Gallery. **May:** Meets Eileen Singer. **June 23:** Accompanies Eileen on a whirlwind trip to Mexico and returns to San Francisco.

1959
February: With pregnant Eileen, briefly moves to Mill Valley. **May 9:** First issue of *Beatitude* published; Kaufman is cofounder and coeditor of this important Beat-era publication. **Summer:** With Eileen, moves in with Bill Margolis at Harwood Alley, San Francisco. **August:** Brutally beaten by SFPD Officer William Bigarani, igniting an intense battle with the North Beach scene, which plays out on the front page of the city's major daily newspapers. Publishes *Abomunist Manifesto* with City Lights Books. **September:** Travels to Hollywood for possible involvement in film version of Jack Kerouac's *The Subterraneans*. Does not pan

out. **October 13:** Son Robert Parker Kaufman born. **October:** Publishes *Second April* with City Lights Books. **November 1 and 12:** Reads at Co-Existence Bagel Shop.

1960

January: Appears in Ron Rice's film *The Flower Thief*, which also has a cameo by the infant Parker. **April:** Publishes *Does the Secret Mind Whisper?* with City Lights Books. **April 18:** Parker is baptized on Bob's 35th birthday. **May:** Invited to read at Harvard and moves back to New York City. Reads often at the Gaslight Café. **June 2:** Eileen and Parker arrive in New York City. They live at 42 St. Mark's Place with musician Dave Pike. **July 24:** Reads with David Amram at the Paperback Book Gallery, located at 90 West 3rd Street, New York City. **August 27:** Reads at the Living Theatre. **September:** Lives at 170 E. 2nd Street, in same apartment building as Allen Ginsberg and Herbert Huncke. **November:** Arrested and taken to Bellevue Hospital.

1961

January 13: Visits Ginsberg's apartment. Timothy Leary is administering a psilocybin dosage to Jack Kerouac and Bob also takes a dose. **March:** Eileen voluntarily checks into Bellevue. **May:** Living at 26 Van Dam Street across the street from opera singer Leontyne Price. **Summer:** Cowrites the song "Green, Green Rocky Road" with Len Chandler. **August:** Eileen leaves for San Francisco, leaving Parker with Bob, and returns to New York City in late November. **October:** Briefly lives with painter Russell Fitzgerald on East 4th Street. **December:** Reads at Les Deux Mégots at 64 East 7th Street. Moves in with Harry Monroe on East 6th Street.

1962

January: Moves to East 3rd Street with poet John Richardson. Eileen has miscarriage at Bellevue. Stays in hospital two months. Upon release moves to Thompson Street. **May 29:** In court for alleged assault at the nightclub Fat Black Pussycat. **May 31:** Imprisoned at Riker's Island. Eileen and Parker leave for San Francisco. **October:** Seen often at the residence of poet John Wieners.

1963

April: Sleeps on the floor at the apartment of recording engineer Richard Alderson, on West 26th Street, near Gramercy Park. **August:** Dave Van Ronk releases his version of "Green, Green Rocky Road" on his album

In the Tradition (Prestige). **September:** Flies back to San Francisco with money provided by Lawrence Ferlinghetti. **November 22:** President Kennedy is assassinated. Two days later, the accused gunman Lee Harvey Oswald is fatally shot by Jack Ruby on live television. Enters a period of silence.

1964

April: Eileen and Parker travel to Mexico where they spend several months while Eileen edits the MS of *Solitudes Crowded with Loneliness*. **Summer:** Admitted to UCSF Langley Porter Psychiatric Hospital and Clinics.

1965

June: Mary Beach reports that Bob is living in San Francisco. **July:** Reportedly incarcerated in SF County Jail for not registering as a narcotics addict. **September 16:** Publishes *Solitudes Crowded with Loneliness* with New Directions. **October:** Bob's "Jail Poems" and an excerpt from the *Abomunist Manifesto* are published in *La Poésie de la Beat Generation*, translated by Jean-Jacques Lebel, Éditions Denoël, Paris.

1966

Solitudes, translated by Mary Beach and Claude Pélieu, published by L'inédit 10/18, Paris. Reviews of this book, by Alain Jouffroy, appear in *L'Express* and *La Quinzaine Littéraire*. Three poems translated by Jean Copans published in the collection *La Poésie Négro-Américaine*, edited by Langston Hughes, Editions Seghers, Paris.

1967

May: Publishes *Golden Sardine*, edited by Mary Beach, with City Lights Books. **Summer:** *Burroughs, Pélieu, Kaufman – Textes*, translated by Beach and Pélieu, published by L'Herne, Paris. This anthology contains poems only seen in French.

1968

Appears in *UMBRA Anthology 1967–68*, edited by David Henderson, published by The Society of Umbra, New York City.

1969

Appears in *The New Black Poetry*, edited by Clarence Major, International Publishers, New York City. **April:** Incarcerated in San Bruno jail for four months. Tells reporter for the San Francisco underground paper *Good Times* that jail doctor claims Bob has Parkinson's disease.

1970
Published in *The Poetry of the Negro: 1746–1970*, edited by Langston Hughes and Arna Bontemps, Doubleday, New York City. Published in *3000 Years of Black Poetry, An Anthology*, edited by Alan Lomax and Raoul Abdul, Dodd, Mead and Co., New York City. Published in *The Voice That Is Great Within Us: American Poetry of the Twentieth Century*, edited by Hayden Carruth, Bantam Books, New York City.

1971
Published in *Black American Literature Anthology*, edited by Ruth Miller, Glencoe, a Division of Macmillan, New York.

1972
April 2: Subject of the broadcast *SOUL! Coming from Bob Kaufman*. PBS WNET, New York, NY. Bob's poems performed by Ossie Davis and Ruby Dee. **September:** "Whatever Happened to Bob Kaufman?" an essay by Barbara Christian, published in *Black World*, Vol. XXI, No. 11, edited by John H. Johnson, Chicago.

1973
May 31: Breaks his silence at the Palo Alto Art Center, during the 1st Photography Invitational, which included the photographs of Jean Dierkes-Carlisle, recites from T.S. Eliot's verse drama *Murder in the Cathedral* and his own new poem "All Those Ships That Never Sailed."

1974
December 6: Gives first public reading, following the end of his vow of silence, at Malvina's, 512 Union Street, in North Beach. Reads poems exclusively from *Solitudes Crowded with Loneliness*.

1975
August 7: Poetry reading at Malvina's for a benefit for *Beatitude* magazine. **September 6:** Bob and Eileen Kaufman renew their vows on Mt. Tamalpais in Marin.

1976

Sardine dorée (*Golden Sardine*) translated by Mary Beach, Claude Pélieu, and Jacques François, published by Christian Bourgois éditeur, Paris. **February 9:** Participates in joint City Lights–*Beatitude* Reading of SF Poets at Little Fox Theater. **May:** Reads, accompanied by saxophonist Charles Lloyd, at *The First Poetic Hoohaw*, a poetry festival in Eugene, OR, produced by Ken Kesey and recorded on film. **August 29:** Poetry reading at Books Plus. **November 1:** Gives poetry reading at Glide Memorial Church for the South African Resistance.

1977

Briefly moves in with photographer Jean Dierkes-Carlisle in San Francisco.

1978

June 9: Reads with Jack Micheline & A.D. Winans at Neighborhood Arts Theatre, 220 Buchanan Street, San Francisco.

1979

May 12–14: With Ror Schenck, gives Rimbaud-themed reading called *A Season in Hell* at the Savoy Tivoli, 1434 Grant Avenue, a benefit for North Beach Community Arts Inc. Reads *Second April* after Schenck recites from Rimbaud. **August 20:** Reads with Philip Lamantia at San Francisco Art Institute. **September 18:** Participates in *Beatitude* benefit reading at Savoy Tivoli. **Autumn:** Living in North Beach at the Hotel Dante, which burns down. Raymond Foye recovers Bob's poems, which become the manuscript for *The Ancient Rain*. Moves in with poet Neeli Cherkovski for six months. Special issue of *Beatitude* (29) devoted to Bob Kaufman, edited by Neeli Cherkovski and Raymond Foye and published in San Francisco.

1980

Publishes three poems in *Beatitude* 30, edited by Neeli Cherkovski and Raymond Foye, San Francisco.

1981

February: Lives in the Swiss American Hotel, 534 Broadway Street. **May:** Publishes *The Ancient Rain: Poems 1956–1978*, edited by Raymond Foye, with New Directions. **September:** Filmed reading his poem "The Poet" at the San Francisco Art Institute for an hour-length documentary

West Coast: Beat and Beyond, by Chris Felver and Gerald Nicosia. **October 21:** Awarded a $12,500 grant, for a Creative Writing Fellowship, by the National Endowment for the Arts.

1982

Eremit in San Francisco: lyrik & prosa, Bob Kaufman, translated by Udo Breger, Eco-Verlag, Zürich. **January:** *With Ossie and Ruby* TV show films in San Francisco for a special program on Bob Kaufman. **August 9:** Poetry reading, at Savoy Tivoli, a benefit for *Beatitude.*

1983

In a letter to Ted Joans, in France, lists the address P.O. Box 1723 in Guerneville, CA.

1984

Documentary *West Coast: Beat and Beyond* is released.

1985

May 15: Gives poetry reading, at a venue on Broadway in North Beach, a benefit for *Beatitude.*

1986

January 12: Dies of pulmonary emphysema in San Francisco. **January 23:** A traditional New Orleans-style funeral parade in Bob's honor marches through the streets of North Beach. His ashes are scattered in the San Francisco Bay as a rainbow emerges over the skyline. **April 26:** *Bob Kaufman, Poet,* a four-hour radio program produced by David Henderson, debuts on KPFA.

COLLECTED POEMS

SOLITUDES CROWDED WITH LONELINESS

POEMS

I HAVE FOLDED MY SORROWS

I have folded my sorrows into the mantle of summer night,
Assigning each brief storm its allotted space in time,
Quietly pursuing catastrophic histories buried in my eyes.
And yes, the world is not some unplayed Cosmic Game,
And the sun is still ninety-three million miles from me,
And in the imaginary forest, the shingled hippo becomes the gay unicorn.
No, my traffic is not with addled keepers of yesterday's disasters,
Seekers of manifest disembowelment on shafts of yesterday's pains.
Blues come dressed like introspective echoes of a journey.
And yes, I have searched the rooms of the moon on cold summer nights.
And yes, I have refought those unfinished encounters.
      Still, they remain unfinished.
And yes, I have at times wished myself something different.

The tragedies are sung nightly at the funerals of the poet;
The revisited soul is wrapped in the aura of familiarity.

AFRICAN DREAM

In black core of night, it explodes
Silver thunder, rolling back my brain,
Bursting copper screens, memory worlds
Deep in star-fed beds of time,
Seducing my soul to diamond fires of night.
Faint outline, a ship—momentary fright
Lifted on waves of color,
Sunk in pits of light,
Drummed back through time,
Hummed back through mind,
Drumming, cracking the night.
Strange forest songs, skin sounds
Crashing through—no longer strange.

3

Incestuous yellow flowers tearing
Magic from the earth.
Moon-dipped rituals, led
By a scarlet god,
Caressed by ebony maidens
With daylight eyes,
Purple garments,
Noses that twitch,
Singing young girl songs
Of an ancient love
In dark, sunless places
Where memories are sealed,
Burned in eyes of tigers.

Suddenly wise, I fight the dream:
Green screams enfold my night.

WALKING PARKER HOME

Sweet beats of jazz impaled on slivers of wind
Kansas Black Morning/ First Horn Eyes/
Historical sound pictures on New Bird wings
People shouts/ boy alto dream/ Tomorrow's
Gold belled pipe of stops and future Blues Times
Lurking Hawkins/ shadows of Lester/ realization
Bronze fingers—brain extensions seeking trapped sounds
Ghetto thoughts/ bandstand courage/ solo flight
Nerve-wracked suspicions of newer songs and doubts
New York altar city/ black tears/ secret disciples
Hammer horn pounding soul marks on unswinging gates
Culture gods/ mob sounds/ visions of spikes
Panic excursions to tribal Jazz wombs and transfusions
Heroin nights of birth/ and soaring/ over boppy new ground.
Smothered rage covering pyramids of notes spontaneously exploding
Cool revelations/ shrill hopes/ beauty speared into greedy ears
Birdland nights on bop mountains, windy saxophone revolutions
Dayrooms of junk/ and melting walls and circling vultures/
Money cancer/ remembered pain/ terror flights/
Death and indestructible existence

In that Jazz corner of life
Wrapped in a mist of sound
His legacy, our Jazz-tinted dawn
Wailing his triumphs of oddly begotten dreams
Inviting the nerveless to feel once more
That fierce dying of humans consumed
In raging fires of Love.

AFTERWARDS, THEY SHALL DANCE

In the city of St. Francis they have taken down the statue of St. Francis,
And the hummingbirds all fly forward to protest, humming feather poems.

Bodenheim denounced everyone and wrote, Bodenheim had
          no sweet marijuana dreams,
Patriotic muscateleer, did not die seriously, no poet love to end with, gone.

Dylan took the stone cat's nap at St. Vincent's, vaticaned beer, no defense;
That poem shouted from his nun-filled room, an insult to the brain, nerves,
Save now from Swansea, white horses, beer birds, snore poems, Wales-bird.

Billie Holiday got lost on the subway and stayed there forever,
Raised little peace-of-mind gardens in out of the way stations,
And will go on living in wrappers of jazz silence forever, loved.

My face feels like a living emotional relief map, forever wet.
My hair is curling in anticipation of my own wild gardening.

Poor Edgar Allan Poe died translated, in unpressed pants, ended in light,
Surrounded by ecstatic gold bugs, his hegira blessed by Baudelaire's orgy.

Whether I am a poet or not, I use fifty dollars' worth of air every day, cool.
In order to exist I hide behind stacks of red and blue poems
And open little sensuous parasols, singing the nail-in-the-foot song,
          drinking cool beatitudes.

CELESTIAL HOBO

For every remembered dream
There are twenty nighttime lifetimes.

Under multiplied arcs of sleep
Zombie existences become Existence.

In night's warped rectangles
Stormy bathtubs of wavy sex
Come hotly drawn.

Everyday, confused in desperate poses,
Loses its hue, to Dada prodigies of black.
There never was a night that ended
Or began.

BATTLE REPORT

One thousand saxophones infiltrate the city,
Each with a man inside,
Hidden in ordinary cases,
Labeled FRAGILE.

A fleet of trumpets drops their hooks,
Inside at the outside.

Ten waves of trombones approach the city
Under blue cover
Of late autumn's neo-classical clouds.

Five hundred bassmen, all string feet tall,
Beating it back to the bass.

One hundred drummers, each a stick in each hand,
The delicate rumble of pianos, moving in.

The secret agent, an innocent bystander,
Drops a note in the wail box.

Five generals, gathered in the gallery,
Blowing plans.

At last, the secret code is flashed:
Now is the time, now is the time.

Attack: The sound of jazz.

The city falls.

BENEDICTION

Pale brown Moses went down to Egypt land
To let somebody's people go.
Keep him out of Florida, no UN there:
The poor governor is all alone,
With six hundred thousand illiterates.

America, I forgive you . . . I forgive you
Nailing black Jesus to an imported cross
Every six weeks in Dawson, Georgia.
America, I forgive you . . . I forgive you
Eating black children, I know your hunger.
America, I forgive you . . . I forgive you
Burning Japanese babies defensively—
I realize how necessary it was.
Your ancestor had beautiful thoughts in his brain.
His descendants are experts in real estate.
Your generals have mushrooming visions.
Every day your people get more and more
Cars, televisions, sickness, death dreams.
You must have been great
Alive.

UNHOLY MISSIONS

I want to be buried in an anonymous crater inside the moon.

I want to build miniature golf courses on all the stars.

I want to prove that Atlantis was a summer resort for cave men.

I want to prove that Los Angeles is a practical joke played
        on us by superior beings on a humorous planet.

I want to expose Heaven as an exclusive sanitarium filled
        with rich psychopaths who think they can fly.

I want to show that the Bible was serialized in a Roman children's magazine.

I want to prove that the sun was born when God fell asleep
        with a lit cigarette, tired after a hard night of judging.

I want to prove once and for all that I am not crazy.

WEST COAST SOUNDS – 1956

San Fran, hipster land,
Jazz sounds, wig sounds,
Earthquake sounds, others,
Allen on Chestnut Street,
Giving poetry to squares,
Corso on knees, pleading,
God eyes.
Rexroth, Ferlinghetti,
Swinging, in cellars,
Kerouac at Locke's,
Writing Neal
On high typewriter,
Neal, booting a choo-choo,
On zigzag tracks.
Now, many cats
Falling in,

New York cats,
Too many cats,
Monterey scene cooler,
San Franers, falling down.
Canneries closing.
Sardines splitting
For Mexico.
Me too.

FRAGMENT

. . . All those dead movie stars, peanut-buttered forever,
Do they kiss famous horses on the nose?
Do they see all of the latest horror movies?
How do they like the exclusive tombs, renaissance mailboxes,
With Bela Lugosi moving around down there
In his capeman Agron suit, sleepless walker,
With his arms full of morphine, his eyes suggesting
Frozen seesaws in cold playgrounds of yesterday.
What came first? The chicken or the spike?
What came last? The needle or the haystack?
That scream was a rumor and remained unscreamed,
Unnoted among narcotic breakfasts and raving love fiends,
Sexy rides on Gothic streetcars and Buddha lost in a phone booth,
Cold talking wind-people, three-dimensional valentines,
Torn from magic tenements in the long Decembers of today.
Easter-faced skylarks, low-flying Mexican birds,
The oracle of the crickets ticking off jazz *Te Deums*,
Our Lady of Nicotine, madonna without child,
Releases her pale balloon, snatched from the folding year,
All the daring young headhunters, traumatic in inflammatory bathing suits,
Shriek grim fairy tales, while convenient needles fall out of haystacks.
Charlie Parker was a great electrician who went around wiring people.

GRANDFATHER WAS QUEER, TOO

He was first seen in a Louisiana bayou,
Playing chess with an intellectual lobster.
They burned his linoleum house alive
And sent that intellectual off to jail.
He wrote home every day, to no avail.
Grandfather had cut out, he couldn't raise the bail.

Next seen, skiing on some dusty Texas road,
An intellectual's soul hung from his ears,
Discussing politics with an unemployed butterfly.
They hung that poor butterfly, poor butterfly.
Grandfather had cut out, he couldn't raise the bail.

Next seen on the Arizona desert, walking,
Applying soothing poultices to the teeth
Of an aching mountain.
Dentists all over the state brought gauze balls,
Bandaged the mountain, buried it at sea.
Grandfather had cut out, he couldn't raise the bail.

Next seen in California, the top part,
Arranging a marriage, mating trees,
Crossing a rich redwood and a black pine.
He was exposed by the Boy Scouts of America.
The trees were arrested on a vag charge.
Grandfather cut out, he couldn't raise the bail.

Now I have seen him here. He is beat.
His girlfriend has green ears;
She is twenty-three months pregnant.
I kissed them both:
Live happily ever after.

BAGEL SHOP JAZZ

Shadow people, projected on coffee-shop walls.
Memory formed echoes of a generation past
Beating into now.

Nightfall creatures, eating each other
Over a noisy cup of coffee.

Mulberry-eyed girls in black stockings,
Smelling vaguely of mint jelly and last night's bongo drummer,
Making profound remarks on the shapes of navels,
Wondering how the short Sunset week
Became the long Grant Avenue night,
Love tinted, beat angels,
Doomed to see their coffee dreams
Crushed on the floors of time,
As they fling their arrow legs
To the heavens,
Losing their doubts in the beat.

Turtle-neck angel guys, black-haired dungaree guys,
Caesar-jawed, with synagogue eyes,
World travelers on the forty-one bus,
Mixing jazz with paint talk,
High rent, Bartók, classical murders,
The pot shortage and last night's bust.
Lost in a dream world,
Where time is told with a beat.

Coffee-faced Ivy Leaguers, in Cambridge jackets,
Whose personal Harvard was a Fillmore district step,
Weighted down with conga drums,
The ancestral cross, the Othello-laid curse,
Talking of Bird and Diz and Miles,
The secret terrible hurts,
Wrapped in cool hipster smiles,
Telling themselves, under the talk,
This shot must be the end,
Hoping the beat is really the truth.

The guilty police arrive.

Brief, beautiful shadows, burned on walls of night.

REFLECTIONS ON A SMALL PARADE

When I see the little Buddhist scouts
Marching with their Zen mothers
To tea ceremonies at the rock garden,
I shake my head. . . . It falls off.

HART . . . . CRANE

They fear you, Crane . . . . you whispered aloft, pains they buried forever. . . .

They hate you, Crane . . . . your sur-real eclipses blot out their muted sun. . . .

They miss you, Crane . . . . your footprints are on their rotting teeth. . . .

They need you, Crane . . . . their walking minds are worn to bony core. . . .

They want you, Crane . . . . stay hidden beneath shadowed bookstore tables. . . .

They call you, Crane . . . . they shout your name in deserted phonebooths. . . .

They beat you, Crane . . . . they draw your mouth on their lovers' bodies. . . .

They know you, Crane . . . . they have memorized the pimples on your soul. . . .

They seek you, Crane . . . . your face is on secret stamps printed on hidden
    envelopes. . . .

They buy you, Crane . . . . your petrified sperm is treasured by marble lovers. . . .

They hear you, Crane . . . . you are screaming from their turned-off radios. . . .

They see you, Crane . . . . you are mirrored in black windows on deserted streetcorners. . . .

They read you, Crane . . . . your books are opened in underground libraries. . . .

They paint you, Crane . . . . your eyebrows are on their glossy calendars. . . .

They teach you, Crane . . . . in secret huddles beneath football stadiums. . . .

They sell you, Crane . . . . you are spreadeagled on grills of poetic eating places. . . .

They celebrate you, Crane . . . . you are a sequined float in clandestine beauty processions. . . .

They worship you, Crane . . . . you are enshrined on suicide altars of pain. . . .

They kill you, Crane . . . . you are electrocuted at breakfast in gas-chamber kitchens. . . .

They are relieved, Crane . . . . you have gone, taking your realities with you. . . .

They deny you, Crane . . . . you are safely dead, but we know, Crane, you never were. . . .

They live you, Crane . . . . ON THE BRIDGE.

EAST FIFTH STREET (N.Y.)

Twisting brass, key of G, tenement stoned,
Singing Jacob's song, with Caribe emphasis.

Flinging the curls of infant rabbis, gently,
Into the glowing East Side night.

Esther's hand, in Malinche's clasped,
Traps the fly of evening, forever.

Ancient log-rolling caps of Caribe waves
Splashing crowded harbors of endless steps.

13

Angry, fire-eyed children clutch transient winds,
Singing Gypsy songs, love me now, love me now.

The echoes return, riding the voice of the river,
As time cries out, on the skin of an African drum.

BIRD WITH PAINTED WINGS

Monet whispered softly,
Drowned love
In pools of light.

Picasso shouted nightmares,
Screaming: Climb inside yourself,
There is a madness there.

Braque gave the echo, precisely.

Mondrian exposed squares.

As the Mexicans roared
In the star-torn Indian night,
Fire lifted Parícutin,
Springing red from black earth.

Modigliani, naked, exposed sadness.

Degas exposed angels in ballet skins,
Smoked behind walls of Marseilles' absinthe dens.

Kollwitz served tears in wooden spoons,
Under dark moons, forever sorrowed.

Rousseau shouted poetry
From his window on that mad world.

A burning bird whistled on high:
Eat it all,
Die!

BLUES NOTE

Ray Charles is the black wind of Kilimanjaro,
Screaming up-and-down blues,
Moaning happy on all the elevators of my time.

Smiling into the camera, with an African symphony
Hidden in his throat, and (*I Got a Woman*) wails, too.

He burst from Bessie's crushed black skull
One cold night outside of Nashville, shouting,
And grows bluer from memory, glowing bluer, still.

At certain times you can see the moon
Balanced on his head.

From his mouth he hurls chunks of raw soul.
He separated the sea of polluted sounds
And led the blues into the Promised Land.

Ray Charles is a dangerous man ('way cross town),
And I love him.

for Ray Charles's birthday
N.Y.C. / 1961

DEAR JOHN:

It has been a lifetime, it seems.
I am no longer what I once was,
So I can't speak with my old eloquence.
I have become less and darker
Than a shadow. Sometimes I think
I've never recovered from Danny's party;
You remember that bash, don't you?

I don't know what happened or when,
But I don't make that scene anymore,
So I just sit here in that new,

Fluorescent lighting, feeling strange
As an old deserted movie set.

There isn't much to do around here
Anymore, so I just sit around,
Thinking about you and Doc and
Those crazy-beauty whores we loved.

I often wonder how Doc would smile
About the lab being turned into a club
Of people; I guess he'd want to bottle a few, for study;
He was crazy enough to do that, you know.

Not much more to say. We've got a media agency,
Whatever that is, two big fashionable eating joints,
For Carmel people and tourists, and a coupla' gift joints.
Only time anything happens is when those poor dreamers
Come down from S.F., but the rents won't let them stay.
Well, so long for now. Here comes a coupla' paisans
Trying out their new Buick. All that gas bugs me.

Yours in warm remembrance,

Cannery Row

PLEA

Voyager, wanderer of the heart,
Off to
          a million midnights, black, black,
Voyager, wanderer of star worlds,
Off to
          a million tomorrows, black, black,
Seek and find Hiroshima's children,
          Send them back, send them back.
Tear open concrete-sealed cathedrals, spiritually locked,
          Fill vacant theaters with their musty diversions,
          Almost forgotten laughter.

Give us back the twisted sons
Poisoned by mildewed fathers.
Find again the used-up whores,
Dying in some forgotten corner,
Find sunlight, and barking dogs,
For the lost, decayed in sorry jails.
Find pity, find Hell for wax bitches,
Hidden in the bowels of male Cadillacs.
Find tomorrow and nexttime for Negro millionaires
Hopelessly trapped in their luxurious complexions.
Find love, and an everlasting fix for hopeless junkies,
Stealing into lost night, long time.

Voyager now,
            Off to a million midnights, black, black,
Seek and find Hiroshima's children,
            Send them back, send them back.

GINSBERG (for Allen)

Ginsberg won't stop tossing lions to the martyrs.
This ends the campaign by leftwing cardinals to elect
        an Eskimo Pope.
The Church is becoming alarmed by the number of people
        defecting to God.
The Holy Intelligence Agency is puzzled: they have proof
        he is broke and his agents
Use spiritual brainwashing in addition to promises
        of quick sainthood.
The holy stepfather cautioned the faithful to emulate none of
        the saints who hide behind the Fifth Commandment
        when persecuted.
There is also a move to cut off Ginsberg's supply of lions.
The poet continues to smoke carnal knowledge knowingly.
I am sure the government can't prove that he is
        stolen property;
I have proof that he was Gertrude Stein's medicine chest.
I am not not an I, secret wick, I do nothing,
        light myself, burn.

Allen passed through that Black Hole of Calcutta
        behind my eyes;
He was wearing rings and hoops of longitude and latitude.
He must have been hurt by real love, and false love, too.
He can cling and fall and clasp eyes with the best,
Design exciting families with no people in them,
Stuffed with bleeding expressions of human form.
Why I love him, though, is equatorially sound:
I love him because his eyes leak.

HOLLYWOOD

Five square miles of ultra-contemporary nymphomania,
Two dozen homos, to every sapien, at last countdown,
Ugly Plymouths, swapping exhaust with red convertible Buicks,
Twelve-year-old mothers suing for child support,
Secondhand radios making it with wide-screen TV sets,
Unhustling junkies shooting mothball fixes, insect junk,
Unemployed pimps living on neon backs of
Unemployed whores.

Bisexual traffic lights, red-faced, with green shades,
Fastest guns in video West slinging lisps with slowest fairies in ivy East,
Unlit starlets seeking an unfilled galaxy, with an opening,
Ranch Market hipsters who lost their cool in grade school,
Yesterday idols, idle, whose faces were made of clay.

Horrible movie-makers making horrors that move,
Teenage werewolves, hot-rockers, rolling with the blows,
Successful screen writers drinking down unsuccessful screams,
Plastic Beatniks in pubic beards, with artistically dirtied feet,
Recreated Jimmy Deans, sport pompadours, looking for sports car mothers,
Sunset strippers, clothed to the hilt—and no further.

San Francisco poets looking for an out place, looking way out of place,
Televised detectives getting waves from television defectives,
Disc jockeys with all-night shows and all-day habits,
Bored Fords, with nothing in their future but grease jobs,

Hindu holymen with police records clear back to Alabama,
Mondrian-faced drive-ins featuring hamburger-broiled charcoal
Served in laminated fortune cookies.

Channel Something piano players down to their last mom,
Down-at-head pot-smokers with down-at-heel eyes,
Death-faced agents living on ten percent of nothing,
Lady painters with three names having one-man shows of expensive framing,
Unemployed Broadway actors with nothing to offer but talent trying to look stupid,

In-group sick comedians, a lot sicker than their comedy, REAL SICK,
No coast Jazz musicians uncommitted, waiting to be committed,
Scoopy columnists, with two punctuation marks, both periods,
Native-son Woodmen of the West, utterly convinced that Donald Duck is Jewish,
Legions of decency borrowing their decency from the legion,
Impatient Cadillacs trading in their owners for more successful models,
Lanky Calypso singers, caught with their fads down, trapped in beat coffee cups
With small-chested actresses, bosomed out by the big breast scene,
Unsympathetic dope-peddlers, who refuse to honor credit cards,
Carping critics refusing to see what's good, just because it isn't present,
Lonely old De Mille-divorced God, seeking a new producer
With a couple of rebuilt commandments . . .
Hollywood, I salute you, artistic cancer of the universe!

SESSION TONGUES

Lost wax process, ear-wax out using vortex from planetarium so
New kind Greek, written more often than hurricanes, in afternoon,
Put it with the whip, or the fear of something or nothing soon.
Take new glowing onion and replace in ice-cube tray, glowing too,
Melt in sun at one million degrees and shape into fish, glowing
In radiation seas and strange unnoticed sensation, death.

MINGUS

String-chewing bass players,
Plucking rolled balls of sound
From the jazz-scented night.

Feeding hungry beat seekers
Finger-shaped heartbeats,
Driving ivory nails
Into their greedy eyes.

Smoke crystals, from the nostrils
Of released jazz demons,
Crash from foggy yesterday
To the light
Of imaginary night.

I, TOO, KNOW WHAT I AM NOT

No, I am not death wishes of sacred rapists, singing
          on candy gallows.
No, I am not spoor of Creole murderers hiding
          in crepe-paper bayous.
No, I am not yells of some assassinated inventor, locked
          in his burning machine.
No, I am not forced breathing of Cairo's senile burglar,
          in lead shoes.
No, I am not Indian-summer fruit of Negro piano tuners,
          with muslin gloves.
No, I am not noise of two-gun senators, in hallowed
          peppermint hall.
No, I am not pipe-smoke hopes of cynical chiropractors,
          traffickers in illegal bone.
No, I am not pitchblende curse of Indian suicides,
          in bonnets of flaming water.
No, I am not soap-powder sighs of impotent window washers,
          in pants of air.
No, I am not kisses of tubercular sun addicts, smiling
          through rayon lips.

No, I am not chipped philosopher's tattered ideas sunk
          in his granite brain.
No, I am not cry of amethyst heron, winged stone in flight
          from cambric bullets.
No, I am not sting of the neurotic bee, frustrated
          in cheesecloth gardens.
No, I am not peal of muted bell, clapperless
          in the faded glory.
No, I am not report of silenced guns, helpless
          in the pacifist hands.
No, I am not call of wounded hunter, alone
          in the forest of bone.
No, I am not eyes of the infant owls hatching
          the roofless night.
No, I am not the whistle of Havana whores with cribs
          of Cuban death.
No, I am not shriek of Bantu children, bent
          under pennywhistle whips.
No, I am not whisper of the African trees,
          leafy Congo telephones.
No, I am not Leadbelly of blues, escaped from guitar jails.
No, I am not anything that is anything I am not.

HIGH ON LIFE

        Floating on superficially elevated streets
secretly nude,
        Subtle forked tongues of sensuous fog
probe and core
        Deliciously into my chapped-lipped pores
coolly whistling,
        Spiraling in hollowed caves of skin-stretched me,
totally doorless,
        Emptied of vital parts, previously evicted finally
by landlord mind
        To make nerve-lined living space, needed desperately
by my transient, sightless, sleepless,
        Soul.

DOLOROUS ECHO

The holey little holes
In my skin,
Millions of little
Secret graves,
Filled with dead
Feelings
That won't stay
Dead.

The hairy little hairs
On my head,
Millions of little
Secret trees,
Filled with dead
Birds,
That won't stay
Dead.

When I die,
I won't stay
Dead.

SAN FRANCISCO BEAT

Hidden in the eye of jazz,
Secretly balling, against time
I see cabbage eye, malignant successes,
Eating plastic ball-shaped benzedrines,
Hiding in the windows of empty doghouses,
Among limb shops, selling breast,
To rookie policemen.

Jazz cops with ivory nightsticks,
Leaning on the heads of imitation Negroes,
Selling ice cubes to returned virgins,
Wrapping velvet Band-aids, over holes
In the arms of heaven-headed junkies.

Hawkeyed baggy-pants businessmen,
Building earthquake-proof, aluminum whorehouses,
Guaranteeing satisfaction to pinstripe murderers,
Or your money back to West Heaven,
Full of glorious, Caesarean-section politicians,
Giving kisses to round half-lipped babies,
Eating metal jazz, from cavities, in father's chest,
Purchased in flagpole war, to leave balloon-chested
Unfreaked Reader's Digest women grinning at Coit Tower.

Dripping harmless flagellations on the scaly backs
Of graduate celibates selling polka-dot diaphragms
To gay young monsters drowning in flowing gutters
Of timely discussions on telemothervisionfather,
Gradually sucking the heads of littlesmallbig people,
Into cathode obedience, demanding all onions
For one flyspeck of love I keep hidden,
In my webbed feet,
Out of Step.

JAZZ *TE DEUM* FOR INHALING
AT MEXICAN BONFIRES

Let us write reeling sagas about heroic movie stars who failed
        and lived.
Let us poetize on twelve-tone prints of Schoenberg and naked
        office girls.
Let us compose Teutonic folksongs on the death of Israel's
        German tribe.
Let us chant those thousand choruses of Nefertiti's funeral
        and desert grief festivals.
Let us pluck lion-gut strings of marble lutes on teak decks
        of Ming junks.
Let us walk through bloody Florentine gates using secret
        Medici keys.
Let us splash in Persian swimming pools among floating shahs
        and dead concubines.
Let us wear robes of legendary eunuchs for lovemaking
        with lewd statues.

Let us wear flaming hats to Mongol dances on mummified
        khans' sacred Gobi.
Let us smoke petrified bamboo shoots in cool waiting rooms
        of Angkor Wat.
Let us wear suttee memories of Bengal widows on holy
        Ganges' burning ghats.
Let us inhale dreamy eternities from alabaster pipes and sail
        glowing solar boats.
Let us walk naked in radiant glacial rains and cool morphic
        thunderstorms.
Let us shrink into pygmy bo trees and cast holy shadows
        on melted cities.
Let us read forbidden Sanskrit on lotus mounds
        of Buddhist nuns.
Let us imitate Homeric Trojans on sea-girt beds
        of Delphic whorehouses.
Let us sing illegal requiems on execution sabbaths
        of sexy Popes and pray.
Let us wail circumcision Jossanas of lost Samaritans buried
        in rumors of love.
Let us carry Inca staves to hawk-priest rituals on altars
        of bleeding suns.
Let us blow African jazz in Alabama jungles and wail
        savage lovesongs of unchained fire.
Let us melt jelly-like into damp caves of lip-biting women
        and feel dew-charred dampnesses of gyrating
        universes of smoke-flavored jazz.

LADIES

How many ladies in how many paintings
Escaped how many snakes?

How many snakes in how many paintings
Escaped how many ladies?

Every lady escaped, but one.
Not one goddam snake ever escaped.

It's a hell of a lot safer
To be a lady
Than a snake.

SONG OF THE BROKEN GIRAFFE

I have heard the song of the broken giraffe, and sung it . . . .
The frozen sun has browned me to a rumor and slanted my navel.
I have consorted with vulgar crocodiles on banks of lewd rivers.
Yes, it is true, God has become mad, from centuries of frustration.
When I think of all the girls I never made love to, I am shocked.
Every time they elect me President, I hide in the bathroom.
When you come, bring me a tourniquet for our wounded moon.
In an emergency, I can rearrange your beautiful wreckage
With broken giraffe demolitions and lovely colorless explosions.
Come, you sex Ferris wheel, ignore my illustrated bathing suit.
Don't laugh at my ignorance, I may be a great bullfighter, olé!
I wanted to compose a great mass, but I couldn't kneel properly.
Yes, they did tempt me with airplanes, but I wouldn't bite, no sir-ee.
Unable to avoid hospitals, I still refused to become a doctor.
They continued to throw reason, but I failed in the clutch again.
It's true, I no longer use my family as a frame of reference.
The clothing they gave me was smart but no good for train wrecks.
I continued to love despite all the traffic-light difficulties.
In most cases, a sane hermit will beat a good big man.
We waited in vain for the forest fire, but the bus was late.
All night we baked the government into a big mud pie.
Not one century passed without Shakespeare calling us dirty names.
With all those syllables, we couldn't write a cheerful death notice.
The man said we could have a birthday party if we surrendered.
Their soldiers refused to wear evening gowns on guard duty.
Those men in the basement are former breakfast-food salesmen.
We had a choice of fantasies, but naturally we were greedy.
If they leave me alone, I will become a fallen-leaf tycoon.
Maybe Peter Rabbit will forgive us our trespasses; one never knows.
At the moment of truth we were dancing a minuet and missed out.
After the nuns went home, the Pope threw a big masquerade ball.
When the hemlock turned rancid, I returned the cup at once, yes sir-ee.

Hurry, the barometer's falling; bring a storm before it's too late.
We shall reserve evenings for murder or television, whichever is convenient.
Yes, beyond a shadow of a doubt, Rumpelstiltskin was emotionally disturbed.

VOYAGERS

Black leather angels of
Pop-bopping stallions searching
In the corners of peace
For violence
That exists
Deep in their
Own sexless breasts,
Creeping away into highway dark,
To find spark-born oblivion
Among the debris of wrecked motorcycles,
Strips of torn metal eagles
Hanging from frames,
Of good-life daddies, transporting
Children's remains
To worn out art corners,
Concealed among the announcements
Of poetry sessions,
Filtering through jazz readings,
Seeking a lost intestine,
Removed by
Good daddy doctor
That day they were
Paroled from their
Mama's belly.
Death's billboard painters
Making gigantic caricatures
Of life,
Minute sounds of belching,
In the backyards of silence,
Betrayed into shouting,
Spotlighting their hiding places,
Revealing cherished murders

To uncaring nonchalant policemen,
Too busy birdwatching
Square of concrete
To notice the public bleedings
On four o'clock streetcorners.
Flowing on the shadow-tread streets,
In shoulder-bumping walktime,
The garrulous street lamps
Report rattlings to each other's
Splintered-wood poems,
Printed on the lost noise
Of dead traffic.
The aging forest is burning itself,
Phoenixlike reborn,
The bush and trees of glass
Silhouette crisply burning stars,
The green glass body
Of phantom women,
Composed of airs of night,
Presses me deeply, crying
Between ruby-quartz thighs,
Neon sperm glows
At the tip,
My poem
Spurting at the thrust
Into tomorrow.

II

Twice-maimed shrews, ailing
In elongated slots
Of pubic splendor
Engulfed by luxurious dogs,
Sniffing curiously,
Among alcohol asylums,
Populated by oversexed
Poverty-stricken brainstorms,
Puberty-stunned explosions
Raging in and out of insane comas,
Spouting word fountains

At the shriveled mouths
Of wildly depraved roses
As Cassandra dances
On the singed eyelids
Of sleepless ants.

Flapping plaid tongues poked
From dying normality faces
Poised to scoop out the
Dirt-filled navels
Of whores and poets
Concealed inside unexploded bodies
Of defective firecrackers, dreaming
Secretly of blowing up
In the face of Time.

III

Be aware of being aware, of been aware,
Of the day the sky cracked up, raining private rain
Inside the heads of circling cats, snapping
Brittle vertebrae, kicking the reality drag.

God, you are
A big black pot
Full of torn handkerchiefs
Mixed with secondhand
Definitions.

IV

Muted explosions in unbowed plastic heads
Of psychotic chessmen illuminate illusions
Held by faint flowing hands, holding
Cut-glass bowls of trapped eyes,
Sprawled among wispy pot-smoke ceilings
Of superimposed accusations;
Punctuated by hooked coughing
Of watery clowns, consecrated idiots,
Sleepy-eyed Christ, aborted Marys.

V

Cynical jazz, blasted from neon intestines,
Electrically had by departed saxophone maniacs,
Noisy artfully contrived screams,
Presenceless souls, trapped
On thin anonymous discs of eroded wax,
Continuous shrieks spearing through
Marbleskin earshaped antennae
Of aesthetic-soaked pincushions,
Springfoot leapers, frozen in flight,
Clinging to shallow bowled spoons,
Twisting in desperately clawed caves
Holding pinkish moisture, dripped
By parched secret needle-sucking mouths
Brooding on stoned cliffs of tarnished arms.
Overlooking underlooking innerlooking
Hysterically conceived combinations,
Of eyes and mother genitals,
Auto-sculpted into ecstatic images
Of long-loved cherished pain.
Digging among reddened lipstained cups,
Of leftover sadness,
Hopelessly hoping hopefully
To find love
Of a dead moon
Or a poem.

WOULD YOU WEAR MY EYES?

My body is a torn mattress,
Disheveled throbbing place
For the comings and goings
Of loveless transients.
The whole of me
Is an unfurnished room
Filled with dank breath
Escaping in gasps to nowhere.

Before completely objective mirrors
I have shot myself with my eyes,
But death refused my advances.
I have walked on my walls each night
Through strange landscapes in my head.
I have brushed my teeth with orange peel,
Iced with cold blood from the dripping faucets.
My face is covered with maps of dead nations;
My hair is littered with drying ragweed.
Bitter raisins drip haphazardly from my nostrils
While schools of glowing minnows swim from my mouth.
The nipples of my breasts are sun-browned cockleburrs;
Long-forgotten Indian tribes fight battles on my chest
Unaware of the sunken ships rotting in my stomach.
My legs are charred remains of burned cypress trees;
My feet are covered with moss from bayous, flowing across my floor.
I can't go out anymore.
I shall sit on my ceiling.
Would you wear my eyes?

MATRICULATION

Big naked professors, standing out in the cold, weary
(that whip festival brings it out, the young more so).

Last year's cotillion instructors with blackjacks and cookies
(refreshments are important when things are slow, you know).

Brawny swimming instructors quivering on canvas life-saving stretchers
(protection of the young is the duty of every orgy-master).

Kilted piano players playing suggestive minuets on gaily decorated triangles
(the music should build to the climax then explode like overloaded creampuffs).

Skinny porters dusting off the heaving bodies with velvet cactus leaves
(the period just after fertilization is important to the victim's future).

SULLEN BAKERIES OF TOTAL RECALL

Sometimes I feel the ones who escaped the ovens where
       Germans shall forever cook their spiritual meals are
       leaning against my eyes.

A wounded margolis in his suit of horror, his eyes of elevated
       Brownsville, that taste of gas in his smile, I could hear
       it when my ears were Mexican weed.

My first reaction is to be angry with Moses for not commit-
       ting suicide; my second reaction is to be furious with
       the Germans for not committing suicide; my third
       reaction is one of total disappointment for not commit-
       ting suicide. I think of Chaplin and roll a mental
       cigarette. I slowly remove my bayonet, write a poem
       about a poetic poem, dedicated to the Aleutian Islands.

The bony oboe doorway beyond the burning nose translates
       me into Hebrew. I know that Faust was actually anti-
       symbolic and would never have married Kate Smith.

And how many Ophelias escaped from Ruth's letter? Are
       teenage cancellations out? . . . Here, here's my brain
       receipt, take my skin check, I want Juliet on the hoof.
       Because of what happened, sex is holy by virtue of
       arithmetic and welcome dampness.

Someone hurled an eyelid at the moon . . . My shadow
       wanders off, lost in the black sidestreets, vulnerable to the
       cooling soft switchblade of light blinking: DON'T WALK.
       . . . Green . . . My footsteps follow me at a distance.

I acknowledge the demands of Surrealist realization. I chal-
       lenge Apollinaire to stagger drunk from his grave and
       write a poem about the Rosenbergs' last days in a
       housing project, how Salvador Agron spread his cape
       for one last snapshot of Jesus speeding through Puerto
       Rico, his car radio blasting, mowing down the tilting
       Hiltons, speeding to the voltage mass of St. Sing Sing,

the famous gothic burning ghats on the banks of the
sacred Hudson . . . And yet when I think of those
ovens, I turn my head in any other direction.

I am doing my best to dry my mind. The brain's a bully.
I go to hospitals named after sadists with diseases that
don't exist and demand famous operations that Dr.
Schweitzer hasn't invented yet; they give me drugs
while I wait for Albert to emerge from the jungle: his
wise organ music may remove this malingering sensi-
tivity before it infects my other organs.

The rabbi across the table from me is also a firm believer in
suicide. He wanted to be an actor on Second Avenue
and eat dinner across from the theater and be insecure
and marry an Adler and talk about Peretz and
Aleichem and Secunda, and wake up to find himself
with an important role in an established theater. He
is holy and eats very little and reads like a scholar and
wants to kill himself. I refuse to tell him the time. If
necessary, I will write the script and we will go
together.

A REMEMBERED BEAT

We heard our beat faintly then,
When John Hoffman hitchhiked with enemy gods
And died in Mexicans' land,
Choked on his dreams of blood and love,
Leaving his poems on dark other side of time,
And first slight hint of a beat.

When Parker, a poet in jazz,
Gave one hundred seventy pounds to a one-ounce needle,
His music, his life,
Six hipsters from uptown
Called it a religious sacrifice
And wore turbans.
Our poet wore lonely death,
Leaving his breath in a beat.

We remember when Max Bodenheim remembered Lorca
And challenged death nightly, with a port pint
Full of mixed-up crazy love and thirty years' bitter
Memory in poet life,
Only to end as hero of a slaughter poem
Written by a maniac, on a Third Avenue night of hell,
And we were there, lost in the sound of a beat.

We remember thin cafeteria Sanskrit scholars
Reading old telephone directories aloud,
Trying to find Buddha or Truth
Among columns of private detectives, private sanitariums
And committees for rehabilitation of bisexual Eskimos,
And the unlisted trace of a beat.

We remember when poets removed tangled brains
To save for a saner time,
When organization men in pink ties declared television love,
Opening the age of electrical stone
As all do-gooders shouted: Punch time clocks,
Or your neighbors, or your youngest boy,
While a warload of young poets
Perished in Pusan's swamp,
Drowned in a flood of matchbook covers from home.
Survivors hid themselves in the folds of a cocaine
        nighttime robe,
As pill time stretched across white powdered deserts
And roots of exotic cactus bloomed in caves of the mind,
As nirvana came dancing, prancing in time to the beat,
Leading new ways through friend-filled narcotic graveyards
To hidden Pacific, big hell, quiet peace of Big Sur
Where that proud pornographer smiles on a redwood throne
As birds pound the air with a beat.

PATRIOTIC ODE ON THE FOURTEENTH ANNIVERSARY OF THE PERSECUTION OF CHARLIE CHAPLIN

Come on out of there with your hands up, Chaplin,
In your Sitting Bull suit, with your amazing new Presto Lighter.
We caught you. We found your fingerprints on the World's Fair.
Give us back the money and start over as a cowboy.
Come on, Chaplin, we mean business.

CAMUS: I WANT TO KNOW

Camus, I want to know, does the cold knife of wind plunge
        noiselessly into the soul, finally

Camus, I want to know, does the seated death wing as
        sudden, swifter than leaden Fascist bullets . . .

Camus, sand-faced rebel from Olympus, brain lit, shining
        cleanly, on far historical peaks . . .

Camus, I want to know, does the jagged fender resemble
        Franco, standing spiked at Madrid's Goyaesque
        wound

Camus, I want to know, the dull aesthetics, rubbery thump of
        exploding wheels, the tick-pock of dust on steel

Camus, I want to know, does it clackety clack like that destiny
        train, shrieking to the Finland station

Camus, I want to know, does the sorrowful cry of unwilling
        companions console the dying air . . .

Camus, I want to know, does the cry of protested death sing,
        like binding vow of lovers' nod

Camus, I want to know, does the bitter taste of jagged glass
        sweeten the ripped tongue, dried

Camus, I want to know, does the sour taste of unfulfilled
　　　　promise flee the dying mouth and eyes and lips

Camus, I want to know, does the liberated blood bubble hotly
　　　　to the soil, microscopic Red Seas

Camus, I want to know, does the cyclop headlight illuminate
　　　　nerve-lined pits of final desires

Camus, I want to know, does the secret hoard of unanswered
　　　　queries scream for ultimate solutions

Camus, I want to know, does the eye of time blink in antici-
　　　　pation of recaptured seasons enriched

Camus, I want to know, does the sliver of quartz sensoulize
　　　　the clash of flesh on chrome and bone

Camus, I want to know, does the piercing spear of death
　　　　imitate denied desire, internal crucifixion

Camus, I want to know, does the spiritual juice flee as slowly,
　　　　as the Saharablood of prophets' sons

Camus, I want to know, does it mirror the Arab virgin, her
　　　　sex impaled on some soldier's wine bottle

Camus, I shall follow you over itching floors of black deserts,
　　　　across roofs of burning palms . . .

Camus, I shall crawl on sandpaper knees on oasis bottoms of
　　　　secret Bedouin wells, cursing . . .

Camus, I shall reach the hot sky, my brown mouth filled with
　　　　fragile telephones, sans rings . . .

Camus, I shall mumble long-cherished gibberish through
　　　　layers of protesting heat, demanding . . .

Camus, I shall scream but one awesome question, does *death
exist? Camus, I want to know* . . .

TO MY SON PARKER, ASLEEP IN THE NEXT ROOM

On ochre walls in ice-formed caves shaggy Neanderthals
        marked their place in time.
On germinal trees in equatorial stands embryonic giants
        carved beginnings.
On Tasmanian flatlands mud-clothed first men hacked rock,
        still soft.
On Melanesian mountain peaks barked heads were reared
        in pride and beauty.
On steamy Java's cooling lava stooped humans raised stones
        to altar height.
On newborn China's plain mythless sons of Han acquired
        peaked gods with teak faces.
On holy India's sacred soil future gods carved worshipped
        reflections.
On Coptic Ethiopia's pimple rock pyramid builders tore
        volcanoes from earth.
On death-loving Egypt's godly sands living sacrifices carved
        naked power.
On Sumeria's cliffs speechless artists gouged messages
        to men yet uncreated.
On glorious Assyria's earthen dens art priests chipped
        figures of awe and hidden dimensions.
On splendored Peru's gold-stained body filigreed temples
        were torn from severed hands.
On perfect Greece's bloody sites marble stirred
        under hands of men.
On degenerate Rome's trembling sod imitators sculpted lies
        into beauty.
On slave Europe's prostrate form chained souls shaped free
        men.
On wild America's green torso original men painted
        glacial languages.
On cold Arctica's snowy surface leathery men raised totems
        in frozen air.
On this shore, you are all men, before, forever, eternally
        free in all things.
On this shore, we shall raise our monuments of stones,
        of wood, of mud, of color, of labor, of belief, of being,
        of life, of love, of sinews, of memories, of mind, of soul,
        of self, of man, expressed in self-determined compliance,

or willful revolt, secure in this avowed truth,
that no man is our master,
nor can any ever be, at any time in time to come.

CINCOPHRENICPOET

A cincophrenic poet called
a meeting of all five of
him at which four of the
most powerful of him voted
to expel the weakest of him
who didn't dig it, coughing
poetry for revenge, beseech-
ing all horizontal reserves
to cross, spiral, and whirl.

TEEVEE PEOPLE

Assuming the posture of frogs, croaking at appointed times,
Loudly treading the plastic floors of copied temples,
The creeping cardboard creatures, endlessly creeping,
In and out of time, eating the clock by the hour,
Poets of the gray universities in history suits,
Dripping false Greek dirges from tweedy beards,
While all the Troys are consumed in mushroom clouds.

The younger machines occupy miles of dark benches,
Enjoying self-induced vacations of the mind,
Eating textbook rinds, spitting culture seeds,
Dreaming an exotic name to give their latest defeat,
Computing the hours on computer minds.

The cold land breathes death rattles, trembling,
The dark sky casts shadows across the wounds
Beneath the bright clothing of well-fed machines,
The hungry heart inside the hungry hearts,
Beats silently, beats softly, beats, beats.

THE EYES TOO

My eyes too have souls that rage
At the sight of butterflies walking,
At the crime of a ship cutting an ocean in two,
At visions of girls who should be naked
Sitting at lunch counters eyeballing newspapers,
At complacent faces of staring clocks
Objectively canceling lives
With ticks.

THE DAY AFTER

Was the day six Hindu holymen
        tore up their sweepstakes tickets.

Was the day six movie stars
        removed their freak suits, disappeared.

Was the day six senile generals
        removed their prostates, reappeared.

Was the day six juvenile delinquents
        removed their brass knuckles, masturbated.

Was the day six shells of burned-out bodies of Hiroshima's
        children crawled across petrified oceans,
        dragging crates of burning philosophies
          over indignant civilized mountain ranges,
        weaved caterpillary among deserted Vaticans,
        paused to take pictures of hollow White Houses,
          wakened sleeping Zhivagos in silent Kremlins.

Was the day six sharkskin-suited oracles
        caused six certified public accountants
          to decide for Christ at the boxing arena.

WAR MEMOIR

Jazz—listen to it at your own risk.
At the beginning, a warm dark place.

(Her screams were trumpet laughter,
Not quite blues, but almost sinful.)

Crying above the pain, we forgave ourselves;
Original sin seemed a broken record.
God played blues to kill time, all the time.
Red-waved rivers floated us into life.

(So much laughter, concealed by blood and faith;
Life is a saxophone played by death.)

Greedy to please, we learned to cry;
Hungry to live, we learned to die.
The heart is a sad musician,
Forever playing the blues.

The blues blow life, as life blows fright;
Death begins, jazz blows soft in the night,
Too soft for ears of men whose minds
Hear only the sound of death, of war,
Of flagwrapped cremation in bitter lands.

No chords of jazz as mud is shoveled
Into the mouths of men; even the blues shy
At cries of children dying on deserted corners.
Jazz deserted, leaving us to our burning.

(Jazz is an African traitor.)

What one-hundred-percent redblooded savage
Wastes precious time listening to jazz
With so much important killing to do?

Silence the drums, that we may hear the burning
Of Japanese in atomic colorcinemascope,
And remember the stereophonic screaming.

MY PRECHANTEUR

In the night he comes, my prechanteur,
Singing the silent songs, enchanting songs
Of purple forest, orange woods
Where yellow flower loves yellow flower,
Green limbs budding, twice yellow
Of ebony maidens with happy eyes
In orange garments, noses that twitch
Singing songs of secret love
In dark sunless places
Illuminated only by the light
Of looks in lovers' eyes,
Witnessed only by silent animals . . .
I awake, yearning, grasping.
He is gone, my prechanteur.

PERHAPS

Should I sing a requiem, as the trap closes?
Perhaps it is more fitting to shout nonsense.

Should I run to the streets, screaming lovesongs?
Perhaps it is more consistent to honk obscenities.

Should I chew my fingernails down to my wrist?
Perhaps it is better to blow eternal jazz.

Maybe I will fold the wind into neat squares.

RESPONSE

for Eileen

Sleep, little one, sleep for me,
Sleep the deep sleep of love.
You are loved, awake or dreaming,
You are loved.

Dancing winds will sing for you,
Ancient gods will pray for you,
A poor lost poet will love you,
As stars appear
In the dark
Skies.

WHO HAS SEEN THE WIND?

A Spanish sculptor named Chirino
Has seen the wind.
He says it is shaped like a coil of hardened copper
And spirals into itself and out again,
That it is very heavy
And can break your toe if it falls on your foot.
Be careful when you are moving the wind,
It can put you in the hospital!

FORGET TO NOT

Remember, poet, while gallivanting across the sky,
Skylarking, shouting, calling names . . . Walk softly.

Your footprint on rain clouds is visible to naked eyes,
Lamps barnacled to your feet refract the mirrored air.

Exotic scents of your hidden vision fly in the face of time.

Remember not to forget the dying colors of yesterday
As you inhale tomorrow's hot dream, blown from frozen lips.

Remember, you naked agent of every nothing.

JAIL POEMS

1

I am sitting in a cell with a view of evil parallels,
Waiting thunder to splinter me into a thousand me's.
It is not enough to be in one cage with one self;
I want to sit opposite every prisoner in every hole.
Doors roll and bang, every slam a finality, bang!
The junkie disappeared into a red noise, stoning out his hell.
The odored wino congratulates himself on not smoking,
Fingerprints left lying on black inky gravestones,
Noises of pain seeping through steel walls crashing
Reach my own hurt. I become part of someone forever.
Wild accents of criminals are sweeter to me than hum of cops,
Busy battening down hatches of human souls; cargo
Destined for ports of accusations, harbors of guilt.
What do policemen eat, Socrates, still prisoner, old one?

2

Painter, paint me a jail, mad water-color cells.
Poet, how old is suffering? Write it in yellow lead.
God, make me a sky on my glass ceiling. I need stars now,
To lead through this atmosphere of shrieks and private hells,

Entrances and exits, in . . . out . . . up . . . down, the civic seesaw.
Here—me—now—hear—me—now—always here somehow.

3

In a universe of cells—who is not in jail? Jailers.
In a world of hospitals—who is not sick? Doctors.
A golden sardine is swimming in my head.
Oh we know some things, man, about some things
Like jazz and jails and God.
Saturday is a good day to go to jail.

4

Now they give a new form, quivering jelly-like,
That proves any boy can be president of Muscatel.
They are mad at him because he's one of Them.
Gray-speckled unplanned nakedness; stinking
Fingers grasping toilet bowl. Mr. America wants to bathe.
Look! On the floor, lying across America's face—
A real movie star featured in a million newsreels.
What am I doing—feeling compassion?
When he comes out of it, he will help kill me.
He probably hates living.

5

Nuts, skin bolts, clanking in his stomach, scrambled.
His society's gone to pieces in his belly, bloated.
See the great American windmill, tilting at itself,
Good solid stock, the kind that made America drunk.
Success written all over his street-streaked ass.
Successful-type success, forty home runs in one inning.
Stop suffering, Jack, you can't fool us. We know.
This is the greatest country in the world, ain't it?
He didn't make it. Wino in Cell 3.

6

There have been too many years in this short span of mine.
My soul demands a cave of its own, like the Jain god;
Yet I must make it go on, hard like jazz, glowing

In this dark plastic jungle, land of long night, chilled.
My navel is a button to push when I want inside out.
Am I not more than a mass of entrails and rough tissue?
Must I break my bones? Drink my wine-diluted blood?
Should I dredge old sadness from my chest?
Not again,
All those ancient balls of fire, hotly swallowed, let them lie.
Let me spit breath mists of introspection, bits of me,
So that when I am gone, I shall be in the air.

7

Someone whom I am is no one.
Something I have done is nothing.
Someplace I have been is nowhere.
I am not me.
What of the answers
I must find questions for?
All these strange streets
I must find cities for,
Thank God for Beatniks.

8

All night the stink of rotting people,
Fumes rising from pyres of live men,
Fill my nose with gassy disgust,
Drown my exposed eyes in tears.

9

Traveling God salesmen, bursting my ear drum
With the dullest part of a good sexy book,
Impatient for Monday and adding machines.

10

Yellow-eyed dogs whistling in evening.

11

The baby came to jail today.

12

One more day to Hell, filled with floating glands.

13

The jail, a huge hollow metal cube
Hanging from the moon by a silver chain.
Someday Johnny Appleseed is going to chop it down.

14

One day Adolf Hitler had nothing to do.
All the Jews were burned, artists all destroyed,
Adolf Hitler was very bored, even with Eva,
So he moved to San Francisco, became an ordinary
Policeman, devoted himself to stamping out Beatniks.

15

Three long strings of light
Braided into a ray.

16

I am apprehensive about my future;
My past has turned its back on me.

17

Shadows I see, forming on the wall,
Pictures of desires protected from my own eyes.

18

After spending all night constructing a dream,
Morning came and blinded me with light.
Now I seek among mountains of crushed eggshells
For the God damned dream I never wanted.

19

Sitting here writing things on paper,
Instead of sticking the pencil into the air.

20

The Battle of Monumental Failures raging,
Both hoping for a good clean loss.

21

Now I see the night, silently overwhelming day.

22

Caught in imaginary webs of conscience,
I weep over my acts, yet believe.

23

Cities should be built on one side of the street.

24

People who can't cast shadows
Never die of freckles.

25

The end always comes last.

26

We sat at a corner table,
Devouring each other word by word,
Until nothing was left, repulsive skeletons.

27

I sit here writing, not daring to stop,
For fear of seeing what's outside my head.

28

There, Jesus, didn't hurt a bit, did it?

29

I am afraid to follow my flesh over those narrow
Wide hard, soft, female beds, but I do.

30

Link by link, we forged the chain.
Then, discovering the end around our necks,
We bugged out.

31

I have never seen a wild poetic loaf of bread,
But if I did, I would eat it, crust and all.

32

From how many years away does a baby come?

33

Universality, duality, totality . . . one.

34

The defective on the floor, mumbling,
Was once a man who shouted across tables.

35

Come, help flatten a raindrop.

Written in San Francisco City Jail
Cell 3, 1959

IMAGE OF WIND

At first extra shadows seemed optical illusions,
Often used to play strange mathematical games.
Self-repeating shadows can be disconcerting to one
Accustomed to creating only one; real madness came
That day shadows began to cast people everywhere.

Only the facelessness of those people, shadow formed,
Made possible the identification most people needed
To prove to themselves that they were themselves, or
At least place themselves among those who counted,
Those who were more than just some shadow's ego, printed.

The fish played games with bows of ships,
As fishermen wove themselves into nets.

Frustrated winds bounced off brick-faced towers,
Whistling over jazzy sobbing in desperate night clubs.

Sometimes, when the wind is blowing in my hair,
I cry, because its coolness is too beautiful.

But usually, I know that rain falls anyway,
Leaving only mud puddles
To catch dead leaves as they fall.
Leaves always fall.
There is nothing to say:
The wind is in charge of lives
Tonight.

SECOND APRIL

*"Be ye not conformed to this world: but be ye transformed by
the renewing of your mind." Romans 12*

O man in inner basement core of me, maroon obliteration smelling
futures of green anticipated comings, pasts denied, now time to thwart
time, time to frieze illusionary motion on far imagined walls, stopped
bleeding moondial clocks, booming out dead hours—gone . . . gone
. . . gone . . . gone . . . on to second April, ash-smeared crowns, perfect,
conically balanced, pyramid-peaked heads, shuddering, beamed on
lead-held cylinders—on granite-flowered windows, on frigid triumphs,
unmolded of shapes, assumed aspects, transparent lizards, shattered
glaciers, infant mountains, formed once, all time given to disappearance,
speculation, investigation of holes, rocks, caught freaks, in skin sandals,
ten million light years dripped screaming, hot dust rotted eyes, ages in
clawing eyes, insanities packed in century-long nights, pointed time-
ward to now. Hollow out trees, release captive satans, explode roses,
sentence grass to death, stab rivers, rage down insane clouds, unchain
snowy lamaistic peaks, dehydrate oceans, suck up deserts, nail sky to
scattered earth, in air, we come, to second April.

O man, thee is onion-constructed in hot gabardine, is earth onion,
too, cat, O poet, they watch, man, they eye a thing, from conception,
Neal knew and it cost questioners' lives. The holy man is pimpy to our
whore, out of America by God, stunned stallion, he, with Einstein on
carbuncled feet, is it stopped, illusionary motion, do we go on, they
watch last night's angels aborted, the sky shot up, death packed up her
old kit bag, they watch, man, everything is even now, the president has
translucent worms in his brain, Sappho, rolling drunks in coffee galler-
ies, cock robin is posthumously guilty, chicken little was right all along,
Vachel's basic savages drive Buicks now, God is a parking meter . . .

Session zero in, is diluted, they watch, diluted that's a thing, we have not
now or ever been a member of diluted, the spoon is a cop, the door is
closed, I hope Rimbaud bleeds all over my stolen pants, pants, that's a
thing, they watch . . . two on four, the ration, now and . . . ever, Dylan
had quadruple nuns, white stainless steel walls, moving out like an

ordinary Puerto Rican, full of love and death, trapped in modern icons, forgetting to rage, as his day died, prosaic night fell, like it always does, they watch, we hide, sneak, make mad in corners, corners, that's a thing, a thing world watches things, world, that's a thing, my negro suit has jew stripes, my yarmulke was lost in a flash flood while i mattered with navajos about peyote.

Session double zero is bare floors, cannery row darkness. San Juan bare whores in young-boy brilliance, discovering balls in sources of pee . . . fried stink was lunch under the bed as the thick-wristed sailor projected Anglo-ness on Maria's wrinkled heaven, I read Sade . . . against the under of the mattress, a thing, that's a thing, they watch, tonight death is blonde, we are bending ice cubes, cubes, that's a thing, cubes, Mondrian dug, they killed him in California, injected natural wood settings and cal tech . . . Modigliani spurting . . . Naked Marys, fucking me out of my mind in triple quarter tones, on my wall sideways . . . a thing they watch, they know we break out, my bending night is ending, one second is value enough, I am forever busted.

Session last zero before one . . . is tin foil, super modern fiddlesticks, they watch, looking for things, I got mine at a one cent sale, I was Mickey Finned with striped tooth paste, caught freak in twisted skin and sandals, covered with angry dust, entrails of lorn . . . women hanging in my alien lips, let me embarrass me, expose self in my self, too cool for the soft blow, hard, not hard enough, they watch, dense bartenders with godhead in legal bodies, they watch, not seeing us in bubblegum wrappers, in hands of future monsters, future, that's a thing, future men with three penises seducing future women with vaginas in their armpits, future children with lavender eyes between their toes, wiping crazy fallout from the ass on their future skulls, a thing, future.

Session golden horn before one . . . is Bayou St. John, Big Sur pornography dipped in, emptied . . . a thing, dipped, dipped in poems, the black child glistened in self-conceived madness . . . dipped in contemporary multiplied generations, played musical electric chairs, dipped in in-jazz the Kansas City maniac found world three, Zulu laughter, good old Fourth of July American heroin, Sumeria, Picasso modern limericks, madness, final mausoleums . . . ah . . . leu . . . cha . . . the time is now . . . is a thing, time is . . . they watch . . .

Session zero before green . . . is head of cows in Montana, Indians push-
ing history on freeways, look out for green, they watch, hidden match-
book covers, secret chronicles of our time . . . a thing, time, pasted on
roof of mouth, time uses needles, hooked time, booming out orgasmic
time, plastered on cottony mattresses, they watch, small private pelvic
mushrooms.

Session semi-zero before inverted fraction . . . is a five thing and strate-
gic incisions, one-o, two-o, three-o, four-o, five-o snips for veal cutlets,
paper signing papas . . . a thing, O god, let me use your library card, I
want the OxforD BooK oF ModerN JazZ . . . I want Baudelaire's De-
nunciation of Moses, I want Ezra Pound's Life of George Washington,
I want Starkweather's Biography of Billy Graham, let me steal James
Dean's suicide note from the film division, I need the Intelligent Wom-
an's Guide to Mongrelism, I need Greenwich Village Novels to wipe me
with, I need New York Times Index to count the murders, I need to talk
with fly pages, that's a thing now, fly pages . . . o fly, o so higho fly, they
watch, put spaghetti in the octane, the new bomb is clean, thank God
for soaP.

Session quarter zero . . . is tubercular leaves, chipped nose saints, ala-
baster sphinx cats . . . burning warehouses, nonchalant cops, pop-bop-
ping black leather angels, fathered fathers, good daddy doctors . . . a
thing, daddies . . . they watch, belly paroles, bareskin eagles . . . numbers
of highway dark things . . . impersonal billboard watches, strips, cut
quilting blocks, torn gloves, long thin drinks of water in bulging sup-
porters, supporters . . . a thing . . . support march of dollar and a halfs,
support sisterhood of Christian and Bantus, it's a thing, they watch
for things, we sand things, before glassthings . . . soon ash things, later
everything, stupid gums bleed needlessly on hard skin apples, is the old
god lying in the cave, pumping stations never close.

Session eight before nothing . . . is bales of cardinal hats, oversexed
rabbis, used car sex, Boston dreams of cobwebs, sobwebs, Himalayan
streetcar tracks, did the mother die of jazz . . . they . . . watch . . . of is
thing, it's all of, pockets full of light years on strange borders, recording
enterings and leaving, hung things, zentree mess of whoring through
tree branches . . . unforgotten bites, mouths full of longhair, wait, don't
break the corduroy, but look out for green, glue the limb first, she too
old to lay on cold, use ladders, take bottle caps, bathing caps and caps of
Caribe waves and when the Fall came, everybody fucked his girl.

Session nothing before nothing . . . is red, look out for green, Dante's blanket too, a thing, lilies burn crisply on green screaming mornings, dogs licking backs of necks, fountains full of sacramental wind and Yom Kippur Good Friday drinking in wet shoes, electric spitballs of lying, Roman night of baby boy dreams, musclebound streets, all our eye, things corkscrewing raindrop pressures, sacrificed goats, queer witch doctors, inventions, frosty gray pocket of peace, linen courtyard of up and down skin piling into cores of new earths, bitch bites and fingernail communiques, God calling and ceiling guffaws, pushed back clots of un-formed nothing, needle me dragged into illusion, God make me a tree.

Session nothing . . . is drunken funerals, pubic breakfasts, football play-er sex in Saturday milk bottles, flight and attempt to raid marble quarry, stone and, on with gold fillings, lost forever in shriveled nipple hyster-ically conceived combination of fingershaped genitals, auto-sculpted explosions of images of explosions exploded.

Session one . . . is hospitalgram, in-group shrieks, narcocomalts, ripped lung leaking coughed air, banana peels, sad significances, unknown fuckers, curly teeth, tea-angry gums holding defeated teeth, fingers holding hands, feet-shaped organs, turning against, inside. Terror-love, falling ceilings, and me you falling too, between legs, arms, members, we are each other's members.

Session two . . . is finally escaped dreams, they watch now, day over night into day—only nuns at night, and light itself is satire time, Tues-day wants out, chickened night, for day, one day this week, no, Jack Karowack, don't break into Mill Valley jails with your shoes on, walls rain all time, but, comic it, baby—love—cool new Indian corn every winter is our lot, and lockos, damn, wham, bamm, cool.

Session three . . . is crazy machine broken, darts not arrived yet, so love, no empty thick concave bottles sing tonight, shadows come too, in new faces, gassed cracked glasses crack, no break, wiser grown kneecaps, third eye remains basic, two birds cheated, punishment until new bath-room arrives, grass will stay, Africa-faced and new mud on the bed-o.

Session four . . . is poor busted Santa Claus, back to hot toys again. They watch, very red, look out for green, eating going on despite no food, facial limp coming back, independent lips, new thing, they watch, ones with babes, boring in judging Colas—screams are rattles to dogs, tears real popular, broken legs have new meaning too—cane on floor, cracking under footprint, horn slurring. Commemorate, question eye-witness pavement, coming is an event, stinging continues.

Session five . . . is in getting out, four times is five, we hope not . . . psychodramatics of long thin stuff calling caterwauling, hoarse whistles in deepness of breathy ears, tonguing old children, flood survivors, deep in jungles, elevating up in flood reactions and objectively conceived esteem, caution, too, is new thing, they watch one with babes, boring in judging is tomorrow . . . more of more is now good, yesterday is tomorrow, thin circles over eyes, trust no longer trusts us, paper is now thick and assy like brown, wrong is good is sad is glad is mad.

Session six . . . is cancered doctors, rejected volunteers, too young, two lungs, too far away for searching, eyes ransacked first, naturalized afterbirths, no problems, fear blows too, strips of mother hate, we get in tonight, problem out now, silver is not spoons only, dress event now, god getting married, funny fun in cassocks, and hoods too, spitballs spiked on ribs are attractive abstracts eating poets, they watch, God eats crying, smooth nine month grave faces, bent, me, you, man, thirsting.

Session seven . . . they watch, we shout, they catch, pushing, bluing, swinging, digging, He won't say, they wash windows, we break them and windows breaking us, fresh lobes to come drunker, they watch, look out for green, we drink drunker fumes, look out for green, smoke god damn soppy wet on the floor toilet paper.

Session eight . . . is Hindu baby in tiger suit, they don't know, see draggy khaki, folded three inside canvas, three pounds of color, three toes flattened, that's a thing now, numbers . . . five cheats, three's goo-o, eight cannot be trusted, ten's the queer count, colors, all. They see . . . numbers, we party, leader died, we commemorate, new on old they see us, multiplication, that's a thing, we be three free, see, be, they see our stained noses, we count up doubled-up hairs, folding near middle, they confer, locking us in our noses, we smuggle, giggle . . . struggle, they guard, they guard God, throwing strips of foreskin, that's a thing, t.b., t.v., t.d., v.d., p.d. . . . . cowboy boots, big busses, signs oleomarginality, stereoriginality . . . hi-finalities, they can't fall us, already we in blank a book, crank a crook, indeed do a deed, turning a key, door faced, mous-ing in, we stay, they manage, we brain out.

Session nine . . . they watch outside suicide, death you is our woman now, look out for green . . . that's a thing, they watch things, reports we can't smash wheat, they make bread, stale crusty bitey bread, we cause, they catch, the bridge, they don't see it, hidden in magazines . . . concealed in blendozines, bleedozines, kilograms, echopium, good, good fish, crocker-faced . . . look out for green, catch a color, look out for numbers, they bite numbers, we bite them . . . they question us, we answer them, spit, black, blue, inside a spiral, a whirl, cross around . . . only one conversation, the world ends, the unworld begins, they watch, we urinate, going . . . now the tiptoe we hear, we all rolling, they unfill the pie, fling oatmeal to the air, breakfast is a new thing, he's new, bleeding hand, prints on a white wall, that's a thing.

Session ten . . . burning burns on burned hand, that's a thing, a thing, down to ten thousand wounds . . . they watch, we swap watches, we chew time, they chew us, chewing, that's a thing, a new thing, chewing, everybody chew somebody; everybody chew a dog, cats exempt, numbers too . . . they watch, a dusty window, hell my eyes, bell my tongue, we are attacking our hair, it waves to neighbors in skies, kinky relatives, wrapped in comets, a thing, comets . . . aluminum cheats, deflects, cities deflected, they watch, we cross breed eyelids, gas helps, it gets us, they get us, we get no getting, we erase ourselves, we smear our board, we are gone, they watch, we cook old chaplinesque shoestrings, they watch, we have never, have we, never ever, never.

Session eleven . . . they conceal our eyeteeth in garter belts, we assume presumptions, report proportions, we tear at his wounds, see, the boy bleeds, but look out for green, they watch, we steal a desert, drown a car, kidnap a mountain, anti-social a girl, they watch, we tar roofs to sit under sun on, a thing, suns, the sun is hot blooded, we o, so cold, cold blood monkeys never kill, not even for food, they bred it out, they bread it out, they bread it . . . new catchy tune, love a chunk of bread, love a hunk of bread, love a funk of dead, head . . . o, me, we, they, trapped in a polka dot . . . caught in porcelain pot, clomping on the floor of ice, that's a thing, floors, ground falling out, indoors, we know they watch, look out for green, they pan out, we go to the great rain forest.

Session twelve . . . a mom pop, on the part they don't see, poor pores sucking in bad air . . . a thing, air, the air, distended air, hard air, air of twin birds on looney peaks . . . air too is a thing, not a goose, they watch, funky circuses parading elephants across airy clouds of air, they watch, we take chances, we give chances . . . they watch, we are raffled off, out, a thing, out, close out, far out, in, out and out, and new is out, too, the first father, on the ship, out in air, cheating at cards of air, all we are is, all we are is, air we are in a hole in space, we put it in, they watch . . . we take it out, the taste of dust on breast is odored air on pricking tongues sticking air and mounds of hair stuck on light, grainless blocks of wood, staggering down the night, they watch the air, we disappear, into a quick dab for clean, splintering, too, now.

Session thirteen . . . is a metal thing, foot-stomach thing, bent prong fork, turning up, on, in, they watch metal, pictures of metal, up through lower holes through stratospheric sex, and metallic jazz, but look out for green, a thing, look, they watch, look, look into the face of a road, see brightly striped freaks paved into dividing lines, a thing, lines, they watch lines, long lines of watchers watching lines, they dig straight, they . . . unbended lines sinking to bottom of earth, we printing many suicide notes on moon-shaped traffic lights, they panel room-shaped metal caves with old skin trophies, we wave dramatic underwear from bent flag poles, they watch, build things, inside trees, clean restrooms in pregnant redwood bellies.

Session fourteen . . . is a roach and happy guts, shorn hair of minor criminals, on floors of prefabricated gas chambers, we mad on Aztec planted turnips, read poems off each others' ass by narrow daylight in New Tex hotel rooms, they watch, we unzip fly, why, gasping into our own interiors, hoping to drag air to strange tomb-like bellies . . . they watch tombs, we throw soggy peanut shells under skidding wheels, we witness God's divorce, the bitch leaves, we cry jazz historical tears, they watch, we lock door on bankrupt, God give us new, we ate fire last time, be cool, God.

Session fifteen . . . is explosive drops of water, on masks, on faces, on nothing, sounds of life strangled in our stomachs, whimpering in our heads, dramatic little realities, through stained glass, rouged Virgin Marys signal a left turn on, a thing on is, they watch On, we overwhelm with mad babies raving down slippery parallelic bars, we go to On museum to see ancient Ons, screaming into Ludwig's cupped ear for a well built death mask, or a four bar get high, or a promise of remembrance in sexy cures, they, watch, on corners, in opinionated, finny, gaudy wombs, power driven, they watch, we wrap each fume in separate paper for the trip we are constantly making, Oh, the god bus has a busted wheel, wheel's a thing they watch, whirling wheels, wailing wheels, steel wheels, cardboard wheels, real wheels, they watch, we crazy and go glowing in pointed spinning soft flames, disappearing into heads of candles, they watch.

We watch them going on watching us going on going, wrapped in pink barley leaves, almost, the time is not near, but, nearer we are to time, and time nearer to ticks. Burning in torch surrender to auto-fantasy, we illuminate the hidden December, seen, flamelit in the on core of the second April, come for the skeleton of time.

> Kissed at wintertide, alone in a lemming world,
> Green bitches, harlequin men, shadowed babes,
> Dumped on the galvez greens, burned with grass.

ABOMUNIST MANIFESTO
BY BOMKAUF

ABOMUNIST MANIFESTO

ABOMUNISTS JOIN NOTHING BUT THEIR HAND OR LEGS, OR OTHER SAME.

ABOMUNISTS SPIT ANTI-POETRY FOR POETIC REASONS AND FRINK.

ABOMUNISTS DO NOT LOOK AT PICTURES PAINTED BY PRESIDENTS AND UNEMPLOYED PRIME MINISTERS.

IN TIMES OF NATIONAL PERIL, ABOMUNISTS, AS REALITY AMERICANS, STAND READY TO DRINK THEMSELVES TO DEATH FOR THEIR COUNTRY.

ABOMUNISTS DO NOT FEEL PAIN, NO MATTER HOW MUCH IT HURTS.

ABOMUNISTS DO NOT USE THE WORD SQUARE EXCEPT WHEN TALKING TO SQUARES.

ABOMUNISTS READ NEWSPAPERS ONLY TO ASCERTAIN THEIR ABOMINUBILITY.

ABOMUNISTS NEVER CARRY MORE THAN FIFTY DOLLARS IN DEBTS ON THEM.

ABOMUNISTS BELIEVE THAT THE SOLUTION TO PROBLEMS OF RELIGIOUS BIGOTRY IS, TO HAVE A CATHOLIC CANDIDATE FOR PRESIDENT AND A PROTESTANT CANDIDATE FOR POPE.

ABOMUNISTS DO NOT WRITE FOR MONEY: THEY WRITE THE MONEY ITSELF.

ABOMUNISTS BELIEVE ONLY WHAT THEY DREAM ONLY AFTER
IT COMES TRUE.

ABOMUNIST CHILDREN MUST BE REARED ABOMINUBLY.

ABOMUNIST POETS, CONFIDENT THAT THE NEW LITERARY
FORM "FOOT-PRINTISM" HAS FREED THE ARTIST OF OUT-
MODED RESTRICTIONS, SUCH AS: THE ABILITY TO READ AND
WRITE, OR THE DESIRE TO COMMUNICATE, MUST BE PREPARED
TO READ THEIR WORK AT DENTAL COLLEGES, EMBALMING
SCHOOLS, HOMES FOR UNWED MOTHERS, HOMES FOR WED
MOTHERS, INSANE ASYLUMS, SANE ASYLUMS, U.S.O. CANTEENS,
KINDERGARTENS, AND COUNTY JAILS. ABOMUNISTS NEVER
COMPROMISE THEIR REJECTIONARY PHILOSOPHY.

ABOMUNISTS REJECT EVERYTHING EXCEPT SNOWMEN.

★   Notes Dis- and Re- Garding Abomunism   ★

Abomunism was founded by Barabbas, inspired by his dying
words: "I wanted to be in the middle, But I went too far out."
Abomunism's main function is to unite the soul with oatmeal cookies.
Abomunists love love, hate hate, drink drinks, smoke smokes, live lives,
      die deaths.
Abomunist writers write writing, or nothing at all.
Abomunist poetry, in order to be compleatly (Eng. sp.) understood,
      should be eaten . . . except on fast days, slow days, and mornings of
      executions.
Abomunists, could they be a color, would be green, and tell everyone to go.
Uncrazy Abomunists crazy unAbomunists by proxy kicky tricks, as
follows:
            By telling psychometric poets two heads are better than none.
            By selling middle names to impotent personnel managers.
            By giving children brightly wrapped candy fathers.
            By biting their own hands after feeding themselves.
            By calling taxis dirty names, while ordering fifths of milk.
            By walking across hills, ignoring up and down.
            By giving telescopes to peeping Toms.
            By using real names at false hotels.

Abomunists who feel their faith weakening will have to spend two
weeks in Los Angeles.
When attacked, Abomunists think positive, repeating over and under:
"If I were a crime, I'd want to be commited . . .
            No! . . . Wait!"

FURTHER NOTES DIS- AND RE- GARDING ABOMUNISM

(This week's notes taken from "Abomunismus und Religion" by Tom Man.)

Krishnamurti can relax the muscles of your soul,
free your aching jawbone from the chewinggum habit.
Ouspensky can churn your illusions into butter and
give you circles to carry them in, around your head.
Subud can lock you in strange rooms with vocal balms
and make your ignorant clothing understand you.
Zen can cause changes in the texture of your hair,
removing you from the clutches of sexy barbers.
Edgar Cayce can locate your gallstones, other organs,
on the anarchistic rockpiles of Sacramento.
Voodoo Marie can give you Loas, abstract horses,
snorting guides to tar-baby black masses.
Billy can plug you into the Christ machine. Mail in your
mind today. Hurry, bargain God week, lasts one week only.

$$ Abomunus Craxioms $$

Egyptian mummies are lousy dancers.
        Alcoholics cannot make it on root beer.
Jazz never made it back down the river.
        Licking postage stamps depletes the body fluids.
Fat automobiles laugh more than others, and frink.
        Men who die in wars become seagulls and fly.
Roaches have a rough time of it from birth.
        People who read are not happy.
People who do not read are not happy.
        People are not very happy.

These days People get Sicker Quicker.
        The sky is less crowded in the West.
Psychiatrists pretend not to know everything.
        Way out people know the way out.
Laughter sounds orange at night, because
        reality is unrealizable while it exists.
Abomunists knew it all along,
        but couldn't get the butterscotch down.

★

Since it is election time, Abomunists are going to frink more, and naturally, as hard core abo's, we will feel the need to express ourselves somewhat more abomunably than others. We will do this simply by not expressing ourselves (abomunization). We will not express ourselves in the following terms:

Excerpts for the LEXICON ABOMUNON

ABOMMUNITY: n. Grant Avenue & other frinky places.
ABOMUNARCOSIS: n. Addiction to oatmeal cookies & liverwurst.
ABOMUNASIUM: n. Place in which abomunastics occur, such as bars, coffee shops, USOs, juvenile homes, pads, etc.
ABOMUNASTICS: n. Physical Abomunism.
ABOMUNATE, THE: n. The apolitical CORPUS ABOMUNISMUS.
ABOMUNETTE: n. Female type Abomunist (rare).
ABOMUNIBBLE: v. 1. To bite a daisy. 2. How poets eat.
ABOMUNICATE: v. To dig. (Slang: to frink.)
ABOMUNICS: n. Abomunistic techniques.
ABOMUNIFICANCE: n. The façade behind the reality of double-talking billboards.
ABOMUNIFY: v. To (censored) with an Abomunette, or vice versa.
ABOMUNIK: n. Square abomuflack.
ABOMUNISM: n. Footprintism. A rejectory philosophy founded by Barabbas and dedicated to the proposition that the essence of existence is reality essential and neither four-sided nor frinky, but not non-frinky either.
ABOMUNIST: n. One who avows Abomunism, disavowing almost everything else, especially butterscotch.
ABOMUNITIONS: n. Love, commonly found in the plural state, very.
ABOMUNITY: n. A by-product of abomunarcosis, also obtained by frinking. (Thus: Frinkism.)

ABOMUNIZE: v. To carefully disorganize—usually associated with frinking.

ABOMUNOID: adj. Having some Abomunistic qualities such as tragictories, pail faces, or night vision.

ABOMUNOLOGY: n. The systematic study of Abomunism; classes every other Frinksday, 2 a.m.

ABOMUNOSIS: n. Sweet breath.

ABOMUNOSOPHY: n. Theoretical Abomunism.

ABOMUNULL: n. 1. They. 2. One who is not quite Here.

ABOMUSICAL: adj. Diggable sounds.

ABOMUTINY: n. Regimentation. v. To impose organization from without, i.e., without oatmeal cookies.

FRINK: v. To (censored). n. (censored) and (censored).

FRINKISM: n. A sub-cult of Abomunism, not authorized nor given abomunitude by Bomkauf.

FRINKY: adj. Like (censored).

—Compiled by BIMGO

ABOMUNIST ELECTION MANIFESTO

I Abomunists vote against everyone by not voting for anyone.

II The only proposition abomunists support are those made to
   members of the opposite sex.

III Abomunists demand the abolition of Oakland.

IV Abomunists demand low-cost housing for homosexuals.

V Abomunists demand suppression of illegal milk traffic.

VI Abomunists demand statehood for North Beach.

VII The only office abomunists run for is the unemployment office.

VIII Abomunists support universal Frinkage.

IX Abomunists demand split-level ranch-type phonebooths.

X Abomunists demand the reestablishment of the government in its
   rightful home at ?

★   Still Further Notes Dis- & Re- Garding Abomunism   ★

(The following translation is the first publication of the Live
Sea Scrolls, found by an old Arab oil well driller. He first saw them on
the dead beds of the live sea. Thinking they were ancient bubble gum

61

wrappers he took them to town to trade in for hashish coupons. As chance would have it, the hashish pipes were in the hands of a visiting American relief official, who reluctantly surrendered them in return for two villages and a canal. We developed the cunic script by smearing it with tanfastic sun lotion, after which we took it down to the laundromat and placed it in the dryer for two hours ($1.20). We then ate four pounds of garlic bread & frinked; then we translated this diary. We feel this is one of the oldest Abomunist documents yet discovered.)

MONDAY—B.C.—minus 4—10 o'sun, a.m.

Nazareth getting too hot, fuzz broke up two of my poetry readings last night. Beat vagrancy charge by carrying my tool box to court—carpenters O.K. Splitting to Jeru. as soon as I get wheels.

TUESDAY—B.C.—minus 3—8 o'sun, p.m.

Jeru. cool, Roman fuzz busy having a ball, never bother you unless someone complains. Had a ball this morning, eighty-sixed some square bankers from the Temple, read long poem on revolt. Noticed cats taking notes, maybe they are publisher's agents, hope so, it would be crazy to publish with one of those big Roman firms.

WEDNESDAY—B.C.—minus 2—11 o'sun, a.m.

Local poets and literary people throwing a big dinner for me tonight, which should be a gas. Most of the cats here real cool, writing real far out—only cat bugs me is this Judas, got shook up when I refused to loan him thirty pieces of silver, he seems to be hung on loot, must be a lush.

THURSDAY—B.C.—minus 1—10 o'sun, p.m.

I am writing this in my cell. I was framed. How can they give the death sentence on charges of disorderly conduct and having public readings without a permit? It's beyond me. O well, there's always hope. Maybe that lawyer Judas is getting me can swing it. If he can't, God help me.

FRIDAY—Neutral—5 o'sun, a.m.

Roman turnkey was around passing out crosses. The two thieves have good connections so they got first crack at them—I got stuck with the biggest one. One of the guards doesn't dig my beard and sandals—taunted me all night. I'm going to be cool now, but tomorrow I'll tell him to go to hell, and what's so groovy is: he will o . . . somebody coming. I feel sort of abomunable. Barabbas gets a suspended sentence and I make the hill. What a drag. Well, that's poetry, and I've got to split now.

BOMS

I   Stashed in his minaret, towering
over the hashish wells, Caliph
Ralph inventoried his popcorn hoard
while nutty eunuchs conced his concubines.

II   Movies about inventors' lives and glass encased historical
documents do not move me as much as drinking or
hiccupping in the bathtub.

III   Filled with green courage we sneezed political,
coughing our dirty fingernails for President.

IV   Ageless brilliant colored spiders webbing eternally,
instead of taking showers under the fire hydrants in summer.

V   Unruly hairs in the noses of statues in public gardens
were placed there by God in a fit of insane jealousy.

VI   Single-breasted suits, dancing in the air,
turned up their cuffs at double-breasted suits
plodding down the street.

VII   Greedy burglars stole my mother and father,
and gave me a free pass to the circus and I like stripes.

VIII   Misty-eyed, knee-quaking me, gazing on the family Home,
realizing that I was about to burn it down.

IX	Waterspouts, concealed in pig knuckle barrels, rumbled, as tired storms whispered encouragement.
X	Angry motives scrambled for seating space shaking their fist at the moon.
XI	Liver salesmen door to doored back pats disturbing chimneysweeps sleeping on roofs.
XII	Daily papers suicide from tree tops purpling the lawn with blueprints.
XIII	Caribou pranced in suburban carports hoofmarking the auto-suggestions.
XIV	Pentagonal merit badges flowed gracefully over the male nurses' heads.
XV	Disordered aquariums, dressed in shredded wheat, delivered bibles to pickles crying in confessionals.

ABOMUNIST RATIONAL ANTHEM

(to be sung before and after frinking)

Derrat slegelations, flo goof babereo
Sorash sho dubies, wago, wailo, wailo.

Geed bop nava glied, nava glied, nava
Speerieder, huyedist, hedacaz, ax, O, O.

Deeredition, boomedition, squom, squom, squom,
Dee beetstrawist, wapago, wapago, loco
          locoro, locoest
Voometeyereepetiop, bop, bop, bop, whipop.

Dearat, shloho, kurritip, plog, mangi, squom pot,
Clopo jago, bree, bree, asloopered, akingo labiop,
Engpop, engpop, boint plolo, plolo, bop bop.

(Music composed by Schroeder.)

ABOMUNIST DOCUMENTS

(discovered during ceremonies at the Tomb of the Unknown Draftdodger)

Boston, December 1773

Dear Adams:

I am down to my last can of tea, and cannot afford to score for more as
the British Pushers have stamped a new tax on the Stuff, I know that
many Colony Cats are as hung as I am, so why don't we get together on
the Night of the Sixteenth and Go down to the Wharf and swing with
a few Pounds. I think it will be cooler if we make the Scene dressed as
Indians, the British Fuzz, will not know who the Tea-Heads are, it will
be very dark so we will have to carry torches, tell the Cats not to goof
with the torches and start a Fire, that would ruin the whole Scene.

Later,

HANCOCK

West Point, December 1778

Dear Wife:

I am trying my best to raise the Money for the Rent, but the Army has
no funds for Personal Hardships, I sounded George about Promotion,
but the Virginia Crowd seems to be in Control so even my hero status
can't be any good. Met a very nice English Cat named André, and he
has offered to see if he can swing a Loan for me, I don't know where
he can get so much money, but since he has been so nice, it would be
traitorous to ask.

P.S. He was telling me how much cheaper it is to live in England. Maybe when this is over we can settle there. I have been doing a lot of drawing in my spare time, and tonight I promised to show André some of my sketches, if I can find them, they are all mixed up with my defense plan and I've broken my glasses. Have to close now. I can hear André sneaking in, the chances he takes. He really loves Art.

Yours, faithfully,

BENEDICT ARNOLD

ABOMNEWSCAST . . . ON THE HOUR . . .

America collides with iceberg piloted by Lindbergh baby . . . Aimee Semple Macpherson, former dictator of California, discovered in voodoo nunnery disguised as Moby Dick . . . New hit song sweeping the country, the Leopold & Loeb Cha-cha-cha . . . Pontius Pilate loses no-hitter on an error, league split over scorer's decisions, Hebrew fireballer out for season with injured hands . . . Civilian Defense Headquarters unveils new bomb shelter with two-car garage, complete with indoor patio and barbecue unit that operates on radioactivity, comes in decorator colors, no down payment for vets, to be sold only to those willing to sign loyalty oath . . . Forest Lawn Cemetery opens new subdivision of split-level tombs for middle-income group . . . President inaugurates new policy of aggressive leadership, declares December 25th Christmas Day . . . Pope may allow priests to marry, said to be aiming at one big holy family . . . Norman Rockwell cover, "The Lynching Bee" from "Post" Americana series, wins D.A.R. Americanism award . . . Russians said to be copying TV format with frontier epic filmed in Berlin, nuclear Wagon Train features Moiseyev Dancers . . . Red China cuts birthrate drastically, blessed events plummet to two hundred million a year . . . Cubans seize Cuba, outraged U.S. acts quickly, cuts off tourist quota, administration introduces measure to confine all rhumba bands to detention camps during emergency . . . Both sides in Cold War stockpiling atomic missiles to preserve peace, end of mankind seen if peace is declared, UN sees encouraging sign in small war policy, works quietly for wider participation among backward nations . . . End of news . . . Remember your national emergency signal, when you see one small mushroom cloud and three large ones, it is not a drill, turn the TV off and get under it . . . Foregoing sponsored by your friendly neighborhood Abomunist . . . Tune in next world . . .

DOES THE SECRET MIND WHISPER?

DOES THE SECRET MIND WHISPER?

Walk back eating peach seeds after she did that I didn't ask her but I couldn't refuse she seemed so intent then her being only out of jail two years and nothing there to caress her head to give some shelter to the moondrip falling from the evening covering images of those dead soldiers on my lawn in the middle of winter with nothing to cover their sins from the frost dripping from the pocket of those professors sitting in the intersection on their knees praying to the virgin whores to present them with a rubber ball to beat out their father's teeth until he screamed go then he gave them the beautifully wrapped boys to play with until the doctor laughed at his needle sitting there under the moss trees with nothing to do but masturbate and think of the beautiful lesbians in the monster's arms wishing their father would come and he would kill them and make them brothers so they could play with those dead little boys at the fountain full of that mental wine used on sad holy days also used to chase away all the ghosts hanging around on the corner waiting for haunted girls to pass so they hide in their shoes anxious to throw peach stones at the whorehouse window for the guys to know that it is time for the policemen to come and get laid for all the hard work they are doing to the children to keep the streets safe for the dust to run up those old white steps in the clouds of coughed sorrow to the roof where mag has her goat milking away beneath the star on the left of the television aerial spitting those electric spit musclebound street to hell and back in time to eat second hand lobsters from the parole board office down at the local church near the middle of the street just as old mag had that goat killed by raindrop pressures on the headbone most painless way to die since the invention of radio got that Italian fellow in trouble up to his neck in messy publicity about politics and the negro vote sticking in his pocket just when jazz jumped out the window and broke the legs of that goddamned old sacrificed goat of mag's lying there waiting for some poor old medicine man to write him a prescription for rock and roll rolling over rocket-burst of clinging forces lashing the reality wall man anti-man again in servile postures grotesque filled skin hunched lanterns cold owl shivering vibrations waiting to wait for waiting death you are now a minor vice your warm lips are far promises forever cold death you are not death yet warmer beds love us human reeling human to you a minor vice life do not leave us till music ends

how else living do we know we live or have lived living among endless
processions of cocteaus gauchos on bucking motorcycles harsh lights
bursting from casual cyclonic winds creeping over strontium landscapes
of scorched anatomies of falling adam birds twisted guitars in greek
hands caressing us back to old crescent formed wharves of michael
faced degenerates whistling over car noises to running statues of fright
and can-can memories of fawning buttocks in flickering autumn's bulbs
gone before in spiked eyes of lady truck drivers on cracked leg roads to
revisited wombs filled with dark brilliant wetness felt in all those sliding
eyes glimmering between rumors of truth shouted from sea shell roofs
of ochre cardboard huts concealing oracles in furry Egyptian cat suits
spitting prophecies out of fat stone books from sanded brains of
timeless deserts of theban prostitutes hidden in time beaten minds of
made mad translators woven into wrought iron ears and eyes of marble
foxes dragging carts of stuffed scented ideas to noiseless suicides behind
walls of animated flesh shells while wild visions crawl on airy knees
through curly forests of nodding heads strewing bits of shattered images
in pointed faces of crepe paper kites flying wildly over petrified idols
kneeling on fat walls of glowing flesh in the black rain dripping silently
in and out of empty stars drooling over nude bodies of dancing planets
celebrating hot birthdays of the sun bannister sliding on twisted bars of
light slanting down marble corpse of twice dead Socrates who begat
Gandhi who begat Krishna who begat Buddha who begat Christ who
begat Einstein who begat Michael who begat Melville who begat
dostoievski who begat Lincoln who begat Bessie Smith who begat
Picasso who begat Charlie Parker who begat Morpheus who begat
Farnsworth who begat Starkweather who begat Geronimo who begat
Whitman who begat hymened women with moist tongues following
chinese funerals escorted by black aeroplanes smokewriting against
patent leather skies beaming soft unbroken rays on glazed foreheads of
spoon eyed painters mourning dead pictures of lost faced girls covered
with tracks of unsuccessful suicides in emptied bays of frantic modern
stonepiles seen plunging into glass faced swamps filled with supersti-
tious alligators crawling among monumental statues of sculptured bone
lying among busy eight o'clock sidewalks bending under constant
shuffling of hard shoes slipping on petrified tears dropped from pocked
eyesacks of ancient seekers of soft thigh love in navels of hard breasted
adding machine girls in store bought curls wallowing in sipped coffee
talking of last night's copulations with certified public computers and
itinerant umbrella peddlers lost in rainless fogs heel and toe and breast
and buttock and crooked neck ballet dancers seducing male nymphs

under cover of secret blankets of brilliant dust blindly flying through
terrified streets of ruined limping vehicles filled with shaggy mouth
youthful gangsters hunting the human dog with stilettos of fear and
dreams of money sex money cars money suits money shoes money
muscles money houses money hair money pearly teeth money pointed
shoes money hats money brains money hate money love twisted into
pimp patterns of money success grasped by money gnarled hands of
lanky editorial writers false teeth credit dentists cheap meat queer
butchers hollow chested bus drivers eye shadow salesgirls all American
football businessmen hollow thigh supermarket clerks money flag
makers money mountain movers money car makers money eye raw
material citizens pulped of money landscapes of holy money timemusi-
cal movies of tiny money children cushion noises of disintegration still
heard in dynastic eras of power skeletons stooped in scooped out offices
of company wife husbands custodians of domestic fear and free terror
for still hearted breathers lurking behind neon tombstones singing out
corpse voice arias while bristling peaks of unclaimed mountain ranges
concealed by sky high forest stretch their necks through newly created
clouds of vibrating breath choked from throats of savage inheritors of
still rivers flowing serenely from shores of death wheezing civilizations
propped on skin shriveled arms of emaciated giants echoing in hollow
bodies futile death rattles beneath dark throbbing of burning drums
heralding spears of lightning hurled by wealthless savages awakened by
the shrill ringing of ceaseless bells tolling the voice of hungry jackals
sticking ancient dog faces stolen from Egyptian gods into pewter
buckets of sour wine drawn from grapes of wrath as bible faced history
chanters creep from ice formed caves wearing belts of heat held by
hands of cool waiting in nighttime republics long hidden beneath
landscapes of memory protected by silk panther stealth satin-finish
jacket boys on rows of corners jangling cold dreams in their fist pockets
hoarding puberty dreams from crushed breast mothers waiting in
kitchen cathedrals for new comings new Christ new cancers new drugs
new nightmares of female beginnings dying like old dehydrated men
sexless at last after nurturing young girl breast in futile hope of love
wishing disasters on doomed lipstick daughters new male body queens
of bed sweat lovemaking suffering from stretched lips of shame of
borrowed contraceptives squirming with giggle noises of skewered pigs
among grunts of satisfaction and eternal disease deposited by sexless
editorials drummed into defenseless pores and wired into never
sleeping ears caught now in moans of fake pleasures murmured over
helpless groaning of elastic flesh as oceans of sperm break on reefs of

human rocks strewn along shores of time slighted by blinking stars in
misty sterile skies silent witnesses to never ending unflinching destruc-
tion committed in those thousand names of god who laughs and orders
death to laugh with him at his withering failures crouched on beds of
earth walls and floors of cork were sucking up our conversation as fast
as we could spit it out through the wordblock o one two why two not a
number a symbol not a symbol a reality oh have you seen my two arms
two legs two heads two brains two horns on my prickly surly head
curling with secrets or is it purring at sun caresses does the secret mind
whisper to secret organs body message me now I am wanting trapped
the new balm tastes of licorice and is shaped like a pickle remember the
first steps first fall all the way to a lone floor waking sleeping dust
remember the lonesome broomstraws on cold linoleum mesas nimble
baby ballet steps pink cuts not quite through the skin deep enough
though for a minor cry a quick lip brush tasting like love tingling
remember sacred parades of imagined desire remember the girls on the
earth one with melted feathers under the crepe de chine curtains the
heaven under the tree the world shut out remember the second breast
oh reality leave them alone alone with memory you are too much up on
trying to terrify me into existing o reality it is so easy to die in dreams
even attend the soul even welcome quiet demise reality don't darken
time's corridor or do you too remember hours minutes shoes vests iced
glasses tables hands and eyes questions questions turning pages music
from warm lips smoky veins on marble tables sinewy wrought iron
tongues flickering threats of unholy candles marijuana dreams of perfect
purpose remember freckles as we smoked wet fire crackers dreamed
rainy day dreams of putting out the sun writing a biography of time on
the head of a pin reconstructing her costumes from the shapes of puffs
covering our heads with laughing reflecting cracked mirrors oh remem-
ber the time on a decadent island ugly whore you mothered then skinny
spaghetti slithering from your belly crawling back of my eyes popping
into my unprepared skull bathing me in thighs and handfuls of live fat
formless bumps little spheres in a new world remember now bury me
feet face arms teeth dreams balls swallow me all make me nothing again
I want to walk through you on every goddamn street in the world
though I see you in dead mind faces of molded brain intellectuals
standing on deserted crusty river piers musing on ghostly forms of gone
ferries and other sad vehicles of mentality nerve peeled images of
transient ecstasies pains of too personal existences private sadnesses hid
in smoky dimensions secret pockets in thought cluttered space where
love stuffed into hungry vortexes of crowded eyes loses its shape

laughter wears torn aspects memory dredged for forgotten visions offers
bitter desire twisted beyond recognition blinded by coppery shadows of
old failures concealed inside fake spires of crumbled plastic chapels
while silent skull dweller mice fatten on decayed noses of tweedy
re-created creatures who shout blasphemy at tigers thrusting ragged
dreams through crashed windows sucking fresh jazz into the cages of
university pink brain circuses circumspectly shielding their manicured
faces from laughing whip eyes of beat oracles doomed to see after bomb
visions of eternity imprinted on flattened objective faces of traceless
cliffs standing more in unhistoried time unchained winds moving
noiselessly through charcoal forest bent staves of burned light darkly
illuminating fluted mountains shrouded in flaky smoke warped cities
filled with a thousand colors of dust web metallic fabric stretched on
frames of powderized towers guarding rivers of jellied earth silent lava
streets humless unformed shadows heat printed on soft marble canvases
gigantic ultimate greek vases posed forever in remembrance of breaths
and odors conceived in now time of scraggly haired frightened girls in
beer mug barrooms of contemporary revolution on barricades of beds
and wine jug bloody fields of screaming no daddy no daddy daddy no
daddy away from home terrors of rape me now rape me now babble
sounds of hypersensitive talk coming in rhythmic breaths saved from
lost evenings memories of paperback conversation with Camus and dry
old Algiers clerks with hidden Wagner records stashed in arab oran
hotels with whiffs of Rimbaud floating in from the holy desert of arab
lovers with thousand year eyes and death and no transfiguration not
ever but hungry truth picking at cadaverous brainy scarecrows down
from the cross forever with handfuls of bent nails screeching martyr
cries for hammers of modern romans for veils of sophomore veronicas
for tears of convent made marys for vacant shells of unholy sepulchers
sealed with blood from anonymous drug stores selling life to death
seeking miscellaneous dehumanized beings floating down the night of
time in power chariots of glass watched by disinterested clots of self
deformed skin and blood with unadjustable souls in torn cellophane
garments blue with blues blue like poems everlastingly blue from inner
explosion self demolished wrecks proclaiming love on hostile street-
corners spewing wordless gasps spinning themselves into minute
histories chapters of crib scenes filled with mother father father sex
mother cry fright wet pants screams of delight hate love daddy love
mother teacher mother shaped all over mother shapes daddy shapes in
clown faces law faces faceless heads in plaster churches of Sunday
bench kneeling before faceless god and cotton candy Sunday night

touch swapping of secret feeling of nothing in first disappointments of no more more stop it hurts it's raw there we are all raw there from fingernails and rough dreams going up in nervy rockets trailing fire tongues clamped in hot-sharp teeth grinding remembrance to ashes for beds for later flames kindled tall green stink weeds growing like legions of sick candles spurting jets of pepper odors into flaring nostrils lips of salty winds kissing cracked realer flesh caught red eyed with banned imaginations offering solitary thoughts on death and other illegal mysteries carried off in hurricane afternoon's warped glimpses of buried events squeezed from pits of stagnant wax ripped from walls of the mind's eye of Goethe taking Faust by the hand across dark teutonic landscapes into Hitler Germanic swamps of twentieth century Bosch daylight pushed by blackened wind from bells of spiked trumpets blasting hun fists through the dead body of whore Europe's culture as Schiller smiled from Beethoven's brain trapped in power as certain as timeless karnak booming over luxor's plain to Tuscan dusky twilights where torchlit Italians carved life in marble mountains ankle deep in severed heads of bloody popes at war with god for rome's remains only to settle for splendored tombs sprung from hands of deathless spirits in tunics of blood and dust crouched in corners of light where creation is master and man does not exist except as tools of art that stern fa-ther-mother of souls not of this earth or in it doomed to disappear in traces of works of beauty and love yet reappear in time abstracts of eternal existence pistons of nature doomed to see those dark trees swaying in forests of pain where Myshkin begged tortured Dostoievski forgiveness in one illuminated flash of remorse for uncommitted sins and deeds left undone cheeks unkissed faith unstated love gone ungiven and an idiot's feet were embraced in that maniacal wood where sarah last Egyptian first saint mother of all gypsies pumped blood of wild rose into Lorca's Andalusian veins where Federico first sang where Mithra in black Spanish robes placed her sword in Ignacio's groin where sweet Lorca weeps bitterly yet lives in the afternoon yet loves in the afternoon that darkly loved wood where all who enter are lost yet live forevermore companion to etruscans and black mountainous shapers of mahogany African breast sucked by old lonely aesthetes looking for lonely women lost on the road to bedrooms of oblivion spreading invisible fingers to steamy corners where athletic gods take all those happy birthday cakes to eat after public showers at baseball games held on heroes' birthdays celebrating lost explorers lost in miserable jungles of old Cambodia with many old statues of slant eyed gods and sleepy eyed virgins sunk in much and lost philosophies dropped by alexander enroute to death in

indian jungles and no conquering of asia today baby greek and other
traveling civilization salesmen tomorrow more jazz and brand new
nook of Hebrew tears cast to western skies of gray and other subdued
colors mixed by mad Mexican painters of old rituals and Aztec virgins'
breasts spouting rusty blood to cold marble pyramids and jazz dear
bitch dear bitch dear bitch dear bitch dear bitch dear bitch where is the
robin's nest where is the final sea of flaming waves seeking last shores
where the sailor sees gulls and other winged creatures but makes no
report for fear of sea god's wrathful eyes filled with painful love and
mistaken death you know the score old veteran remover old flickering
floozy of destroyed angels and ancient dreams of old embryonic wonder
dreams of glory on rounded fields of strange bellies with sandpaper
skins bruising tender hands holding other lives cherished from memory
of yesterday and today giving communion for all time in new year
noises of hopes and forgotten fears blow blow blow blowing through
shadow canyons where we stand on wounded feet filled with muddied
toys and bones of phantom friends lost in swirling clouds of broken
storms flying in heads of adult children left over from illegal xmas
forbidden now that space is the thing of momentous impact and drivers
of last year's bomb haunting tin littered launching pads enveloped by
crushed hopes of unescaped visionaries hung from dying rockers in
hidden lunatic afternoons of probe and thrust and naked skies beckon-
ing with ammonia fingers to rooftree wanderers lost to pursuit of
womanly earth writhing under rabbit couplings of hurried lovers
anxiously disappearing into each other seeking the ultimate bomb
shelter deep inside desperate wombs filled with wet butterflies and
shells of deserted silkworms gone forever to weave Hiroshima's shroud
and spin flowers into her burned sod dead of shame and fire great gift of
Kansas Orpheus and god smuggled aboard as co-pilot later seen at
survivors victory celebrations a lone mourner at his family's funeral
unnoticed with his eyes of flame amid sheets of swirling vapors of belief
in insane embraces with blind animals exhaling hot death breath puffing
through laughing playground searing cheeks of children chewing
chocolate rockets and no silverbells evermore in times of earache
commercials vomited from radioactive radios every minute on the
minute sandwiched edgewise between wireless seductions of virginal
charity nurses with vaginas of old gold and silver and no doctor
appendix can't go to menopause party with you must attend lobotomy
sale with four out of five leading new york maniacs on channel last
chance for other cathode orgies flowing into wall-to-wall tombs
demanding save that poor pregnant wonder horse tragic disguised

survivor of apocalypse good I want to count down for the camera and
for all cold breasts everywhere in captivity in living rooms dying rooms
lonely rooms rooms of hot heads under chrome in beauty parlors
whores rooms in duty palaces good schoolgirls rooms of friendly
masturbations reverberating with father shouts and anthropology
dreams of new guinea bush love plucked from savage genitals and men's
rooms of leftover sadness on grooved dry whimpering torsos and board
rooms where people are split two for one those rooms of frigid suprem-
acy and rooms of followed hearts suddenly filling with human mud
rising from bowels of blood pumped from painful rooms of rock-eyes
poets whispering into their own ears curses too valuable for sealed ear
drums of well tailored successes hiding inside scooped paper-filled
bellies of concrete giants kneeling at all the proper moments counter-
pointing fragmented peon noises of it did not happen it did not happen
that paul's canary ate radioactive seeds that morning and now only
meditates refusing to admit that his song is gone that we sold our blood
in hospital butchers shops only to be busted for dangerous needle
marks by a cop who knew god that we stayed in bed all christmas week
for fear of offending jesus at gift shops that we were so depressed by the
suicide rate we read old newspapers and contemplated suicide it did not
happen it cannot happen because it always happens while we hide in
Buddha's smiling breast drifted to sweeter peaks of self and all seeking
those elusive koans hidden in crevices of other navels dug in behind
venus mounds of girls who glide onto the spike yet contain no answer
but offer only gates of jellied lips opening on other softer queries
answered with wet friction and cries of deeper deeper deeper stab me
through impaled on that bony question answers fly to the loins and life
is stabbed into existence as orgasmic silence bathes the room in peace
as questions disappear rolling down ballooning bodies in milky crystals
of sex odored sweat drowning interhooked feet in pools of giving taking
giving never what is asked taking many times more until empty of self
free of self until possessor of self in this time of sour bees and honey we
are not flowers no lilies grow in our eyebrows and our skulls are
potential ash trays for those fires smothered in cores of men smoldering
hot coals fuming to burst into flame yet we shall stand naked and cool
them with angry love songs.

GOLDEN SARDINE

Carl Chessman (Reel I, II, III, IV)

CARL CHESSMAN INTERVIEWS THE P.T.A. IN HIS SWANK GAS
CHAMBER BEFORE LEAVING ON HIS ANNUAL INSPECTION OF
CAPITAL, TOUR OF NORTHERN CALIFORNIA DEATH UNIVERSI-
TIES, HAPPY.

Carl Chessman is in sickly California writing death threats to the Wiz-
ard of Oz, his trial is being held in the stomach of Junipero Serra, at last
the game starts, chessman steals all the bases & returns to his tomb to
receive the last sacraments from Shirley Temple.

Silence, oyegas, oyegas, f.ms, the corpsey bailiff, atones, ready, ALL
STAND, AL HITCHCOCK PRESENTS, CARL CHESSMAN OF THE
UNIVERSE OF CALIFORNIA VS. THE PEOPLE'S GODLY GAS
BIRTHRIGHT.

chessman draws an impressionistic picture of vinnie van go with three
beautiful stink flowers stuffed into his vacant ear, declares mothers' day
out of bounds for spacemen, discusses cute gas stove being put in the
game room by the gold star mothers, feels their meters, pronounces
them queer, & offers to slap their bosoms into exotic shapes without
charge, free.

Chessman names the last week in December national week. offered
Jesus free room & board.

CARL CHESSMAN KNOWS, THE GOVERNOR OF CALIFORNIA
KNOWS, GOOD JOHNNY THE POPE KNOWS, SALVATORE AGRON
KNOWS & ALL THE LEAKY EYED POETS KNOW, IN THEIR PORES.
NO ONE IS GUILTY OF ANYTHING AT ANY TIME ANYWHERE IN
ANYPLACE, ASK THOSE HEBREW ECSTATICS UP THERE ON THE
TREES OF SORROW, MYSTIC BLOODFRUIT PICKED IN THE SEA-
SON OF THE DAMNED, LIVE FROM THE AMAZON, THE MARTYRS'
DAUGHTER . . . . FOUR MIDWESTERN SAINTS, GIVE HEADS
. . . RATHER THEMSELVES TO LUSTY, PAGAN, RAW, CLOTH-
INGLESS JIVARO TEENAGER, SWEETHEART OF THE YOUNG
HEADHUNTER.

CHESSMAN CALLS UP GOD, WANTS TO KNOW AT ONCE, DOES
SANTA CLAUS BELIEVE IN CHILDREN? GOD GETS PANICKY &

PUTS DOWN HIS GUITAR, BEGINS TO MAKE GREAT SIMULTA-
NEOUS PHONE CALLS TO EVERYONE HE CAN THINK OF & IS
GIVING OUT UNTRUE ADDRESSES UNTIL CHESSMAN ACCUSES
HIM OF FELONIOUS DEISM, GOD COPS OUT & GIVES CHESSMAN
A LITTLE RED DEW LINE TELEPHONE, GOD ACCUSES CHESSMAN
OF . . . . BEING GOD, CHESSMAN DENIES EVER HAVING
BEEN GOD, REMINDS GOD OF THEIR DUSTBOWLING YEARS,
CHESSMAN WINS WEEKEND PASS TO HOME FOR UNWED STEP-
MOTHERS, & WINS VILLAGE HORSESHOE CONTEST,

> chessman announces new butane concept of humility, chess is going
> around lifting skirts of manacled altar boys at religious monastery of
> deliberate unsexual design,

> now old curveballer carl, great san quentin on mangashouse gang
is going to throw out the first president of the season, old carl tells an
anecdote about god's wild youth.

> This is a poem about a
> nobody, twenty something
> years old, whose parents
> sent him to a good college
> but, who instead read buddhist
> magazines & of course became god,
> he is now standing in front of his
> parents' house saying, they think I've been in school for four years,
> how can I walk in cold and tell them I am god, I think I'll go over
> to chessman's little studio & sleep.

Now the march of the wire sculpture poets in old collector carl's san
quentin word saloon, cool wind litanies, as they unwrap their image
patches, surrealist post card day at carl's & now the poets fearlessly
unscrew their heads, & carl sketches their brain in the nude . . . & now
carl long distance chessman gets a call from a leper colony that wants
his autograph, carl flies to the leper nation in his indian aeroplane &
signs baseballs for the kids, dances. Ah old left bank carlos is throwing
a party for genet's new anthology subjective laughter cures, Now carl in
his pink maryland riding habit sings the new hit tune, going goer going
for gone, Now carl begins to write ballads & think immortal & comb his
hair into a peak that had snow on it, How sudden the memory of the
beethoven quartets, the agonies, returned to man, totaled on a dark ear.

& now chessman cites the bull, manolete glowers, chessman reminds him that he is dead, blacked out, old aficionado carlito warns manolo to stay away from dead movie stars, sudden death for dead . . . . bull fighters, chessman invents a new drug that cures kleptomania, & locates nuns arabia.

Now the pat o'brien leading man demands that stonewall chessman cop out, the idiot . . . . the worried football player tried to fumble, but old gentleman jim chessman is telephoning . . . . & now chessman predicts the arrival of the damp movie stars, not included in the tarot . . . . & with them is the brightest of these year round christmas trees, orphans of the camus storm, & the celebrated subliminal com- mercial blinking across their sincere suits, VICTIM, WILLING & now doctor von stroheim is explaining how the two miniature atom bombs set each other off in that little gray pail that the guards are putting a coat of lipstick on right now . . . . & the committed slide along the bagel shop walls, satirical quentical of the mind.

Here, Chessman, is the message to all garcias everywhere, lon- gitude people, beyond the margin,

I am glad now, sad now, home, in TIME FOR THE MURDER, guilty California is quiet

Alien winds sweeping the highway
fling the dust of medicine men,
    long dead,
        in the california afternoon

Into the floating eyes
    of spitting gadget salesmen,
    eating murdered hot dogs,
        in the california afternoon.

The ancient hindu guru
dreams of alabama,
gingerbread visions,
    of angry policemen,
    as he waves a sacred raga,
    over the breast of
    frigid sunworshippers,
    in the california afternoon

A sad-eyed mexican,
   sacrifices an easter-faced virgin,
      to a cynical god,
         beneath an ancient sun,
         in the california afternoon.

   thin fluted riddles . . . .
      yogi blown through lost ages . . . .
      discreet puddles, seeping . . . .
         down the back, of giant time . . . .
         caught in ankle deep theories . . . .
         of wind blown love . . . .

All those
floodlight monumental
      conceptions, along the road, laughing in wounded
               air,
         crying to paint me blue, in the california
               afternoon.

         The Enormous Gas Bill At The Dwarf Factory.

         A Horror Movie to be Shot with Eyes.

         (Dedicated to the Mothers of America.)

(REEL I)

Carl Chessman interviews San Quentin P. T. A. before leaving on his
. . . . annual tour of California Death U-niversities.

Caryl Chess- Man is in sickly California writing death threats to the
Wizard of Oz, the green giant announces his trial will be held in the
stomach of . . . . Junipero Serra.

Charlie Chaplin & Sitting Bull walk hand in hand through the World
Series, Chest- Mann steals all the bases except Home & receives the last
sack-o-men from KING KONG.

Oyez, Oyez, Oyez, the people of the state of Call CHEZ- Main vs CALI-
FORNIA. Caul enters the plaza dressed in blinking RED- LIGHTS sing-
ing clap hands . . . . . here comes the lindberg baby, presents the Judge
with an impressionistic . . . . . picture of Sebastian with three beautiful
stink flowers growing in his ear . . . declares MOTHERS DAY out of
bounds for spacemen, winks at the GOLD STAR . . . . FATHERS,
offers to sculpt their souls into exotic shapes, without charge . . . .

End of reel one.

ALL BOOM SHOOTING TO BE DONE FROM FAR OUT . . . .
CLOSEUPS TO BE SHOT ZOOMING IN . . . CAMERA PANS THE SET
ON THE WAY BACK OUT . . . . . .

Film to be used in shooting reel one. BLACK OR WHITE OR COLOR,
NOT YET DEVELOPED OR DEVELOPED ALREADY.

Props to be used on this location . . . . ONE RUSTY OFFICIAL
BUCKET, ONE SAWED OFF HIGH CHAIR.

(REEL II)

As the scene opens wave after wave of twin-engined attorney generals
fly past . . . . . . dipping their wings as tho' passing over the tomb of the
unknown gas meter . . . .

Caryl Mellville writes first book on new butane concept of humility
. . . . CELL No. Pennsylvania 6-5000, Waitun Place.

CARL DARROW APPEARS IN COURT WITHOUT SUSPENDERS
OR MAKE-UP & a brilliant monkey . . . . perched on each eyelid,
submits STARTLING legal brief on bailiff's unshined shoe . . . . . Prima
Faeces Nolo Contendere Argument on old little known decision in
. . . . obscure criminal case, "THE PEOPLE OF MARIN COUNTY
VS. I. SOCRATES" . . . . forgotten trial hinged on whether or not
the prosecutor was plugged into proper wall . . . . socket while
preparing case, ended in hung plaintiffs, daring move wins populautor
new trial, judge sets new hearing for opening day of famous salinas
rodeshowdown session to be held in castroville, "artichoke capital of the
world" . . . .

(MONTAGE SEQUENCE):

OPENS ON DAVY CROCKETT IN COONSKIN KNICKERS STANDING
IN FRONT OF A SHOOTING . . . . GALLERY ON FORTY SEC-
OND STREET BUYING ONE HUNDRED ROUNDS FOR A QUARTER,
CLOSE-UP OF A GRIM-FACED CONGRESSMANSHOOTING AT LIT-
TLE CAST IRON BEARS, CLUSTERS OF LITTLE UNCRACKED LIB-
ERTY BELLS DANGLE FROM HIS EARS, THREE UNLIT BIRTHDAY
CANDLES GROW SLOWLY FROM HIS HEAD AS THE LAST BEAR
KNEELS DOWN & EXPENSIVE RAIN FALLS, EMERGING FROM
THIS FRAME SUDDENLY WE SEE GAYLY DECORATED LANDING
CRAFT . . . . BULGING WITH FIERCE LOOKING PENGUINS
ALL WEARING SHINY NEW WRIST WATCHES & . . . . SMOK-
ING ROLL YOUR OWN CIGARETTES, THE SMOKE FORMING A
HUGE CLOUD THAT TURNS . . . . . INTO A GIGANTIC, LUSTY,
RAW, PAGAN, JIVARO TEENAGER PURSUED BY FOUR MIDWEST-
ERN ALBINOS THROWING PEPPERMINT JAVELINS AT HER RE-
VOLVING BREAST BEFORE BEING FELLED BY A NUCLEAR TIPPED
SNOWBALL. THROWN BY NANOOK OF THE NORTH., SCENE ENDS
WITH NANOOK PASSING OUT SOUVENIR POLAR BEARS AT THE
GRAND OPENING OF THE NEW ARNOLD SHOENBERG SUPER-
MARKET, WHILE OUTSIDE IT IS RAINING BLACK VOLKSWAGENS
(END OF MONTAGE SEQUENCE) FILM RETURNS TO ENORMOUS GAS
BILL.

(AT THIS POINT FILM SHOULD ANNOUNCE THAT IT IS VERY CROWDED AT
DISNEYLAND).

It is now summertime for the one Billionth consecutive time & once
more Caruso sings take me out to the ball game as Yankee Stadium
fills up with Zionist & . . . . hardware store owners, old southpaw
Caryl watches as jane darwell throws out the first telephone booth,
the air is filled with invisible home runs & the . . . . crowd cheers
as the bleachers go up hometown flames, & Gertrude Stein arrives in
her private underground railroad car, surrounded by know something
intellectual WITH STILL LIFES in their eyes, & no navels, WATCH-
ING LEARNEDLY AS OLD CARL RUTH, LAST OF . . . . . THE OLD
GAS-HOUSE GANG GOES DEEP INTO LEFT FIELD, HIS BACK TO
THE WALL, ALL EYES GLUED TO HIS DIFFICULT BREATHING,
AS HE WALKS INTO THE GRANDSTAND & THE BALL FALLS,
OUTSIDE THE FOUL LINE, OUT OF PLAY, THE UMPIRES ORDER

LEFTY CHESSMAN OUT OF THE STADIUM, BACK TO HIS SWANKY
BACHELOR APT, IN THE EL MUERTO HOTEL. WE LEAVE F.
SCOTT CHESSMAN SITTING IN HIS WRITING DEN ON GLAMOR-
OUS DEATH ROW, HE IS LEANING INTENTLY OVER THE TOI-
LET BOWL NEAR HIS TYPEWRITER IN WHICH HE IS SECRETLY
TRAINING HIS PET GOLD FISH, BROWNIE, TO SWIM THE EN-
GLISH CHANNEL, & NOW & THEN LOOKING UP TO COUNT THE
LIFELIKE BLACK WIDOW SPIDERS ON WALLPAPER DONATED
BY THE SATURDAY EVENING POST, & SO AS QUAINT 'LIL OLE
WESTERN CIVILIZATION . . . . . . SINKS SLOWLY IN THE WEST,
WE LEAVE FUN-LOVING CALIFORNIA WITH ALL OF ITS . . . COL-
ORFUL DEATH FESTIVALS, & SET SAIL FOR EXOTIC NEBRASKA,
CAREFREE GOTHIC ISLE, BIRTHPLACE OF THE FAMOUS INDIAN
BONE SCULPTORS, ORIGINATORS OF THE CUSTER OPEN AIR
HEAD, PAT. PENDING

(*REEL III*)

The scene opens with Dim Pictures of Animal Sadness, the Deathbed
of the last Buffalo in Nebraska, he is dying of lonesomeness, (strange
Plague Brought by The Ghost People), Weeping Beneath His Holy
White Hide, he recalls cherished Memories of his past, Remembering
when Indians were Red, recalling the Arrows Arc, Flamer the Soft Bull
of the Skies, assuming his Bison Dignity, He refuses to be pitied or
accompanied, Finally alone he unlocks the Acres of Unscarred Ameri-
can Love . . . . hidden in the boney caves of his great Mountainous
Shaggy Godhead, Across the Green Centuries of his Eyes, his Soul
walks the slaughtered plain His sheen of released Contempt illuminates
the one hundred million hushed Crucifixions buried in the bloody
weave of triumphant Blue, Indigenous Murder cloth, His spirit erupts in
punctual Geysers, unseen by the Roman eyes of Cold . . . Ohio People
spreading Picnics & circuses, smearing katsup on the holy Playground
His ancient Dream pounds with life, long vanished into leather Jackets
. . . . His Fuming Wounds Burn in Indignation, kindled by jets of
hateful greed. The winds of lamentations carry his grief to be impaled
on Grand Tetons Arrowhead crown His Iconed Hide decorated forever
with the Christmas Bullets of America . . . . . Arkward his Clean Beast
Speech calls to his teeth, now hanging from the . . . . venereal
wrist of the latest celluloid Madonna, grinning behind her prize-win-
ning scabs . . . . Childlike Breezes Singing on the Rug of Skull
Breathe the old litany of . . . Buried America's retelling Tribal Woes of

ingenuously executed thin-lipped Pogroms. On the Rim of Ice White Exctinction The Dying Buffalo Becomes the Scorned . . . . Image of Christ, His Compassionate Pawing uncovers the Mass Graves long . . . . concealed by Cowboy Death Games, Played by Men, America's Deadly Children . . . .

Emptied at last Chains of Lifeless Nebraskas string beadlike over the Stolen Landscape, Flat in emulation of its spidery soul, The Gaunt Stretches of Arid Guilt tints the surface of America's Pride, Sick pasted Repairs define those Terrifying Craters dug from the Confiscated Souls of Destroyed Giants Stashed behind Christian . . . . Altars, to be dragged out on Trophy days in Honor of Ancestral Kills . . . . Grinning in Consumptive Triumph, Sub-dividing the Happy Hunting Ground . . . . Clothed in Unfitting Garments peeled from Red Bodies of Wild Peace-Pipe Saints, Martyred by their Undying faithfulness to the caressing Earth, & This America's own Secret Deaths . . . . The bitter Nebraskas are finally dipped in the Blood, & no Lambs Bless Them, Leafless Nebraska's Stolen pool feeds on Laughing Springs drilled out of the Papoose Eyes of Black Banged Familiar Infants, The Native Baptism Stains America's Ragged Soul With Black Water . . . . & Gothic Hate Festivals of Rotted Conscience, suffocate the Vanishing Ambition, CARYL CHESSMAN WAS AN AMERICAN BUFFALO, THUNDERING ACROSS CALIFORNIA'S LYING PRAIRIES, RACKED WITH POISON THE ARROWS OF AUTHORITY, GUARDING THE BRILLIANT . . . . VISIONS OF MILLIONS OF GENOCIDED RED CRAZY HORSE PEOPLE, DEAD IN THE MAKESHIFT GAS CHAMBERS OF SUPPRESSED HISTORY, CARL CHESSMAN WAS AN AMERICAN BUFFALO FILLED WITH GLISTENING EMBRYOS, FLYING WITH ZULU KINGS TO THE BOTTOMLESS PITS OF AMERICA'S SOUL, CARYL CHESSMAN WAS AN AMERICAN BUFFALO, & OUR VOMITTING ASSASSINS KILLED HIM, & DESTROYED THEMSELVES IN THEIR REPUBLICAN-DEMOCRAT HASTE TO EXTINGUISH HIS BURNING. COME MY SMALL BROWN SON, TASTE HIS BREATH, SHINING US WITH TRUTH

(REEL IV)

The Natural Gass Ballard & The Germ At its Source.

The scene opens with dim silhouettes of animal sadness, trapped in echo chambers of time. We are standing at the death bed of the last

Buffalo in Nebraska. he is dying of onesomeness, strange disease brought by the new mirror people with no sky in their faces, unseen red fingers clutch at his snowy white hide holy in the light of love willful destruction.

Saturated with the rusty terra cotta dignity of Bisons, he refuses pity, & embarks on his dusty voyage alone.

Comforted by the promised shadows of the Great Divide, he unlocks the final hoard of raw American love, whispering it on the winds, blessed with the scars of terror.

Battering with his monumental hooves he grinds the remains of his injected fear into the dust of multiplied generations, releasing the inhibited future.

Across the layers of centuries stacked in his eyes, his soul traverses the newly slaughtered brain, singing benedictions learned from holy birds.

He bathes in geysers pushed from yesterday to zombie congregations of cold Nebraska people, alarm clocks in their claws, timing the orgasm of earth.

His streaming eyes seek out familiar caves to receive his hide, having seen his race become leather jackets on pimply backs of Nebraska masturbators.

His wounds become inflammatory beacons, ignited by Nebraska's matchbooks.

Damp winds of tomorrow carry his grief to impalement on Grand Tetons Arrow.

His hide becomes the brown Christmas tree of remorse, lit by America's blinking Christmas bullets.

His golden beast tongue screams for his stolen teeth, now hanging from the venereal wrist of Hollywood's latest madonna, posing in her glamorous scabs.

The eternal chorale of the breeze sings the litany of the red Phoenix
. . . . the falling waters chant of nations of woe, the horror song cycle
. . . . desperate retellings of the thin-lipped Nebraska pogroms
. . . .

TIDAL FRICTION

Tidal Friction . . . Comments At Real Movie . . . . Something
KNOWS PITY CAN THROW US ERECTERS, SEEING-EYE MEN FOR
. . . . BLIND DOGS . . . ENTERFECTUALS

Tidal Power . . .

> . . . Jack-Hammering the Mind Mine . . .
> Digging the Hole in the Soul . . . . . .
> Turn in your seals & number the
> dust . . . . I want to ask a terrifying
> question What time is it going to
> be . . . . . The Tragedy is, an over
> abundance . . . . of color, & a total
> lack of black . . . . & between the
> screams, Rancid function & America
> boying you to manless death, no, not
> even the great American novel of dis-
> play, You bought That Death on . . .
> time, & your only legacy is surplus . . .
> & your America is a tinted mother
> whose breast you have never sucked
> for all your mimed lust, & the literature
> of your suicide note is the significant
> arithmetic of the remaindered calendar
> that mark the filling of your hole in this
> American place, from which you have
> been gone a truly long time, & walked
> here since, the trousered whore of your
> face, that hand-painted mirror, stained
> with your neutral presence, & the holes
> you call eyes, & as you go endlessly
> Pin-striped to wherever it is that you go,

remember I have never refused you my
own humaness, tho' yours are but
nerveless . . . . bites, for which I am
in your perverse debt, for you have al-
lowed me to taste my blood, red with
my own hot living, & it cooled my
soul & I leave your own sawdust
within, for who . . . would bite the
dead, not even a know-nothing in-
tellectual, happy enough to point his
laughing finger at millions postered
sams, in fake star suit, & shout i want
you, while dancing on exotic beds, but
watch it scout, I can see those gothic
brain surgeons weeping over the re-
mains of destroyed american love
machines, & those know something
intellectuals hang around together, &
swap commentaries.

A TERROR IS MORE CERTAIN . . .

A terror is more certain than all the rare desirable popular songs i know,
than even now when all of my myths have become . . . . & walk around in
black shiny galoshes & carry dirty laundry to & fro, & read great books
& don't know criminals intimately, & publish fat books of the month &
have wifeys that are lousy in bed & never realize how bad my writing is
because i am poor & symbolize myself.

A certain desirable is more terror to me than all that's rare, How come
they don't give an academy award to all the movie stars that die? they're
still acting, ain't they? even if they are dead, it should not be held against
them, after all they still have the public on their side, how would you
like to be a dead movie star & have people sitting on your grave?

A rare me is more certain than desirable, that's all the terror, there are
too many basketball players in this world & too much progress in the
burial industry, lets have old fashioned funerals & stand around & for-
give & borrow wet handkerchiefs, & sneak out for drinks & help load

that guy into the wagon, & feel sad & make a date with the widow &
believe we don't see all of the people sinking into the subways going to
basketball games & designing baby sitters at Madison Square Garden.

A certain me is desirable, what is so rare as air in a Poem, why can't i
write a foreign movie like all the other boys my age, I confess to all the
crimes committed during the month of April, but not to save my own
neck, which is adjustable, & telescopes into any size noose, I'm doing
it to save Gertrude Stein's reputation, who is secretly flying model air-
planes for the underground railroad stern gang of oz, & is the favorite in
all the bouts . . . not officially opened yet Holland tunnel is the one who
writes untrue phone numbers.

A desirable poem is more rare than rare, & terror is certain, who wants
to be a poet & work a twenty four hour shift, they never ask you first,
who wants to listen to the radiator play string quartets all night. I want
to be allowed not to be, suppose a man wants to swing on the kiddie
swings, should people be allowed to stab him with queer looks & drag
him off to bed & its no fun on top of a lady when her hair is full of shiny
little machines & your ass reflected in that television screen, who wants
to be a poet if you fuck on t.v. & all those cowboys watching.

SHEILA

CAST

OUT OF RAINCLOUDS

LOCUST

IN DAMPENED WINGS

MADE

LEWD CAUSTIC REMARKS

TO

THIRSTY OLD MEN

RIDING

WHEEZING GREY HORSES

ON

WARPED, FADED CAROUSELS

REFLECTED EYES OF SWANS, EMPTY AT LAST

SHE IS GONE IN CAVES OF GREY MARBLE AND FORMS
SHE IS GONE IN BLUE TRUCKS PAINTED WITH SECRETS
SHE IS GONE IN TAXABLE PUBLIC SHEETS
SHE IS GONE IN CADAVER-INFESTED MUNICIPAL FILING CABINETS
SHE IS GONE IN STILLED WHIRLPOOLS PITTED ALONG HER ARMS
SHE IS GONE IN OBSCURE CONSIDERATION OF LOST EVENTS
SHE IS GONE IN COLD METROPOLITAN STATISTICS
SHE IS GONE IN SILENCE TO SILENCE FROM SILENCE
SHE IS GONE IN SHOES, IN SOCKS IN FABRICS OF BLACK
                RIDING HORSES INTO NOTHING
                DRAGGING UNNOTICED ASPECTS OF US ALL

MOUNT THE TROPHY, THE WINNERS ARE WAITING
                IN LIVING ROOMS.

HEATHER BELL   Chorus

You know Heather Bell, she lives around the corner from everybody,
Heather's problem is not staying around the corner . . . she is an unusual
girl, she has no desire to sleep with her father, partially because her
father is dead. It may also be said of her that she has never willingly
submitted to her stepfather . . . until she had received everything she
had been promised.

Heather is cool for a schoolgirl, she prefers the company of hipsters,
beats, homosexuals—impotent novelists . . . and a beat girl who looks
very much like a view of her as seen from the inside . . . Heather loves
jazz as much as she hates her mother who no longer loves . . . Heather
is an American matador. Heather's mother is an American bull. Heather
needs a cape to tire her bull and prepare it for the kill . . . Heather fights
rough, her cape is apt to be ripped, but how important is a cape when
you know the important thing is to kill. Heather is cool & needs a cool
cape.

WALKING HOT SEASONS

From walking hot seasons, through unmarked years of light,
My face is moonburned, EVERYTHING THAT NEVER HAPPENED IS MY
        FAULT.

BLACK CARROT OF DENIAL, BURNED IN THE TOASTERS OF
        MEMORY
THAT SUMMER NEVER CAME AGAIN, WE LIE IN THIGHS, SPEAKING
        IN TONGUES, HOLY
BENT TURTLE OF REMORSE LOCKED IN STEP, CHASING THE HARE
        OF WHIMSY,
EUPHORIC FIXER, UNCALL MY NAME, TEAR UP MY EYES, I REFUSE
        TO APPEAR
        THOSE THINGS DONE IN COMPASSION & TOTAL DISREGARD.
        THOSE THINGS DONE BY PEOPLE I DIDN'T KNOW & PEOPLE
            WHO KNEW ME,
        EVERYTHING I PLANNED CAME AS A COMPLETE SURPRISE
        THERE WERE NO INTERMISSIONS SO I WALKED OUT BEFORE
            THE END.
        THEY SAY MY LIFE IS EXCITING, BUT I DON'T BELIEVE THEM.

RESULTS OF A LIE DETECTOR TEST

From the sleeping calendar I have stolen a month
I am afraid to look at it, I don't want to know its name
Clenched in my fist I can feel its frost, its icy face
I cannot face the bewildered summer with a pocketful of snow
I imagine the accusing fingers of children who will never be born
How to shut out the cries of suffering death wishers, awaiting
      the silent doors of winter tombs. Deprived of cherished exits,
I shall never again steal a month . . . or a week or a day or an hour
  or a minute or a second, unless I become desperate again.

COME

Come let us journey to
      the Sky.
I promised the Moon.

All that I come from
All that I have been,
All that I am
All that I come to
All that I touch,
Blossoms from
      a thorn,
AROSEAROSE

Love is the condition
of Human Beings
Being Humans.

To be beloved
Is all I need
And whom I love
Is loved indeed,
There never was a Night that
Ended, or began,
Forms breaking
Structures imaged,
Come love,
Love come.

SARASWATI

May Saraswati give thee
            intelligence
Entwined with the Lotus . . .
      Thou art produced from
      Limb by limb,
But of the heart thou art
      born!

Thou indeed art the
          self called son!
So live a hundred autumns

UNHISTORICAL EVENTS

APOLLINAIRE
          NEVER KNEW ABOUT ROCK GUT CHARLIE
          WHO GAVE FIFTY CENTS TO A POLICEMAN
          DRIVING AROUND IN A 1927 NASH

APOLLINAIRE
          NEVER MET CINDER BOTTOM BLUE,
          FAT SAXOPHONE PLAYER WHO LAUGHED
          WHILE PLAYING AND HAD STEEL TEETH

APOLLINAIRE
          NEVER HIKED IN PAPIER MACHE WOODS
          AND HAD A SCOUTMASTER WHO WROTE A SONG ABOUT
          IVORY SOAP AND HAD A BAPTIST FUNERAL

APOLLINAIRE
          NEVER SAILED WITH RIFF RAFF ROLFE
          WHO WAS RICH IN CALIFORNIA, BUT
          HAD TO FLEE BECAUSE HE WAS QUEER

APOLLINAIRE
          NEVER DRANK WITH LADY CHOPPY WINE,
          PEERLESS FEMALE DRUNK, WHO TALKED TO SHRUBS
          AND MADE CHILDREN SING IN THE STREETS

APOLLINAIRE
          NEVER SLEPT ALL NIGHT IN AN ICEHOUSE,
          WAITING FOR SEBASTIAN TO RISE FROM THE AMMONIA TANKS
          AND SHOW HIM THE LITTLE UNPAINTED ARROWS.

COCOA MORNING

Variations on a theme by morning,
Two lady birds move in the distance.
Gray jail looming, bathed in sunlight.
Violin tongues whispering.

Drummer, hummer, on the floor,
Dreaming of wild beats, softer still,
Yet free of violent city noise,
Please, sweet morning,
Stay here forever.

PICASSO BALCONY

Eaten with remains of torn flowers,
Overwhelming afterthoughts of binding loves, classic pains,
Casting elongated shadows of early pieces of blue,
Stringing hours together, in some thin melodic line,
Wrapped around the pearl neck of morning,
Beneath the laughter of sad blue seabirds.

"MICHELANGELO" THE ELDER

I live alone, like pith in a tree,
My teeth rattle, like musical instruments.
In one ear a spider spins its web of eyes,
In the other a cricket chirps all night.
This is the end,
Which art, that proves my glory has brought me.
I would die for Poetry.

BLUE SLANTED INTO BLUENESS

NO SEBASTIAN, NOT AGAIN, NOR A FIRST TIME EITHER
WHO WILL BE THE FIRST ONE TO BREAK THE ICE,
REST FOREVER IN THE AMMONIA TANK, IN AN ICE HOUSE
HUNG BY THE THUMBS.

I AM NOT A FORM,
I AM ME, SACRED & HOLY,
I AM UNIMPALABLE,
THE FORM THAT MEMORY TAKES
HAS BLED ON ME,
AND BURNED RIMBAUD TO ASHES,
NO ONE ELSE CAN EVEN THINK OF THAT FORM
BLEEDING THEMSELVES OR OTHERS.

EARLY LOVES

Slippery driftwood, icebreaking mudpacks.
Garfish, mothers of cajun whores,
Laughing blood noises, at comic shrimps.
Gliding on leaves of sunken trees.

Dying love, hidden in misty Bayous
Red love, turning black, brown,
Dead in the belly, brittle womb
Of some laughing crab.

A father. Whose, mine?
Floating on seaweed rugs.
To that pearl tomb, shining
Beneath my bayou's floor.

Dead, and dead,
And you dead too.

No more arm twisting,
Heart twisting laughter.
Dead moss, colors of sorrow.

Later in hot arms, hers,
Between sweaty lovemakings.
Crying will wet moss swamps,
Hidden beneath her arms.

Tears will wash her dirty murdered soul.
God will be called to atone for his sins.

ROUND ABOUT MIDNIGHT

Jazz radio on a midnight kick,
Round about Midnight,

Sitting on the bed,
With a jazz type chick
Round about Midnight,

Piano laughter, in my ears,
Round about Midnight.

Stirring laughter, dying tears,
Round about Midnight.

Soft blue voices, muted grins,
Exciting voices, Father's sins,
Round about Midnight.

Come on baby, take off your clothes,
Round about Midnight.

JAZZ CHICK

Music from her breast vibrating
Soundseared into burnished velvet.
Silent hips deceiving fools.
Rivulets of trickling ecstasy
From the alabaster pools of Jazz

Where music cools hot souls.
Eyes more articulately silent
Than Medusa's thousand tongues.
A bridge of eyes, consenting smiles
Reveal her presence singing
Of cool remembrance, happy balls
Wrapped in swinging
Jazz
Her music . . .
Jazz.

TEQUILA JAZZ

The party is on.
People are on,
Too.
Are you on too?

Who crouches there in my
Heart?
Some wounded bird,
Hidden in the tall grass
That surrounds my heart.

Unseen wings of jazz,
Flapping, flapping,
Carry me off, carry me off.
Dirt of a world covers me,
My secret heart,
Beating with unheard jazz.

Thin melody ropes
Entwine my neck,
Hanging with
Tequila smiles,
Hanging, Man,
Hanging.

HARWOOD ALLEY SONG (San Francisco)

Oh the God-bus has a busted wheel
Oh Atlantis died of venereal disease
Caesar's hung on Pandora's box
Mexico Mexico, fill my nostrils.

Rimbaud, you brilliant maniac, desert turtle.
Stop flirting with camels, turn in your pike,
we are late for the lotus affair, sacrifice,
after Bacchanal, the form shall bleed, on us.

Remnants of neo-classical witch doctors,
hurling jagged missives of flame-sheeted bone,
affecting space cures, on curved people,
standing in themselves, up to their necks.

Inside my cave-eyes the desperate cock
fled shrieking, deserting my handless clock.
God, you are just an empty refrigerator;
with a dead child inside, incognito,
in the debris of the modern junkpile.

Nut-brown hands, hot from pushing Parícutin
from smoky core, to exploding light, reddened,
must yet calm vibrant nerves of dead gods,
yet tear Montezuma, from dark skies,
to chant the song of time, for us.

Warm-blooded petitions, demanding unnoticed existence,
voided by sudden accusations, abstract dares,
trapped in moist webs of atoms, secreted,
in folds of wind, caught hanging in time.

HIS HORN

Swinging horn softly confirming
Anguished cries of eternal losers
Whose gifts outgrow their presence.
We hear this lonesome Saxworld dweller
Swing higher—
Defiantly into a challenge key
Screamed over a heartbeat
Shouting at all beat seekers
To vanish into soft sounds of jazz
And walk with him to smoky ends
While his jazz walks forever
Across our parched heartstrings.

THE BIGGEST FISHERMAN

singular prints filed along damp banks,
supposed evidence of fouled strings, all;

breached dikes of teeth hewn agate statues
scaly echoes in eroded huts of slate and gristle.

mildewed toes of pastoral escapes, mossy charades,
cane towered blind, smooth blister on watern neack

angry glowing fish in eniwetok garments and pig tusks
alarmed horror of black croakers, finned hawks sinking.

collectors of fish teeth and souls of night vision demons
taxidermy fiesta of revolutionary aquatic holidays lost.

breeding hills of happy men, of no particular bent, or none,
condemned to undreamlike beauty of day to day to day to day,
deprived of night, ribbon bright streams die parched deaths
baked by fissioning waves of newly glowing fish.

INSIDE CONNIE

INNER LIT, TWISTED TREES,
SNARLING.
CURTAINS OF THE MIND,
DRAWN.
EXPOSING MADNESS,
ILLUMINATING DEATH,
DANCING,
AROUND HER HEAD.

LOST WINDOW

Tall strips of carrion moonlight.
sparing only stars.
Giant bees gliding along the sidewalks,
Lonely insects, stinging each other.
Unknowing victims, mounting feathery scaffolds.
Lines of tired aprons dancing mobile-like.
Across lit stages of air.
Minute pieces of death, flinging themselves
Across crowded intersections.
Muted sobbing of a hidden child,
Filters over the sill,
Of a secret window, hidden
In the dark corner
Of evening.

CROSS WINDS (Song for Paul Swanson)

Cross wind, eat lost mad ones,
Cactus, grow them over.
Dig small graves, shallow,
Lay them gently
In the soft earth.
Speak the dead words,
Tell of life, lost.

Give places to the wanderers,
Corners, where they might crawl.
In the end, in beginnings,
Give love, give life,
At last, give death,
Cross winds.

BELIEVE, BELIEVE

Believe in this. Young apple seeds,
In blue skies, radiating young breast,
Not in blue-suited insects,
Infesting society's garments.

Believe in the swinging sounds of jazz,
Tearing the night into intricate shreds,
Putting it back together again,
In cool logical patterns,
Not in the sick controllers,
Who created only the Bomb.

Let the voices of dead poets
Ring louder in your ear
Than the screechings mouthed
In mildewed editorials.
Listen to the music of centuries,
Rising above the mushroom time.

BLUE O'CLOCK

Seven Floating lead moons,
      Red up night skies,
      Seven twisted horns,
      Mouth blown seven times.
Seven shaking angels
      Shadowed stripe,

Night.
Seven ice white suns,
White down day skies,
Revealing our pains
To each.

[BUT AS LOVE]

BUT AS LOVE
IS
LONG-WINDED
THE MOVING WIND
DESCRIBED ITS
MOVING COLORS
IN SOUND &
LIGHT.

THE CAT IS SLEEPING ON A POEM

A Lady cigarette fixed in the ash trays of history
I shall unremember last night's humorous junk tragedies
In honor of personal survival I turn my back to the mirror
The sun is an oatmeal cookie, the moon a blue glass eye
Hooked on fake wisdom, the owl's wing hides his eye in the light.

Sometimes a sacred dream is wrapped in scarf,
Thrown around an anonymous neck, & chest,
As smoking worlds emerge, hot flickering signals
From Indian nerves, in bonfires of Aztec surprises.

There is a season in there is a season in the mind when
The toadstools change color.
Not hot, not cold,
It comes at no known
Times
Perhaps that china plate was

Exaggerating, maybe
The gingham dog, & the calico cat
Got married,
And lived happily ever after.

SUN

Sun, Creator of Suns,
Sun, which makes Men,
My eye fails me,
Longing to see Thee
I touch stone.
For the sole desire to know
Thee
Might I know thee
Might I consider thee
Might I understand
Look down upon me
Sun, Moon, Day, Night,
Spring, Winter,
Are not ordained in vain.

THE MIND FOR ALL ITS REASONING

The mind for all its complicated reasoning,
Is dependent on the whim of an eyelid,
The most nonchalant of human parts,
Opening and closing at random,
Spending its hours in mystique,
Filled with memories of glimpses
            & blinks.

An eyelid hurled at the moon,
An exhausted nude woman,
Damp kimonas flowing from her pores.

A red poem can be a
   Hairy fire-extinguisher
   Hanging from the ears of
   A divine burglar,
My eyes opened on closed windows, a curved man.

CROOTEY SONGO

DERRAT SLEGELATIONS, FLO GOOF BABEREO
SORASH SHO DUBIES, WAGO, WAILO, WAILO

GEED BOP NAVA GLIED, NAVA GLIED, NAVA
SPEERIEDER, HUYEDIST, HEDACAZ, AX, O, O

DEEREDITION, BOOMEDITION, SQUOM, SQUOM, SQUOM
DEE BEETSTRAWIST, WAPAGO, WAPAGO, LOCO, LOCORO, LOCOEST
VOOMETEYEREEPETIOP, BOP, BOP, BOP, WHIPOP

DEARAT, SHLOHO, KURRITIP, PLOG, MANGI, SQUOM POT
CLOPO JAGO, BREE, BREE, ASLOOPERED, AKINGO LABIOP
ENGPOP, ENGPOP, BOINT PLOLO, PLOLO, BOP BOP

SLIGHT ALTERATIONS

I climb a red thread
To an unseen existence,
Broken free, somewhere,
Beyond the belts.

Ticks have abandoned
My astonished time.
The air littered
With demolished hours.

Presence abolished
I become a ray

From the sun
Anonymous finger
Deflected into hungry windows
Boomerang of curved light
Ricocheted off dark walls
The ceiling remembers my face
The floor is a palate of surprise
Watching me eat the calendar.

I SIGH A MARBLED SIGH AH, AT LAST

WE FLY AHEAD INTO THE PAST, GOOD, WE DEFEAT PROGRESS,
PROGRESS HAS BECOME BALD GALL & STOLE GOLD GROWN BE-
NEATH A FALL OFF OF THESE WALLS OF NOW
          SO NEW, A DISAPPEARED YEBREAISHE, SO LONG AS WE
          SHOW A PROPHET.
                    ANY LOSS WE GAIN IS HOURS, WHICH MULTIPLY AND DI-
VIDE US INTO THE SEASONS OF APRIL, MONTH IN WHICH MONTHS
WERE BORN, & GO IF THEY REMEMBER NOT TO REMEMBER ALL THOSE
MEMORIES UNMARKED IN SEEDS & ARROWS.

I HAVE MET THE ARTIST OF THE MOUNTAIN OF BLOCKS THAT THIN
THEMSELVES OUT INTO AN EYELINE DANCING COLOR MOBILES
STRETCHED FROM ONE EYE OF THE MIND TO ANOTHER, & GOD FOR-
BID, SHE IS NOT FORBIDDING, & THAT OMNIPOTENCE I FEARED WAS A
PAINTING'S REVENGE FOR ALL THE STARING IT HAS ENDURED AT THE
HAND OF MY EYE, (TOUCHE, ME COLORS & STRUCTURES & ARTKEY
TEXTURES WE ALL WIND)

WHY WRITE ABOUT

WRITE HUNG THINGS, MAD MESS
ZEN TREE JOY, DAD, LIKE, YOU KNOW?
SWUNG OUT CATS, HUNG,
ON PUBLICITY, LIKE, YOU KNOW,
SICK MIDDLE CLASS CHICKS,
NYMPHO, CACAUSOIDS, EATING SYMBOLS,

LITTLE OLD BOYS, IN MONDAY BEARDS,
ATTENDING, ALL THE, SCHOOLS,
OF SELF PITY,
SELLING THEIR RIGHT
TO REVOLUTION,
TO A PIECE OF,
LIKE, YOU KNOW MAN,
ITS, A SCENE,
LIKE, YOU KNOW,
THE, MOTHER BIT,

GENETIC COMPLICATIONS.
LIKE MAN, LIKE
MAN, LIKE,
LIKE.

WAITING

SOMEWHERE THERE WAITS, WAITING
A BOOK IS WAITING, WAITING,
TO BE WRITTEN.
COLD COLD PAGES, WAITING,
TO BE WRITTEN,
MAN SEEKS GOD,
IN A BOOK.

SOMEWHERE THERE WAITS, WAITING
A PICTURE WAITS, WAITING,
WAITING TO BE PAINTED
COLD COLD CANVAS, CANVAS.
WAITING TO BE PAINTED.
MAN SEEKS GOD IN A PICTURE.

SOMEWHERE THERE WAITS, WAITING
A WOMAN WAITING, WAITING,
TO BE LOVED, WAITING,
COLD COLD WOMAN,
WAITING TO BE LOVED,
MAN SEEKS GOD IN A WOMAN.

SOMEWHERE THERE WAITS, WAITING
A MAN IS WAITING, WAITING,
COLD COLD MAN, WAITING,
TO BE WANTED, WAITING.
MAN SEEKS GOD
IN MAN

SOMEWHERE THERE WAITS, WAITING
A BABY IS WAITING, WAITING.
WAITING, WAITING TO BE BORN,
COLD COLD BABY, WAITING,
TO BE BORN, BLOOD OF EARTH,
WAITING TO BE.
MAN SEEKS GOD,
IN A BABY.

WIND, SEA,
SKY, STARS,
SURROUND
US.

HEAVY WATER BLUES

The radio is teaching my goldfish Jujitsu
I am in love with a skindiver who sleeps underwater,
My neighbors are drunken linguists, & I speak butterfly,
Consolidated Edison is threatening to cut off my brain,
The postman keeps putting sex in my mailbox,
My mirror died, & can't tell if i still reflect,
I put my eyes on a diet, my tears are gaining too much weight.

•

I crossed the desert in a taxicab
only to be locked in a pyramid
With the face of a dog
on my breath

I went to a masquerade
Disguised as myself
Not one of my friends
Recognized

I dreamed I went to John Mitchell's poetry party
in my maidenform brain

Put the silver in the barbeque pit
The Chinese are attacking with nuclear
Restaurants

The radio is teaching my goldfish Jujitsu
My old lady has taken up skin diving & sleeps underwater
I am hanging out with a drunken linguist, who can speak butterfly
And represents the caterpillar industry down in Washington D.C.

•

I never understand other peoples' desires or hopes,
until they coincide with my own, then we clash.

I have definite proof that the culture of the caveman,
disappeared due to his inability to produce one magazine,
that could be delivered by a kid on a bicycle.

When reading all those thick books on the life of god,
it should be noted that they were all written by men.

It is perfectly all right to cast the first stone,
if you have some more in your pocket.

Television, america's ultimate relief, from the indian disturbance.

I hope that when machines finally take over,
they won't build men that break down,
as soon as they're paid for.

i shall refuse to go to the moon,
unless I'm inoculated against
the dangers of indiscriminate love.

After riding across the desert in a taxicab,
he discovered himself locked in a pyramid
with the face of a dog on his breath.

The search for the end of the circle,
constant occupation of squares.

Why don't they stop throwing symbols,
the air is cluttered enough with echoes.

Just when I cleaned the manger for the wisemen,
the shrews from across the street showed up.

The voice of the radio shouted, get up
do something to someone, but me & my son
laughed in our furnished room.

WHEN WE HEAR THE EYE OPEN . . .

When we hear the eye open, there, in that place,
There, a whisper is a scream,
Breathing there, in that place,
A breath is the birth of sound,
We shall see our reflections
On the gigantic thighs of a giant,
There, in that place,
My head is a bony guitar, strung with tongues, plucked by fingers & nails,
The giant is only his legs, the rest of him will be gone far on,
And blinking cities will fly from his knees,
        And in a future, in that place, there,
            I was a nut in a chocolate bar,
                And I melted in a soft hand,
                    And we sang a luna tune,

The ear hears fear, the eye lies, the mind dies, the teeth curl,
And Runic stone alone, weeps at the death of sleep,
Colder than a frozen nun, chilly accusations point,
Naked river, screamer on lonely poet corners,
Yes, and bugs with lights another crime of mine

How else walk against these black winds of mind death,
Blowing down these lonely streets,
They have found a way to disturb the moon,
The sun burns at love's two ends,
On the eternal launching pad.

FALLING

Cool shadows blanked dead cities, falling,
Electric anthills, where love was murdered.
Daily crucifixions, on stainless steel crosses,
In the gardens of pillbox subdivisions, falling.
Poets, like free reeds, drift over fetid landscapes,
Bearded Phoenix, burning themselves, falling.
Death patterns capture the eyes, falling.
A saving madness, cast by leafless trees, falling,
Cushions the songs, filtered through smoking ruins,
From the nostrils of unburied dead gods.
Cool shadows, fall over drawn eyelids, falling,
Cutting off the edge of time, falling, endlessly.

I WISH . . .

I wish that whoever it is inside of me,
would stop all that moving around,
& go to sleep, another sleepless year
like the last one will drive me sane,

I refuse to have any more retired burglars
picking the locks on my skull, crawling in
through my open windows, i'll stay out forever,
or at least until spring, when all the wintered
minds turn green again,

It's all right fellows, it's just a joke,
you had me scared for a moment God, i thought you were serious,
i was beginning to believe that this was really your idea of life,

i know second fifth, but you made it sound so unbelievable,
You're the only one in this whole big universal gin mill, believe me god,
who could get away with it, even that oldest boy of yours
& yet even he, your own
fleshlessness & bloodlessness, was helpless when it came to dirty jokes.

SUICIDE

Big Fanny & stromin vinne deal,
all that's left of the largest colony
of the new world, who coulda guessed it
no one in his right mind.

Poets don't sneak into zoos & talk with tigers anymore,
even though they read Blake & startle all by striped
devices, while those poems of God pout, lurking & sundried torn tree jungles
William Blake never saw a tiger & never fucked a lamb.
you get off at fifty ninth street, forever

The first man was an idealist, but he died,
he couldn't survive the first truth,
discovering that the whole
world, all of it, was all his, he sat down
& with a little piece of string, & a sharp stone
invented suicide.

THE LATE LAMENTED WIND, BURNED IN INDIGNATION

TONTO IS DEAD, TONTO IS DEAD, TONTO IS DEAD
        RUN HIDE IN SUBWAYS.
        ELECTRIC ARROW OF PENITENT MACHINES & FOOTSTEP
        HORROR
LET THE FLEA CIRCUS PERFORM, TONTO IS DEAD—

THE BEST PLACE TO JUDGE A TAP DANCE CONTEST,
        IS FROM BENEATH THE STAGE.

TONTO IS DEAD, HIDE IN SUBWAYS.
HEAVY WATER MUSIC, SPILLED FROM PUBLIC HARPSICHORDS,

AT GALA LAUNDERMAT CONCERTS, FEATURING SONATAS FOR
DEFEATED OBOES,
BETWEEN DOOR SLAM OVERTURES, & SOGGY BALLETS,
EXITING INTO KEY EYES OF LONELY JAZZERS,
TONTO IS DEAD, TONTO IS DEAD,
MUSEUMS ARE EXEMPT FROM MARTIAL LAW,
HIDE IN THE SUBWAY, QUICK
BEFORE IT MELTS.

NIGHT SUNG SAILOR'S PRAYER

Voyager now, on a ship of night
Off to a million midnights, black, black
Into forever tomorrows, black
Voyager off to the time worlds,
Of life times ending, bending, night.

Pleader on the ship of the children night
Begging a song for children still in flight
Sing little children, sing in the empty cathedrals
Sing in the vacant theaters,
Sing laughter to the twisted sons
Poisoned from the mildewed fathers
Sing love to the used up whores
Dying in some forgotten corner.
Sing sunlight and barking dogs
To the born losers, decaying in the sorry jails.

Sing pity and hell, to the wax biches
Buried in the bowels of the male cadillacs
Sing tomorrow and tomorrow and sing maybe next time
To the negro millionaires, trapped in their luxurious complexions.

Sing love and an everlasting fix
For the hopeless junkies, stealing into night's long time
Sing yes, and yes, and more and more

113

To the cloud borne bohemians
Afloat in their endless fantasies.

Sing love and life and life and love
All that lives is Holy,
The unholiest, most holy all.

THE UNDER WEIGHT CHAMPION

What goes up is bound to come down . . .
What goes down is bound to come up.
For god's sake, stop all the stop
God is missing & is out trying to launch his own rocket.
Hooray for mrs. Rasputin.
Burnt eskimos to the rear march.
Adam & Eve went up the hill to fly a drunken garter,
Mrs. Jack horner sat in a corner eating her son's last pie,
Jack & Jill are guilty of eating stolen apples,
A kleptomaniac steals from bees, & has a many-armed mind,
Little miss muffet sat on a tuffet waiting for a taxi-cab.
Shear the hot cakes clean, the locust people are painting my
head, one beard explodes succession burned comedies inside a head.

PLEA

Voyager, wanderer of the heart,
Off to
                a million midnights, black, black
Voyager, wanderer of star worlds,
Off to
                a million tomorrows, black, black,
Seek and find Hiroshima's children,
                Send them back, send them back.
Tear open concrete sealed cathedrals, spiritually locked
                Fill vacant theaters with their musty diversions,
Almost forgotten laughter.

Give us back the twisted sons
Poisoned by mildewed fathers.
Find again the used up whores,
Dying in some forgotten corner,
Find sunlight, and barking dogs,
For the lost, decayed in sorry jails.
Find pity, find Hell for wax bitches,
Hidden in the bowels of male Cadillacs.

Find tomorrow and next time for Negro millionaires
Hopelessly trapped in their luxurious complexions.
Find love, and an everlasting fix for hopeless junkies,
Stealing into lost nights, long time.

Voyager now,
          Off to a million midnights, black, black
Seek and find Hiroshima's children,
          Send them back, send them back.

DRUNK TIME

Free reeds drift in the weeping morning,
Here on the liquid floor of hell.
Phoenix, burn sunlight, to dead gods,
As concrete patterns capture eyes.

Poet madness aglow in the shadows,
Breathing songs amid the smoke
From the eyes of long dead gods,
Tall weeds walk on air,
Between your breath & mine.

Naked flint-eyed women,
Goddesses of nothing,
Brightly lit flesh,
Eaten, in rooms of the dead.

Cool shadows fall on drawn eyelids,
Drunken memories, weave in, out of times past,

Times of pear-shaped arguments,
Of intent & purpose,
Lost among crashing noises,
Cynical laughter,
Echoes of tears,
As the air ends

GENEOLOGY

Great-Grandfathers, blessed by great-grandmothers,
Shaped recently cooled buried stars, downed moons.

Creating hawk-beaked hatchets, phallic pikes, fire,
To tear out stubborn determined cells, clinging to
Other great-grandfathers, other great-grandmothers.

Proudly survived fathers, goaded by proud mothers,
Rolled lead drippings into skull piercing eternities.

Sent to stamp death on final presences, life forms,
Of other survived fathers, other proud mothers.

Sons, grandsons, daughters, granddaughters, bastards
Rolling the atmosphere into sinister nuclear spheres,

Insane combustions, to melt the bones, ivory teeth,
Of other sons, grandsons, daughters, granddaughters, Bastards.

Here, Adam, take back your God damn rib.

ON

On yardbird corners of embryonic hopes, drowned in a heroin tear.
On yardbird corners of parkerflights to sound filled pockets in space.
On neuro-corners of stripped brains & desperate electro-surgeons.
On alcohol corners of pointless discussions & historical hangovers.
On television corners of literary corn flakes & rockwells impotent America.

On university corners of tailored intellect & greek letter openers.
On military corners of megathon deaths & universal anesthesia.
On religious corners of theological limericks and
On radio corners of century-long records & static events.
On advertising corners of filter-tipped ice-cream & instant instants.
On teen-age corners of comic book seduction & corrupted guitars.
On political corners of wanted candidates & ritual lies.
On motion picture corners of lassie & other symbols.
On intellectual corners of conversational therapy & analyzed fear.
On newspapers corners of sexy headlines & scholarly comics.
On love divided corners of die now pay later mortuaries.
On philosophical corners of semantic desperadoes & idea-mongers.
On middle class corners of private school puberty & anatomical revolts.
On ultra-real corners of love on abandoned roller-coasters.
On lonely poet corners of low lying leaves & moist prophet eyes.

O-JAZZ-O

Where the string
At
Some point,
Was some umbilical jazz,
Or perhaps,
In memory,
A long lost bloody cross,
Buried in some steel calvary.
In what time
For whom do we bleed,
Lost notes, from some jazzman's
Broken needle.
Musical tears from lost
Eyes,
Broken drumsticks, why?
Pitter patter, boom dropping
Bombs in the middle
Of my emotions
My father's sound
My mother's sound,
Is love,
Is life.

O-JAZZ-O WAR MEMOIR: JAZZ, DON'T LISTEN TO IT AT YOUR OWN RISK

In the beginning, in the wet
Warm dark place,
Straining to break out, clawing at strange cables
Hearing her screams, laughing
"Later we forgave ourselves, we didn't know"
Some secret jazz
Shouted, *wait, don't go.*
Impatient, we came running, innocent
Laughing blobs of blood & faith.
To this mother, father world
Where laughter seems out of place
So we learned to cry, pleased
They pronounce human.
The secret Jazz blew a sigh
Some familiar sound shouted *wait*
Some are evil, some will hate.
"Just Jazz, blowing its top again"
So we rushed & laughed.
As we pushed & grabbed
While jazz blew in the night
Suddenly they were too busy to hear a simple sound
They were busy shoving mud in men's mouths,
Who were busy dying on the living ground
Busy earning medals, for killing children on deserted street corners
Occupying their fathers, raping their mothers, busy humans we
Busy burning Japanese in atomicolorcinemascope
With stereophonic screams,
What one hundred per cent red blooded savage, would wasted precious time
Listening to jazz, with so many important things going on
But even the fittest murderers must rest
So they sat down in our blood soaked garments,
and listened to jazz
          lost, steeped in all our death dreams
They were shocked at the sound of life, long gone from our own
They were indignant at the whistling, thinking, singing, beating, swinging,
They wept for it, hugged, kissed it, loved it, joined it, we drank it,
Smoked it, ate with it, slept with it
They made our girls wear it for lovemaking

Instead of silly lace gowns,
Now in those terrible moments, when the dark memories come
The secret moments to which we admit no one
When guiltily we crawl back in time, reaching away from ourselves
They hear a familiar sound,
Jazz, scratching, digging, blueing, swinging jazz,
And listen,
And feel, & die.

OCT. 5TH, 1963

Chronicle
Letters to the Editor
5th & Mission
San Francisco, Calif.

Gentlemen:

Arriving back in San Francisco to be greeted by a blacklist and eviction, I am writing these lines to the responsible non-people. One thing is certain I am not white. Thank God for that. It makes everything else bearable.

The Loneliness of the Long Distance Runner is due to the oneliness of the Long Distance Runner, that uniqueness that is the Long Distance Runner's alone, and only his. The Loneliness of the Long Distance Runner is the only reason for the Long Distance Runner's existence. Short distance runners run, they finish neither first nor last, they finish, that is all that can be said about them, nothing can be said for them, an ordinariness that is their closest proximity to the truly unique. Men die, as all men come to know, sooner or later, at any rate either way, men die. On that all men can depend.

To answer that rarely asked question. . . . Why are all blacklists white? Perhaps because all light lists are black, the listing of all that is listed is done by who is brown, the colors of an earthquake are black, brown & beige, on the Ellington scale, such sweet thunder, there is a silent beat in between the drums.

That silent beat makes the drumbeat, it makes the drum, it makes the beat. Without it there is no drum, no beat. It is not the beat played by who is beating the drum. His is a noisy loud one, the silent beat is beaten by who is not beating on the drum, his silent beat drowns out all the noise, it comes before and after every beat, you hear it in beatween, its sound is

Bob Kaufman, Poet

THE ANCIENT RAIN

PRIVATE SADNESS

Sitting here alone, in peace
With my private sadness
Bared of the acquirements
Of the mind's eye
Vision reversed, upended,
Seeing only the holdings
Inside the walls of me,
Feeling the roots that bind me,
To this mere human tree
Thrashing to free myself,
Knowing the success
Of these burstings
Shall be measured
By the fury
Of the fall
To eternal peace
The end of All.

LORCA

   Split ears of morning earth green now,
Love and death twisted in tree arms,
    Come love, throw out your nipple
to the teeth of a passing clown.

Spit olive pits at my Lorca,
Give Harlem's king one spoon,
At four in the never noon.
Scoop out the croaker eyes
    of rose flavored Gypsies
Singing García,
In lost Spain's
Darkened noon.

DEAR PEOPLE

We cut our teeth on oyster shells,
We were suckled on father's milk,
So what?
Broken homes,
Don't cop out,
Buying diamonds
Off the backs of
South African Negroes
The wax bitches
Are well dressed tonight,
Dear people,
Let us
Eat jazz.

[THESE DAYS AND WEEKS]

These days and weeks
That cannot be found on any calendar,
These hours and minutes unknown to the clock,
When all those rusting ships of the past, long gone
To the bottom of life, guarding the sunken dreams
Cast up their sorrows to swell this grief with memory.

Terror is around us both my soul. Nothing else will come.
I cannot describe the horrors, and worse, I cannot flee.
A wall is all.
I am hacked by knives I do not see, stung by stinging bee,
I can only bleed in silence, my pains are numb with admiration.

Where do you keep them all, my soul? How long can you stand?
What question is this being asked, can humans ever know?
Mad teeth are in the forms of man and chew my love to bits,
And I can do nothing, my soul, but wait their clawing cut,
            Ask only that my flesh holds
            & my anguished mind's reassurance in surprise,
            & my love survive these brutal enigmas,
            That I please you, my Soul . . . if only you alone.

AWE

At confident moments, thinking on Death
I tell my soul I am ready and wait
While my mind knows I quake and tremble
At the beautiful Mystery of it.

PICASSO'S BALCONY

Pale morning light, dying in shadows, loving the earth in midday rays,
casting blue to skies in rings, sowing powder trails across balconies.
Hung in evening to swing gently, on shoulders of time, growing old, yet
swallowing events of a thousand nights of dying and loving, all blue.
Gone to that tomb, hidden in cubic air, breathing sounds of sorrow.

Crying love rising from the lips of wounded flowers, wailing, sobbing,
breathing uneven sounds of sorrow, lying in wells of earth, throbbing,
covered with desperate laughter, out of cool angels, spread over night.
Dancing blue images, shades of blues past, all yesterdays, tomorrows,
breaking on pebbled bodies, on sands of blue and coral, spent.

Life lying heaped in mounds, with volcano mouth tops, puckered, open,
sucking in atoms of air, sprinkling in atoms of air, coloring space, with
flecks of brilliance, opaline glistening, in eyes, in flames.

Blue flames burning, on rusty cliffs, overlooking blue seas, bluish. In
sad times, hurt seabirds come to wail in ice white wind, alone, and wail
in starlight wells, cold pits of evening, and endings, flinging rounds of
flame sheeted balls of jagged bone eaten, with remains of torn flowers,
overwhelming afterthoughts, binding loves, classic pains, casting elon-
gated shadows, of early blue.

Stringing hours together, in thin melodic lines, wrapped around the
pearl neck of morning, beneath the laughter of sad sea birds.

RUE MIRO

MIRO . . . THE FLOWERS ARE UP THERE ON THE WALL WHERE I LAST
SAW THEM & THE TIME BEFORE THAT, VARIOUS, WITH HOT
DOTS STICKING OUT ALL OVER, PRANCING DARKLY IN THEIR
WOODEN FRAME, THEIR WALL, DANCING LIKE GYPSIES ON THE
ROOF OF A DRUM . . .

MIRO . . . THERE IS A STREET WITH YOUR NAME, NAMED BEFORE YOU,
AFTER YOU, THEN AND NOW IT FLOATS IN DROPS AND SHAD-
INGS, STRANDED IN A FAKE SPAIN, FARTHER THAN MONTRO-
ICH, WAY OFF, A WET PLACE, OF HOT RAINS, & YELLOWED
LONG LEAF PLANTS, NAMED FOR A BROKEN SUN KING, LOU-
ISIANA, RHYMES WITH YESTERDAY, GONE, PAST, MOVED ON,
GHOSTLY, BROWN WISHES . . .

MIRO . . . YOUR NAME IS A BLACK RIBBON IN A STABBED LANDSCAPE,
RAVED COLD FORMS SLANTED AGAINST A STEW OF BURNING
SYMBOLS & EYES. BLATANTLY HONKING DUCKS GO UNNOTICED
IN EXPENSIVE FEATHERS, A FACELESS PLACE OF CURVING
BLOOD & FINGERING MOTIONS . . .

MIRO . . . EMPTY TURTLES, GLIDE BETWEEN A DIVIDE OF BAROQUE
HOTELS, FLEEING TO SHELLY NEST DEEP INSIDE A SCOOPED
OUT TRUTH, A SCOPE OF THINNING CRIES, A CHORUS OF GRIN-
NING OYSTERS, HEAVY DRAPERIES FROM TOULON, & ROOMS
OF DROWNING FURNITURE, DANGLING IN THE MIND'S EYE, A
WALK THROUGH THE BERSERK AIR,

MIRO . . . I WAS BORN ON YOUR STREET, FORTY THOUSAND YEARS AGO
IN A YEAR OF APRILS & SCREAMED A FLOCK OF DAZED GEESE
STAGGERED.

MIRO . . . ON THAT STREET, I HEARD A FEVER & SAW A WHITE
MOON, BY THE GALVEZ GREENS, BROKEN INTO MILLIONS OF
TRANSPARENCIES.

INQUIRY INTO A DECEMBER BECAUSE

The descendants of dinosaurs are quicksand men, holy crime
minds, dripping fake myths.

Those germinal wise men circumcised trees, demolished time,
invented mushrooms, those rubber toes of God.

I am being followed by hot butterflies and pickpockets have
lifted my navel. Stony crows have wakened me cawing at the moon.
My eyes leak, dripping sight all over my collar.

Fake mystics, who photograph
God, while ecstatic pygmies
Burped the Christ child.
Murmuring, smile, baby,
It's your birthday.

COUNTESS ERIKA BLAISE: CHORUS

Erika Blaise began life with several established truths in her mouth, one
was that her father owned three governments and held options on two
more. The other was that she was ugly; the aesthetics of her physical
make-up had been poorly handled by her maker, and as though in
remorse, he had endowed her with all the appetites he had not lavished
on the Marquis de Sade. It would not do to bore one with the education
and girlhood of an aristocratic European girl, as their lives do not begin
until all that is done with, stored with bloomers. Erika, being Count-
ess Blaise, was not allowed to destroy ordinary people, that is, people
whose annihilation is handled on a corporate scale. This placed her in
the uncomfortable position of having to find two people who were not
already spoken for, which is no small task today. Of course, after poking
around the flabby corners of humanity, she discovered that the only
group still available and in plentiful supply were artists; what's more,
they seemed to enjoy it, even demanding wounds that no one was pre-
pared to inflict, as though their diet was pain—flavored with self-taught
self-pity. Erika would not let such hungry people starve, for that would
not be civilized. Neither would she turn her back on any who seemed
worthy of such historical attentions. She began by collecting major

works by artists whose triumphs had placed them outside her game preserve, unearned trophies, but useful lures for less wily game stalking the well-framed jungle. Indiscriminate in her choice of charms to dangle from her social bracelet, she concocted a hodgepodge of self-immolators, unique only for its variety, angelic American girl refugees from Nebraska Victorianism, grateful for the chance to buy Sorbonne dreams in her richly lavendered armpits, English prose writers fleeing Berlitz concentration camps, New York painters pining for one-man shows, which she allowed them to put on so long as they didn't hang pictures, stone cutters, pastel chewers, wire benders, Arab boys with mosaic buttocks, inventors of new artistic movements that lasted one week, unless they became exhausted before the week was out—and fled to Marseilles. Blond German Faustian youth swearing to paint Nietzsche while tripping over borrowed evening gowns amid superman Teutonic giggles, hot-blooded Spaniards who had to be reheated every hour, who painted only their lips, sexy South Americans who slept in boots, and only with each other, explosive Mexicans who would paint only mountains and made love to kill time, Andalusian Gypsies with Flamenco dripping from their fingertips, who would not sin in the same room with a crucifix. African giants hired by the foot, with secret orders to kill Picasso, Italian futurists, who possessed nothing, but a past. Endlessly through the Louis Quinze bush, Erika led that vermilion safari in artistic circles until dizzy with the realization that she was bored, bored open to a new sound, one complete as yet unexplored world, jazz, Africa's other face, stranded—in America, yet to be saved. No Erika anywhere could ignore such a situation; who else can bring the silence so completely? Many. But one must lead.

[AS USUAL]

As usual
   the usual axe
      falls on the usual neck
         in the usual place
           at the usual time
as usual.

TELEGRAM TO ALEX/BAGEL SHOP, NORTH BEACH SF

DEAR ALEX, TOMORROW I AM GOING TO EAT ALL OF THE SUEZ
AND PANAMA CANALS, SO PLEASE DO NOT USE YOUR LIGHT &
GAS AND REFRAIN FROM EYEBALLING FOR TWO SECONDS, WE
HAVE A NEW DEAL FOR CHUCK BAUDELAIRE, THE NEW FRENCH
JUNKIE KID TO PAINT SOME TENDER BATHING SUITS ON MA &
PA KETTLE AND BEARNOG BAROOCK AND CARNAL SPELLMAN
CAN'T COME, SO THERE.

CLAP HANDS, HERE COMES THE LINDBERGH BABY

I reject those frozen
injections
of last night's junk
tragedy,
memory,
blotted survivor
no longer remembers
chromed elbows,
rosy highways,
pinned submission,
eyeless skull faces,
socketless eyes
screwed in,
eyes that have no history,
eyes that darken brows,
eyes that have no lids,
eyes that never blink
broken into &
entered eyes.

Sometimes a sacred dream
is wrapped in a scarf,
circling an anonymous
neck,
hung on a hook.
Sometimes are smoked times,
ambitiously obscured times,

frail times of the long pipe,
Mandarin by implication.

Maybe the young poets
wanted to be popes
or kings
of Mexico.

UNANIMITY HAS BEEN ACHIEVED, NOT A DOT LESS FOR ITS ACCIDENTALNESS

Raga of the drum, the drum the drum the drum the drum,
        the heartbeat
Raga of hold, raga of fold, raga of root, raga of crest, raga
        before coming,
Raga of lip, raga of brass, raga of ultimate come with yesterday,
        raga of a parched tongue-walked lip, raga of yellow,
        raga of mellow, raga of new, raga of old, raga of blue,
        raga of gold, raga of air spinning into itself,
I ring against slate and shell and wood and stone and leaf
        and bone
And towered holes and floors and eyes—against lone is lorn &
        rock & dust & flattened ball & solitudes of air & breath &
        hair & skin fed halves & wholes & bulls & calves & mad &
        soul & new & old & silence & saves & fall wall & water
        falling & fling my eye to sky & tingle & tangle.
I sing a mad raga, I sing a mad raga, a glad raga for the ringing
        bell I sing.
A man fishing with old clothes line, shouting bass drum
Sometimes in extravagant moments of shock of unrehearsed
        curiosity, I crawl outside myself, sneaking out through the
        eyes, one blasé, one surprised, until I begin to feel my own
        strangeness; shyly I give up the ghost and go back in until
        next time.

I can remember four times when I was not crying & once when
        I was not laughing.
I am kneaded by a million black fingers & nothing about me
        improves.

Gothic brain surgeons, weeping over the remains of destroyed
love machines.
Diggers, corkscrewing cleanly in, exhilerausted, into the mind
mine, impaled on edgeless shafts of subtle reminiscence,
green-walking across the belts and ties.
Slanted dark-walked time, wet with ages of dryness,
Raga of insignificance & blessed hopelessness.
Raga of sadness, of madness, of green screamed dreams,
mile-deep eyes.

The greatest men have gone unknown: Buddha was the twenty-
fourth.
A beggar is the body of a God-ness, come to shoot movies
with his eye,
Movies of people who do not beg, ragged, broke eagles,
hummed into the wheels turning, some in, others out,
rarely ever in or out, or vice versa, half open.
A string begins where a man ends a string, a man begins where
a string ends. A man bereft of string, falls all walls, be-
comes a screamed baby, raved.

FRAGMENT FROM PUBLIC SECRET

REBELS, WHAT ARE REBELS, HERE IN THIS LAND OF REBELLION,
THIS LAND THAT BEGAN WITH REBELLION—ARE THEY THOSE
WHOSE ACTIVITIES CAN OBJECTIVELY BE ABSORBED OR AS-
SIMILATED INTO THE PATTERING TIME, REMEMBER, IT IS NOT
IMPORTANT, FOR IN THE END, THE REBEL IS TIMELESS, AND IT
IS ONLY IN THE PASSAGE OF TIME THAT WE CAN DISCERN THE
REBEL FROM THE DISSENTER.

AMERICA, WHO ARE YOUR REBELS, WHAT SHORES HAVE THEY
BEEN CAST UPON? IS IT BECAUSE YOU HAVE DISCOVERED A
USE FOR EVERYTHING THAT THEY HAVE FOUND THEIR ONLY
RECOURSE IS TO SEEK AMONG NOTHING, HOPING TO FIND
COMPONENTS WHICH, IN THE FINALITIES OF CONSTRUCTION,
MIGHT ASSUME THE POSTURES OF PRINCIPLES, AND DISCOV-
ERING THE HORROR OF FRUSTRATION, TURN TO DEATH AS
THE FOUNT OF THE CREATIVE ACT? FROM THERE TO WHERE?

WHERE DO SEEKERS GO—SEEKERS WHO HAVE NO GERMAN
PHILOSOPHER TO LEAD THEM THROUGH THE HALLS OF DOOM,
WHOSE WHITELIKE WALLS ARE INVISIBLE TO THE NAKED
EYE? SEEKERS OF THE TRUTH HAVE ALWAYS WAKED EYES, AND
ALWAYS WILL, AND IN TIME SHALL BE NAKED IN THEIR OWN
LIGHT.

HERE IS A REBEL, ONE LARGE, MONSTROUS REBEL, WHO FIRST
TEARS DOWN HIMSELF, AND SNEAKS LIKE FIREWORKS INTO
THE PATHS OF OTHERS, HOPING TO EXPLODE, OFTEN SHOW-
ERED, EXISTENT TO THE END.

EVERY TIME I OPEN MY BIG MOUTH
I PUT MY SOUL IN IT.
IT TAKES SO MUCH TO BE NOTHING,
TO SHROUD THE MIND'S EYE
FROM THE GAUDY THEATER
OF THE HEAD.
FALLNESS NOON OF THE MIND
CLUTTERED WITH DISCARDED FANTASIES
NERVE PANELED CORRIDORS OF IMAGINATION
OPENING ON HIDDEN UNIVERSE
GLIMPSED IN THE ECHO
OF A SCREAM.

SCENE IN A THIRD EYE

on the gray shadow of the darkened city
in lost photographs of other sad visions,
ferrying images of transient ecstasies,
pains, private sadnesses, hid
in smoky towers, secret pockets in clandestine
nations.

what? pushed into hungry mouths of crowded buildings
retains its form, reason is too unreliable,
memory screwed into hoped-for visions, desire,
twisted beyond recognition, detected in echoed
sound.

shouting crossviews from worn cliffs, dug down
in the wake of violent earthworms, blinded in
refracted corkscrew glares, from coppery phantom
silhouettes of fake existence, pinned into air, stuck in
time.

NOVELS FROM A FRAGMENT IN PROGRESS

RETURN TRIP SEATED ERECT ON THE SINGING TRAIN IN DELIB-
ERATE ATTEMPT NOT TO FALL ASLEEP, USE OF IMAGINATION
TO AVOID SWAYING PEOPLE, UNREAL VISIONS OF MURALS ON
RED RESTROOM FLOORS, SLEEP URGE GETTING STRONGER,
SCREWING UP THE EYES TO A PERFECT BREAST, ROUGH STOP,
STRONG WISH FOR EROTICISM DEPARTING NATIONS CARRYING
BIG PAPER BAGS, WONDERING ABOUT THE DENTS IN BOXER'S
FACES, REJECTION OF THE SEXUAL ASPECT OF SWEAT, PIC-
TURE OF THE MOTORMAN AS THE MYSTIC FERRYMAN, HIS FACE
WOULD EVER BE DESCRIBED IN NOVELS, AWARENESS OF MUSIC
OUT BY THE WHEELS, SERIOUS ATTEMPT TO WRITE SONGS,
SURPRISED AT MY OWN NAIVETE, AMUSED BY SOUNDS LIKE
ONE I CAN'T WRITE, APPROACHING STATION, EYES OF SLIDING
DOOR, WAITING FOR IT TO OPEN, MORE PEOPLE, ANOTHER
STOP. IT ALWAYS HAPPENS, BRING THIS OFF WITHOUT ANNOY-
ING. ALWAYS WATCH THEM GET OFF BEFORE THE BIG EVENT,
I ALMOST GIVE UP AT TIMES LIKE THESE. HOW TO SAVE IT.
REPETITIOUS FRUSTRATION, NOW, MYSTIC HOURS WITHOUT
LOSING A GRIP ON MY SANITY & FREQUENTLY, WOMEN REAL-
IZE MY CONCENTRATION TO MASTER THIS TRICK, WILLING TO
RIDE PAST THEIR DESTINATION.

SECONDLESS

Secondless, minute scarred, hourless, owless, sourness,
    flowerless, for a statement, FOR GOD
the Pygmies are ECSTATIC.
            FICKLE TIME GONE FROM TIME INTO TIMELESSNESS,
Sometimes are tickless times,

BILLIE HOLIDAY, UNFUNNY LAUGHTER TIME & HOT WORLDS
FRECKLED TROPHY TIME
slanted & faded cloudy times,
white stain powdery rock times,
MOUTHMARKED ROCKLESS TIMES
Morning times, salamandered time,
MINUTE AGES OF TIMELESS TIME & CLOCKLESS CLOCKS, &
COCKLESS COCK.
Times of many colored afternoons,
WHEN MORNING BECAME A STRANGE HOSPITAL, & DE-TIMED
THE NEEDLESS DREAM,
time's brilliant alcoves, unbelled,
where brown shadows, snap like slivers
of widowed icycles . . . iced cycles . . .
pale times of riding the crippled horse,
to untimed farthest dry lips of the mind,
hazy latitudes of desperate hours, flattened
into stretching landscapes tickless cinemas,
technicolored on silently curved screens
of the mind.
BROKEN BY QUIET BLACK LAKES & NERVY GEYSERS &
NOTHING CONTINUED.
A GREAT PAINTING IS HUNG UP ON THE SKY.
THE ARTIST HIDES IN A JUNGLE OF WRECKED CLOCKS.

[DARKWALKING ENDLESSLY]

DARKWALKING ENDLESSLY, THESE ANGUISHED FLOORS OF EARTH
THROUGH RAINFULL SEASONS OF THE MIND, PAST THE FOAMING WAVE
OF BROKEN INTO AND ENTERED EYES, RIDING BLACK HORSES TO THE
THIN LIPS OF THE MIND. IN A YEAR OF BREAKING APRILS, I COME TO
THAT PLACE THERE. MY SOUL IS MOONBURNED. MY BODY A SINEWED
HURT FOR ALL THE NOTHING THAT I AM, THE NOTHING THAT IS ALL
MY MINGLES OF AFRICAN HAIR. SPEAK FOR ME. I WEAVE THE WINDS
AND KISS THE RAINS, ALL FOR LOVE.

I DREAMED I DREAMED AN AFRICAN DREAM. MY HEAD WAS A BONY
GUITAR, STRUNG WITH TONGUES, AND PLUCKED BY GOLD FEATHERED
WINGLESS MOONDRIPPED RITUALS UNDER A MIDNIGHT SUN, DRUM-
MING HUMAN BEATS FROM THE HEART OF AN EBONY GODDESS, HUM-
MING THE MELODIES OF BEING FROM STONE TO BONE AND FROM SAND
ETERNAL. BLUE RAIN FALLING IN SOFT EYEDROPS FROM NUDE BODIES
OF DANCING PLANETS, BEATS OF SCIENCE PLAYED ON VIBRATED TEETH
OF OPEN-MOUTHED AFRICAN HARPSICHORDS.
VENUS, THE STAR JAZZER IN TRANSIT, ON FLUTED BARS OF BLACK
LIGHT, DANCING IN THEATERS OF BIRDS STREAMING BEAUTY'S NAME
BEYOND THE BELTS. MAHOGANY GOLDFISH BLOSSOM IN THICKLY
    LOADED
SKIES DOWN FROM THE INTIMATE DISTANCE BY A RIVER WHERE PEACE
IS GREEN IN THE FOUNTAIN. ROSES DISAPPEAR INTO EACH OTHER.
THE SUN AND THE MOON CREATE THE BALLAD AT ITS SOURCE, AND
ALL THOSE FIRES OF LOVE I BURN IN MEMORY OF.

HIGHER THAN THE TALLEST PEAKS
DEEPER THAN THE STEEPEST CLOUDS
FARTHER THAN THE FARTHEST SEAS
STANDS THE SERENE KINGDOM OF THE TRULY FAIR
WITH HER IMMORTAL CHILDREN OF
                THE MIND.
THE GREAT ROSE OF TIME TURNS SLOWLY.
THE DREAM FLOWN ON WINGS OF SILVER BELLS, BEYOND HARPOONS
    AND SCREECH OWL,
GONE FAR ON BEYOND BEYOND.
THE DREAM IS ON THE HEIGHTS AND RISING.

[I WANT TO ASK A TERRIFYING QUESTION]

I want to ask a terrifying question,
"What time is it going to be?"
That Sunday never came,
He lied, speaking in tongues,
Hot walking New York, in smoky Januaries,

My back is moonburned,
And my arm hurts,
The blues come riding,
Introspective echoes of a journey,
Truth is a burning guitar,
You get off at Fifty-ninth Street forever.

[THE TRAVELING CIRCUS]

The traveling circus crossed the unicorn
with one silver dollar & pederasty eyes.

If i can't be an ugly rumor i won't be the good time had by all.

A certain terror is more rare to me than desirable
than publishing two volumes of my suicide notes,
there are too many lanky baseball players,
newspapering my bathroom floor, and too much
progress in the burial industry, let's go back,
to old-fashioned funerals, & sit around &
be sad, & forgive one another, & go outside
to bury the bottle, & borrow stiff handkerchiefs,
& help load the guy in the wagon & flirt with the widow,
& pretend not to see all those people sinking
into subways, going to basketball games,
going to those basketball games.

A certain desirable terror is more desirable to me than rare
than the thought that i could die right in the middle of
sexual intercourse, & with my new all-purpose transistor
blanket go right on pumping away, with no emotional letdown
if you stop, you're dead, the jakov syndrome, tell the kids,
don't mess around with the light switch, tell them they'll
     be shocked
if they unplug daddy.

A terror is more certain that's rare, & more desirable.

THERE ARE TOO MANY UNFUNNY THINGS HAPPENING TO THE
        COMEDIANS.
Why don't the monasteries serve hot & cold hero sandwiches &
all kinds of split pea soups, & bring the guys to the village
once a week to get laid, & make them stop printing all those fat
books with god's picture on the cover,
& all that subway mystery stuff.

A certain desire is more rare than terror,
than that happy shop, home of free association,
where i breakfasted with the suicidal rabbi,
& the world's champion padlock salesman, who
wore impeccable seersuckers, & whose only
oversight is cannibalism, & who is someday going
to eat himself and get busted if he stays in the
flesh game.

All bicycle seats beatified & take on appearance of north poles,
        other things
certain are real to me, but what is so rare, as air is a poem.

It's all right real, it's just god playing dirty jokes again,
that was the old universal gin mill story, with chopin &
amelia earhart floating down the suez canal with dueling pistols
in their hair, as the great symphony of fish play beethoven's
        teeth.

TRANSACTION

TO BREAK THE SPELL OF SUNDAY
I OFFERED THE GANGSTER A SILK EAR
AND FIRST COPIES OF FAMOUS HOROSCOPES.
HE DEMANDED AN UNWRITTEN CONTRACT
WITNESSED BY A GYPSY QUEEN.

BLUES FOR HAL WATERS

My head, my secret cranial guitar, strung with myths plucked from
Yesterday's straits, it's buried in robes of echoes, my eyes, breezeless flags,
    lacquered to present a glint . . .
My marble lips, entrance to that cave, where visions renounce renunciation,
Eternity has wet sidewalks, angels are busted for drunk flying.
I only want privacy to create an illusion of me blotted out.
His high hopes were placed in his coffin. Long paddles of esteem for
    his symbol canoe.
If I move to the stars, forward my mail c/o God, Heaven, Lower East Side.
Too late for skindiving and other modern philosophies, put my ego in storage.
The moon is too near my family, and the craters are cold in winter,
Let's move to the sun, hot water, radiant heating, special colors,
Knife-handle convenience, adjacent to God, community melting free.
Eskimos have frozen secrets in their noses and have chopped down
    the North Pole.
The Last Buffalo will be torpedoed by an atomic submarine, firing
    hydrogen tiepins.
God is my favorite dictator, even though he refuses to hold free elections.
That gate around me will hold, I worry about the padlock I painted on.
My hair is overrun with crabgrass, parts of my anatomy are still unexplored.
No more harp sessions for me; I am going to hell and hear some good jazz.
Do you hear the good news, Terry and the Pirates are not really real.
If you value the comfort of your fellow worshippers, don't die in church.
Why ruin our eyes with TV, let's design freeways after dinner tonight.

He might have lost some friends, but Jesus could have made a fortune on
    that water to wine formula.
History is the only diary God keeps, and somebody threw it on the bonfire.
The day of the Big Game at Hiroshima. The moon is a double agent.
This year the animals are holding their first
    "Be kind to people" week.
The Siamese cats will not participate and will hold their own
    convention in Egypt. The civilized world fears they may
    attempt to put Pharaoh back in place on the throne.
For God's sake, Hal, jam the radio. Trip them with your guitar.

A TIGER IN EACH KNEE

White tiger I hear you
Hum on the drone
Flowing on beds of
Fresh snow on springs
Flowing back to the nether
     source,
The truth is an empty
     bowl of rice
Those cathode men who cage
  you shall melt
In the summer sun,
For they are ugly bars
Who echo the sting of
Unholy rivers in their dried cracked
Bed.

WALK SOUNDS

Soft noise, where crystalline sap dwells.
Tree bark houses, tree bark shoes.
Long green journeys, into sounds of death.
Cries of who blows, who blows, who blows,
Rings of raindrops, on damp streets.
Quietly disappearing, in fearmottled night,
Sweeping over asphalt mesas, to long gutters,
Where gray birds lie, gone time is buried,
Safe from hideous laughter, babblings,
Of sidewalk fools, tongues straining,
Flicking, on steps of air, nervously.
Glowing blue, black, blue, black,
In the shapes of night.

WAR MEMOIR: JAZZ, DON'T LISTEN TO IT AT YOUR OWN RISK

In the beginning, in the wet
Warm dark place,
Straining to break out, clawing at strange cables
Hearing her screams, laughing
"Later we forgot ourselves, we didn't know"
Some secret jazz
Shouted, wait, don't go.
Impatient, we came running, innocent
Laughing blobs of blood and faith.
To this mother, father world
Where laughter seems out of place
So we learned to cry, pleased
They pronounced human.
The secret jazz blew a sigh
Some familiar sound shouted wait
Some are evil, some will hate.
"Just Jazz, blowing its top again"
So we rushed and laughed.
As we pushed and grabbed
While Jazz blew in the night
Suddenly we were too busy to hear a sound
We were busy shoving mud in men's mouths,
Who were busy dying on living ground
Busy earning medals, for killing children on deserted streetcorners
Occupying their fathers, raping their mothers, busy humans were
Busy burning Japanese in atomicolorcinescope
With stereophonic screams,
What one-hundred-percent red-blooded savage would waste precious time
Listening to Jazz, with so many important things going on
But even the fittest murderers must rest
So we sat down on our blood-soaked garments,
And listened to Jazz
                    lost, steeped in all our dreams
We were shocked at the sound of life, long gone from our own
We were indignant at the whistling, thinking, singing, beating, swinging
Living sound, which mocked us, but let us feel sweet life again
We wept for it, hugged, kissed it, loved it, joined it, we drank it,
Smoked it, ate with it, slept with it
We made our girls wear it for lovemaking

Instead of silly lace gowns,
Now in those terrible moments, when the dark memories come
The secret moments to which we admit no one
When guiltily we crawl back in time, reaching away from ourselves
We hear a familiar sound,
Jazz, scratching, digging, bluing, swinging jazz,
And we listen
And we feel
And live.

ARRIVAL

Bitter rose blood from dead grapes,
Miniature rivers, flowing on cracked lips.
Old men fighting death in secret corners,
Time rushing wildly through terrified streets.

Odors of laughter reach the nostrils,
Pure poetry from the mouths of children,
Waves of dark flames batter the dawn.
The crawling day arrives, on skinned
Knees.

LIKE FATHER, LIKE SUN

Come, Love,
Love, Come,
Sing a river, Federico . . . García . . . Lorca . . .
In Sarah's tents a Gypsy moon . . . Godless Spain's burning noon . . .
I wrote my first poem in brown gravy, my best friend was a green candle,
Orleans . . . New Orleans . . . the bend in the river cleaves to the sky . . .
Louisiana, named for a broken sun king, bequeathed to a star jazzer,
Miro . . . the flowers are still up there on that wall, stem, petal, all,
Their roots playing the silences, between Babatunde's drumbeats,
Feeding pongee petals to green breezes, flying in darting wonder.
Crane, the flowers have crossed your bridge, beyond, beyond; gone far on
When the wind is blowing through my hair, I cry breath, its coolness loves.

The great rose of time turns on her redding breast, Pocahontas's here,
The land is Apache, Kiowa, and Sioux ranges.
Colorado brings a horse.
The white tiger's horn growls—the drone, the man he killed who caged him . . .
They are ugly bars, who echo the sting of unholy rivers, zoos of death,
The poet in Easter-faced boots, walks from my chest, mystic bloodfruit.
Be the hum in the cluster.
Muddy Mississippi flowing to the thickly hooded skin, cross the bar,
Andean the Delta counts the teeth in the Buddha's smile, vanishing directions,
Whispers, the great rain forest grows mahogany goldfish, Africa's stolen babes,
Coming from ages of impalement, ages wet with dryness, awesome of soul.
Their right eye is a sun, their left eye is a moon.
Their blue eyes come walking, introspective echoes of a journey, soaring,
Of the first generation, the first humans, their cradle the shape of
The human heart, its sound comes in color of the moon, the sun
Returns their golden crown, wrapped in the aura of familiarity, bathed
In want and care, dank bare, safe in compassion's attic.
Beyond harpoons and screech owls and ringless bells.
Europe, the hornless bull, eunuch rapist of infants, man and God,
Whines stench of king time as Joan's light flickers, and goes out,
Gone to herald her father's shore,
Who in her descent from the peak, found the summits in
        mankind's suffering breast.
The liars who stole the soul do not notice, their hearts no longer beat,
        they cannot die, they are in hell now,
Their Power, fungus and rainless soon,
Michelangelo screaming in lonely triumph,
The sound that probes to the
Otherside.
The poem comes
Across centuries of holy lies, and weeping heaven's eyes,
Africa's black handkerchief, washed clean by her children's honor,
As cruelly designed anniversaries spin in my mind,
Airy voice of all those fires of love I burn in memory of.
America is a promised land, a garden torn from naked stone,
A place where the losers in earth's conflicts can enjoy their triumph.
All losers, brown, red, black, and white; the colors from the Master Palette.

MORNING JOY

Piano buttons, stitched on morning lights.
Jazz wakes with the day,
As I awaken with jazz, love lit the night.
Eyes appear and disappear,
To lead me once more, to a green moon.
Streets paved with opal sadness,
Lead me counterclockwise, to pockets of joy,
And jazz.

BONSAI POEMS

I
I remember those days before I knew of my soul's existence.
I used to be able to step on bugs and steal flowers.

II
All those well-meaning people who gave me obscure books
When what I really needed was a good meal.

III
Lately, since formulating mystic parables of my own,
People ask me what do I know all about China—
And do I think Surrealism will spread to Iowa—
Or would winning the Pulitzer Prize have saved Chessman,
When I answer that I am writing the Great American Suicide Note,
They sniff my clothes and leave.

IV
Men who love women
Should never go swimming.

V
Every time I see an old man carrying a shabby cardboard suitcase,
I think he is an eternity agent on some secret mission.

VI
I never understand other people's hopes or desires
Until they coincide with my own; then we clash.

VII
Yes, there was a time when I was unsure of myself,
But that was before I was Me. I barely knew him.

VIII
The culture of the cave man disappeared, due to his inability
To produce a magazine that could be delivered by a kid on a bicycle.

DEMOLITION

They have dismantled
The Third Avenue El;
It's still the same though,
They haven't removed
Those torn-down men.

QUERY

New? Leftovers, overlooked by hurrying death.
Rejects with unadjustable souls,
Love-specked clots, of modern blood.

Marks, all over inside,
Traces of explosions,
First God's, then man's.

Color? Blue, jazz blue.
Blue like love,
Blue like poems,
Blue like blues.

Old? Whole university loads,
Tons of cellophane giants.

Book-end minds, bent backs,
Carrying heavy styles,
Lead forms, tradition colored.
Shouting barbarian, blasphemy,
But quite polite.

New:
    Laughter on exotic beds.

SPLICED REFLECTIONS

Diverse remarks on what is truly dead
    (Success and crime, two equal values).

Historical departure (Cain's refusal to slay Abel)
    Persistence of women who still love.

Voice of unseen commentary heard through plugged ears,
    Obscure history of grass fires (Niagara of Soul).

Grunt passage (navigating in blocked wombs).

Sudden conference with imaginary Indian chiefs
    (Ritual smoking, floors of white buffalo skins).

Innocent criminals buried under avalanches of cactus needles
    (Great philosophical question: Was Geronimo turned on?).

Inca arrival, sun-faced jaguars, hammered-silver evidence,
    Testimonial rockets launched (commemoration of
        Baudelaire's whims).

Cold penetration is unison (arid tests of burning mollusk)
    Ritual murder and levitation, semiweekly mating dances.

    Light the wind, drag the rain in.

THE CELEBRATED WHITE-CAP SPELLING BEE

THE CELEBRATED WHITE-CAP SPELLING BEE WAS WON BY A
    SPELLING BEE.
A STAR ASKED A POINTED QUESTION: CAN A CIRCLE WRAP AROUND
    ITSELF?
A STILLED PYGMY ANSWERS, FROM THE BACK OF MY MIND, ARE WE
    DEEP DWARFS
AND HAVE OUR SAY IN THE AFFAIRS OF FLOWERS. A MISSPELLED BEE
    MAKES A SIGN.
BLUE IS ONE OF THE MANY FACES OF BLUE. HOW QUICK A RED WHALE
    SINGS THE BLUES.
WHEN AN OUTBOARD SOLAR BOAT SINKS, I WILL WALK THE SUN'S
    PERIMETER, CURVING UP.
ONCE I PUT MY INITIALS ON A MAGNIFICENT CROCODILE.
WE WALKED A RIVER'S FLOOR. A BIRD I HEARD SING IN A TREE IN THE
    GULF OF MEXICO . . .
BIRD SONG OF LOVELY SALT, A LOVE SONG.
I CHANGE MY MIND, AND THE NEW ONE IS OLDER . . . A DRUM BEATS
    BEHIND MY RIBS.

SOMEONE DREW A PORTRAIT ON A WAVE . . . IT WOVE AS WE
    PASSED, DOING KNOTS, RUST HANDS.
SWELLS STOP WHEN THE SEA IS ALARMED. HELL COOLS ITS FIRES OF
    ANTICIPATION.
WHEN OCEANS MEET, OCEANS BELOW, REUNIONS OF SHIPS, SAILORS,
    GULLS, BLACK-HAIRED GIRLS.
THE SEA BATHES IN RAIN WATER, MORNING, MOON & LIGHT, THE
    CLEAN SEA.
GREAT FARMS ON THE OCEAN FLOOR, GREEN CROPS OF SUNKEN HULLS
    GROWING SHELLS.
SEAS THAT GROW FROM A HOLE BORN IN A TURTLE'S BACK, A SEA IN
    A TORTOISE SACK.
FISH GO NAKED ALL THEIR LIVES. WHEN CAUGHT, THEY DIE OF
    EMBARRASSMENT.
MANY, MANY YEARS AGO, THERE WERE MANY, MANY YEARS TO GO
    & MANY, MANY MILES TO COME.
THE LAND IS A GREAT, SAD FACE. THE SEA IS A HUGE TEAR,
    COMPASSION'S TWINS.

IF THERE IS A GOD BENEATH THE SEA, HE IS DRUNK AND TELLING
    FANTASTIC LIES.
WHEN THE MOON IS DRINKING, THE SEA STAGGERS LIKE A DRUNKEN
    SAILOR.
POETS WHO DROWN AT SEA, THEMSELVES, BECOME BEAUTIFUL WET
    SONGS, CRANE.
A LOOKOUT MAKES A LANDFALL, A FALLING LAND MAKES A LOOKOUT.
AT THE ENDS OF THE WATER, THE HOLY MARRIAGE OF THE HORIZONS.
THE SEA, DILUTED CONTINENTS LOVING FALLEN SKIES, TIME BEFORE
    TIME, TIME PAST, TIME COMING INTO TIME. TIME NOW, TIME
    TO COME, TIMELESS, FLOWING INTO TIME.
EVERYTHING IS THE SEA. THE SEA IS EVERYTHING, ALWAYS . . .
    ETERNALLY, I SWEAR.

THE SECRET LIFE OF ROBERT FROST

FROCK-COATED SHERPA GUIDES DISTRIBUTING (MONOGRAMMED
    GOLDFISH)
TO NEGLECTED MIDWIVES AT SECRET TRYST ON DESERTED ROLLER
    (COASTERS)

DEMENTED ELEVATOR OPERATORS IN SPACE SUITS SINGING HYMNS
TO GOTHIC BRAIN SURGEONS WEEPING OVER REMAINS OF DESTROYED
LOVE MACH(I)NES, O ULTIMA THULE (NO) MORE OAT(ME)AL.

DEVOTED TUNE PICKERS WHINING OF VANISHED TRIUMPHS
DRESSED IN SURREALIST TUNICS OF GAUZE AND IVORY
RUBBER PHANTOMS TAPPING UNFANTASTIC CRIMINAL FEET
TO WARPED RHYTHMS SHOT FROM OPEN-SKULLED HARPSICHORDS
GALA LAUNDRY CONCERTS FEATURING SONATAS FOR DIRTY OBOES
    BETWEEN MUSHROOM RONDOS' SOGGY BALLETS
SERVED WITH PERFUMED MARSHMALLOWS FROM KEY EYES OF
    LONELY JAZZERS.

TORN ASPHALT MATTRESS OF UNIVERSAL RODENTS (PSYCHIC
    IMPOTENCE)
COLLEGE FACES OF GRANITE ANTIQUITIES STALKED BY LAZY TIGERS
    (STRIPES)

SMELLY BROADCASTS OF COMIC TRAGEDIES BURST FROM FLOWER
    DUST (SKULLS)
COOL DAMP TONGUES SLIPPED FROM LIPS OF SKINNY (LOUDSPEAKERS)
CROUCHED BEHIND CLASSIC FACES OF MYSTIC (TRAFFIC) LIGHTS
    BLAZING
HARD COLD WAVES OF TINSEL FROM BEADS OF KIDNAPPED LAMAS
BURNING OLD PRAYER WHEELS IN ABANDONED (PHONE BOOTHS)
ACHING TEMPOS DRIPPING FROM MOANING (AFRICAN (FINGERS OF ART
                        ART)   BLAKEY)
ABSTRACT BOMBS DROPPING FROM SWOLLEN BELLIES (OF BLASTED
    EGGSHELLS)
FLOATING DOWN BLACK WATER CANALS IN MARBLE BOATS, HIGH ON
                        (SAINTLY   (DESTRUCTION
                         RED DIRT)   MARIJUANA)

[POEMS POETICALLY]

Poems poetically
pole the Poet into a
balancing axis
for endlessly revolving surfaces,
tender leaves are forest gifts
to represent the earth
growing out of decay,
the minds' youngest buds
live on the revolving transformation
of live enduring mountains of thought, and
clear their pores in the melting sea.
And open fields spawn
their harvest in the passing
rain of the plain, as
the spring divines its
collections to the ocean,
and the great waters
continual upheavings speed toward subtle gatherings.
Shepherds with light fingers,
staff guided by the winds,
spinning their
auras into the
sun.

ALL HALLOWS, JACK O'LANTERN WEATHER, NORTH OF TIME

A PLACE CALLED LONELINESS, A SOFT TOWN IN THE OCTO-
BER COUNTRY AN UNIMAGINARY LANDSCAPE THAT EXISTS IN
A REAL UNREAL WORLD, ARTERIAL LAVA STREETS CLICKING A
SOUND OF LOUDLY WALKED BRUISES THICK STRING UNBEINGS,
POURING THEMSELVES INTO EACH OTHER, FILLING THEM-
SELVES WITH EACH OTHERS' EMPTINESS, SHOUTING SILENCES
ACROSS THE SCREAMING ROOMS, VISUALLY BROKEN UNRE-
CORDS STITCHING ILLUSIONARY HUMS, AS THE GREAT MAR-
BLE FEATHERED STONE BIRDS CRACK THE SOLID AIR, FLYING
FROM THE DRUM OF ROCK, ETERNAL STONE POEM OF THE
SUN . . . I KNOW OF A PLACE IN BETWEEN BETWEEN, BEHIND
BEHIND, IN FRONT OF FRONT, BELOW BELOW, ABOVE ABOVE,
INSIDE INSIDE, OUTSIDE OUTSIDE, CLOSE TO CLOSE, FAR FROM
FAR, MUCH FARTHER THAN FAR, MUCH CLOSER THAN CLOSE,
ANOTHER SIDE OF AN OTHER SIDE . . . IT LIES OUT ON THE
FAR SIDE OF MUSIC . . . THAT DARKLING PLANE OF LIGHT ON
THE OTHER SIDE OF TIME, AND IT GOES ON GOING ON BEYOND
BEYOND . . . IT BEGINS AT THE BITTER ENDS.
I KNOW STARNESS . . . I KNOW LOSTNESS . . . MOVE OUT
MOONLIGHT.

RONDEAU OF THE ONE SEA

DEEP ROLLING GALILEE, ETERNAL SEVEN OCEAN NAMED SEA
ENDLESSLY FLOWING HOLY SEA, SEA NEVER STILLED, ALL
FLOWING SEA, SEA DESTROYER OF BAAL AND MAMMON, DRIED
AND FOREVER DIED SEA, SEA, ERASER OF SEA DARKS, REMOV-
ER OF SEA VALVES, EVAPORATOR OF THE EVIL ONES PARENT
OCEAN SEA, SEA BREAKER OF RA'S SEA, BROKEN AND DEHY-
DRATED FOREVER BY DEEP ROLLING GALILEE, SWEET GREEN
WET BLUE SALTLESS SEA: BELOVED GALILEE, THE GREEN
WALKING, BLUE WALKING JESUS CHRIST, SEA.

BLOOD FELL ON THE MOUNTAINS

BLUENESS, THE COLOR OF LOVE, BLUE SLANTED TO A CRACK-
LING AND BLUE COLOR, THE COLOR OF COLORS AS SWEET
BLUE NOCTURNES OF THE VOID. SOLITUDES FILLED WITH
LONELINESS, BLACK RAIN TWISTED HAIL, WOUNDED SNOW.
THE MOUNTAIN CRIED DRY, TEAR OF STONE AMONG THE TALL
TREES, THE SLEEPWALKER WALKED THE BRIDGE OF EYES,
AMIDST COLORS OF THE DAY.

      IN THE LEFT HAND IS THE DREAMER
      THE BALLAD AT THE SOURCE
      THE SINGER AND THE SONG,
      POEM FOR EILEEN ON MY
      RETURN HOME,

I   AM   A   LOVER
          BOB
ME   TO   YOU.

SMALL MEMORIAM FOR MYSELF

Beyond the reach of scorn, lust is freed of its vulgar face.
No more blanch of terror at reality's threat of sadness.
No blend of grief can cause the death of laughter now.

In remembrance of certain lights I have seen go out,
I have visualized pathetic rituals and noisy requiems,
Composed of metaphysical designs of want and care.

[ALL THOSE SHIPS THAT NEVER SAILED]

All those ships that never sailed
The ones with their seacocks open
That were scuttled in their stalls . . .
Today I bring them back
Huge and intransitory
And let them sail
Forever.

All those flowers that you never grew—
   that you wanted to grow
The ones that were plowed under
   ground in the mud—
Today I bring them back
And let you grow them
Forever.

All those wars and truces
Dancing down these years—
All in three flag-swept days
Rejected meaning of God—

My body once covered with beauty
Is now a museum of betrayal.
This part remembered because of that one's touch
This part remembered for that one's kiss—
Today I bring it back
And let you live forever.

I breathe a breathless I love you
And move you
Forever.

Remove the snake from Moses' arm . . .

And someday the Jewish queen will dance
Down the street with the dogs
And make every Jew
Her lover.

[MY MYSTERIES CREATED FOR ME]

MY MYSTERIES CREATED FOR ME
BY GOD ARE UNKNOWN TO
ME, YET I LIVE EACH ONE
PERFECTLY, GOD IS MY GREEN-
EYED ONE, WHOSE POWER IS
ENDLESS. I ASK GOD,
OH GOD . . . TO THE COWARD, GIVE A HORSE
THAT HE MAY FLEE GOD FOREVER,
GIVE CAIN NO FORGIVENESS
FOR WHAT WAS DONE, I ASK GOD,
MY GREEN-EYED ONE, BEFORE THIS
EARTH STOPS SPINNING, THINK OF ME.
REMEMBER, I AM HERE TOO, MY GREEN-
EYED ONE WHOSE POWER IS ENDLESS, AFTER
WHAT WAS DONE TO YOU, WHAT FORGIVENESS . . .
O GOD, MY GREEN-EYED ONE
COME UPON THE EARTH
AND STRIKE THE GLOBE
WITH YOUR WRATH, FOR
WHAT HAS DIED IN THE SUN.
O GOD, MY GREEN-EYED ONE,
PUT YOUR SHARP STARS IN
THE SKY. SEND ORION
THE HUNTER STAR TO HUNT
THE KILLERS OF THE DREAM,
TO HUNT THE SLAYERS OF
THE DIVINE INCUNABULA, O
MY GREEN-EYED ONE, BEFORE THIS EARTH STOPS
SPINNING.

OREGON

You are with me Oregon,
Day and night, I feel you, Oregon.
I am Negro, I am Oregon.
Oregon is me, the planet
Oregon, the State Oregon, Oregon.

In the night, you come with bicycle wheels,
Oregon you come
With stars of fire. You come green.
Green eyes, hair, arms,
Head, face, legs, feet, toes
Green, nose green, your
Breast green, your cross
Green, your blood green.
Oregon winds blow around
Oregon. I am green, Oregon.
You are mine, Oregon. I am yours,
Oregon. I live in Oregon.
Oregon lives in me,
Oregon, you come and make
Me into a bird and fly me
To secret places day and night.
The secret places in Oregon,
I am standing on the steps
Of the holy church of Crispus
Attucks St. John the Baptist,
The holy brother of Christ,
I am talking to Lorca. We
Decide the Hart Crane trip, home to Oregon
Heaven flight from Gulf of
Mexico, the bridge is
Crossed, and the florid black found.

UNTITLED

THE SUN IS A NEGRO.
THE MOTHER OF THE SUN IS A NEGRO.
THE DISCIPLES OF THE
SUN ARE NEGRO.
THE SAINTS OF THE
SUN ARE NEGRO.
HEAVEN IS NEGRO.

[THE NIGHT THAT LORCA COMES]

THE NIGHT THAT LORCA COMES
SHALL BE A STRANGE NIGHT IN THE
SOUTH, IT SHALL BE THE TIME WHEN NEGROES LEAVE THE SOUTH
    FOREVER,
GREEN TRAINS SHALL ARRIVE
FROM RED PLANET MARS
CRACKLING BLUENESS SHALL SEND TOOTH-COVERED CARS FOR THEM
TO LEAVE IN, TO GO INTO
THE NORTH FOREVER, AND I SEE MY LITTLE GIRL MOTHER
AGAIN WITH HER CROSS THAT
IS NOT BURNING, HER SKIRTS
OF BLACK, OF ALL COLORS, HER AURA
OF FAMILIARITY. THE SOUTH SHALL WEEP
BITTER TEARS TO NO AVAIL,
THE NEGROES HAVE GONE
INTO CRACKLING BLUENESS.
CRISPUS ATTUCKS SHALL ARRIVE WITH THE BOSTON
COMMONS, TO TAKE ELISSA LANDI
NORTH, CRISPUS ATTUCKS SHALL
BE LAYING ON BOSTON COMMONS,
ELISSA LANDI SHALL FEEL ALIVE
AGAIN. I SHALL CALL HER NAME
AS SHE STEPS ON TO THE BOSTON
COMMONS, AND FLIES NORTH FOREVER,
LINCOLN SHALL BE THERE,
TO SEE THEM LEAVE THE
SOUTH FOREVER, ELISSA LANDI, SHE WILL BE
GREEN.
THE WHITE SOUTH SHALL GATHER AT
PRESERVATION HALL.

THE AMERICAN SUN

THE AMERICAN SUN HAS RISEN,
THE OTHER SUNS HAVE LEFT
THE SKY, THE POEM HAS ENTERED
THE REALM OF BLOOD. BLOOD IS

NOW FLOWING IN ALL SKIES AND
ALL THE STARS CALL FOR MORE
BLOOD, THE OLD EMPIRES HAVE
BEEN BROKEN BY THE AMERICAN
SUN AND SHALL CEASE TO EXIST
AS THE POLITICAL ENTITIES THEY
ONCE WERE, AND CAN NEVER BE
AGAIN, THE AMERICAN SUN
BRINGS DEATH TO ALL ENEMY
EMPIRES, THE AMERICAN SUN BRINGS
DEATH BY FIRE TO ALL WHO DARE
OPPOSE THE AMERICAN SUN, EMPIRES
OF THE PAST ARE BREAKING FROM
THE CONSTANT POWER OF THE AMERICAN
SUN, THE AMERICAN SUN CHALLENGES
ALL OTHER EMPIRES AND DEMANDS
THEY RESPOND TO THE CHALLENGES
OF THE AMERICAN SUN, THOSE THAT DO
NOT RESPOND ARE TO BE BROKEN AND
BURNED, THE AMERICAN SUN
OPENS THE GRAVES OF EMPIRES
THAT FALL TO THE AMERICAN SUN,
ALL FORMER KINGS AND QUEENS
OF EMPIRES CRUSHED BY THE
AMERICAN SUN ARE TAKEN FROM
THEIR GRAVE AND TOMBS TO EXIST
IN THE NIGHT OF THE LIVING
DEAD AND SUFFER THEIR
FALL TO THE AMERICAN SUN,
THE PRIESTS OF THE AMERICAN SUN
ARE STARS IN THE SKIES OF
ALL ENEMY EMPIRES, THEY ADMINISTER
THE LAWS OF THE AMERICAN SUN,
THE AMERICAN SUN DOES NOT GIVE
MERCY TO EMPIRES FALLEN TO
THE AMERICAN SUN,
THE AMERICAN SUN DOES NOT PERMIT
DISOBEDIENCE, ANY ATTEMPT TO
DISOBEY THE AMERICAN SUN
IS PUNISHED BY DEATH AND TOTAL
DESTRUCTION OF THE OFFENDING EMPIRE,

THE AMERICAN SUN IS THE
ONLY SUN, ALL OTHERS ARE
BROKEN AND TORN FROM THE
SKY BY THE AMERICAN SUN,
THE DARK STAR THE ENEMY SUNS
HAVE BECOME HAS BEEN
THROWN DOWN ON THE ENEMY'S OWN LAND
BY THE AMERICAN SUN.
THE LANGUAGE OF THE AMERICAN
SUN IS SPOKEN BY STARMEN
AND STARWOMEN OF AMERICA,
THE AMERICAN SUN IS AMERICA, AND
ALL AMERICANS. NO OTHERS
ARE PERMITTED ON OR IN THE
AMERICAN SUN. THE AMERICAN
SUN IS THE ONLY FIRE. ALL OTHERS
ARE PUT OUT BY THE AMERICAN
SUN. THE MOON IS THE AMERICAN
MIDNIGHT SUN AND MUST BE
OBEYED BY ALL OTHER EMPIRES,
THE AMERICAN SUN DOES NOT FORGIVE
ANY ENEMY, BUT PUNISHES EVERY OFFENDER
WITH DEATH AND DESTRUCTION.
THE AMERICAN SUN IS AMERICAN
HOLINESS, THE AMERICAN SUN IS
THE SUN OF HEAVEN, THE AMERICAN SUN
IS THE AMERICAN CHURCH, THE AMERICAN
SUN IS AMERICAN RELIGION, THE
AMERICAN SUN IS THE LAW, IN ALL
SKIES, THE AMERICAN
SUN IS AT WAR WITH ALL ENEMIES
OF THE AMERICAN SUN, THE AMERICAN
PLANETS, MARS JUPITER, SATURN VENUS,
PLUS THE OTHER PLANETS OF
THE AMERICAN UNIVERSE ARE
AT WAR WITH ALL OTHER UNIVERSES,
THE AMERICAN SUN CREATES ALL AMERICAN LIFE.
THE AMERICAN SUN CREATES ATOMIC
DEATH ON ALL ENEMIES OF THE SUN, THE AMERICAN
SUN CALLED THE ATOMIC BOMB IS
BEING DROPPED ON ALL ENEMY

CITIES BY THE AMERICAN SUN,
CALLED THE SPIRIT OF ST. LOUIS,
THE AMERICAN SUN CALLED
THE HYDROGEN BOMB, IS BEING
DROPPED ON ALL ENEMY EMPIRES
BY THE AMERICAN SUN, CALLED
THE SPIRIT OF ST. LOUIS, THE
ENEMIES OF THE AMERICAN
SUN ARE NOT PERMITTED TO
SURRENDER, THE AMERICAN SUN
IS DESTROYING ALL ENEMY EMPIRES,
WHEN THE AMERICAN SUN
HAS COMPLETED THE DESTRUCTION
OF ALL ENEMY EMPIRES, THE
AMERICAN SUN SHALL CREATE
THE FIRES OF WAR, BURNING
ALL OVER AND UNDER THE SKIES
OF THE CRUCIFIXION, AT THE
AMERICAN SUN CALLED THE
CROSS, THE BUDDHA HAS BEEN
TOPPLED AND HAS BECOME AN
EASTERN IDOL WITH NO WESTERN
SKY, THE BUDDHA IS NOW STANDING
IN FRONT OF THE AMERICAN SUN CALLED
R.C.A. VICTOR, LISTENING TO HIS MASTER'S VOICE.
THE BUDDHA HAS A BLACK SPOT ON ONE EAR NOW.
THE AMERICAN SUN CALLED
ARTHUR FARNSWORTH TELEVISION
HAS TORN DOWN THE TEMPLE'S
WALLS AND DRIVEN THE MONEY-
LENDERS FROM THE WESTERN
SIDE OF THE RHINE RIVER TO
THE EASTERN SIDE OF THE RIVER
THAT DIVIDES THE GERMAN EMPIRE.
INTO TWO SEPARATE BUT EQUAL
STATES, THE AMERICAN SUN HAS
MADE THE MONEYLENDERS
ERECT A WALL OF THE TORN-DOWN
TEMPLE OF THE EAST BANK OF THE RIVER
TO SHIFT THE MONEYLENDER'S POWER
TO THE SIDE OF THE RIVER THAT IS NEAR

VIENNA.
THE AMERICAN SUN CALLED
THE CATHOLIC CHURCH HAS
EXCOMMUNICATED SAVONAROLA
VLADIMIR ILYICH LENIN AND HAS
FORBIDDEN THE RUSSIAN EMPIRE
TO HAVE A CHURCH, OR A CHRISTIAN
RELIGION, THE RELIGIOUS COURT
OF HEAVEN HAS PRONOUNCED HIS
BEHEADING OF THE LADY POPE
ST. JOAN, AN UNFORGIVABLE SIN,
HEAVEN FORBIDS RUSSIA TO HAVE
A CATHOLIC CHURCH, HEAVEN UNDRESSES
THE BODY OF LENIN IN THE TOMB AND
DISCOVERS THE LEGS HAVE TURNED BLACK,
RUSSIAN COMMUNISM IS REFUSED THE
SACRAMENT BY HEAVEN, PRINCE MIKE ROMANOV
OF HOLLYWOOD IS THE ONLY RUSSIAN HEAVEN ALLOWS
IN HEAVEN'S CATHOLIC CHURCH
THE AMERICAN SUN CALLED
THE AMERICAN FLAG IS THE
ONLY FLAG FLYING AT CRUCIFIXION
CALLED THE EARTH NOW IN THE
SKIES OF HEAVEN.
THE AMERICAN SUN IS NOT
PART OF ANY PEACE MOVEMENT.
THE AMERICAN SUN IS A
SUN OF WAR, THE DAYS OF
PEACE ARE DRAWING
TO AN END. THE ENEMIES OF
THE AMERICAN SUN ON THE
EARTH SHALL SOON BE ATTACKED
BY THE PURE POWERS OF THE
AMERICAN SUN. THE ENEMIES OF
THE AMERICAN SUN IN AMERICA
HAVE ALREADY BEEN SENT TO
HELL AT THE AMERICAN
CRUCIFIXION. HELL IS CALLED
THX 1138, THE ENEMIES OF
THE AMERICAN SUN ARE SHOWN
THEMSELVES ON TELEVISION,

IT IS FILMED INSIDE THE CROSS
BY THE AMERICAN SUN.
UNLIKE BIRTH OF A NATION,
IT IS NOT IN PUBLIC DOMAIN,
AT THE CRUCIFIXION,
THE AMERICAN SUN HAS
ATTACKED RUSSIA WITH
NUCLEAR WEAPONS AND MOSCOW
IS IN FLAMES, THE TOMB OF
LENIN HAS BEEN DESTROYED,
THE BODY OF LENIN IS BEING CARRIED THROUGH
THE CITY . . .

UNTITLED

THE EARTH MOVED, AND CHANGED ITS
ANGLE IN RELATION TO OTHER UNIVERSES,
THE SPHINX OPENS THE DOOR, HORUS ENTERS
HIS BEAK EMERGES FROM THE SUN OF
HIS HEAD, HORUS ARMS OUTSTRETCHED
GIVES THE POEM A SUBSTANCE, SET GOES OFF.
THE TIME OF SET WAS SHORT, HORUS IS
HERE FOREVER, HORUS ADMIRES THE
GOLD KING, PHARAOH TUTANKHAMUN,
AMON RA STANDS WITH OSIRIS AT KARNAK,
HORUS DIRECTS BOY HORUS TO
THE FLIGHT, PYLON GENTLE FLIGHT,
PRUFROCK ENTERS THE
DOOR TO THE ORIENT
AND EMERGES SWIMMING.

FROM A PAINTING BY EL GRECO

I AM THE ETERNITY THAT WAS HELD
BY THE OSTRICH EGG.
THE MAGNIFICENT DECEMBER IS NOW
NO LONGER HIDDEN.
THE SUN, I AM ALONE, IS PRESENT FOREVER.

THE POET

FROM A PIT OF BONES
THE HANDS OF CREATION
FORM THE MIND, AND SHAPE
THE BODY IN LESS THAN A SECOND.
  A FISH WITH FROG'S
  EYES,
   CREATION IS PERFECT.
THE POET NAILED TO THE
BONE OF THE WORLD
COMES IN THROUGH A DOOR,
TO LIVE UNTIL
HE DIES,
WHATEVER HAPPENS IN BETWEEN,
IN THE NIGHT OF THE LIVING
DEAD, THE POET REMAINS ALIVE,
  A FISH WITH FROG'S
  EYES,
   CREATION IS PERFECT.
THE POET WALKS ON THE EARTH
AND OBSERVES THE SILENT
SPHINX UPON THE NILE.
THE POET KNOWS HE MUST
WRITE THE TRUTH,
EVEN IF HE IS
KILLED FOR IT, FOR THE
SPHINX CANNOT BE DENIED.
WHENEVER A MAN DENIES IT,
A MAN DIES.
THE POET LIVES IN THE

MIDST OF DEATH
AND SEEKS THE MYSTERY OF
LIFE, A STONE REALITY IN THE
REALM OF SYMBOLS, FANTASY, AND
METAPHOR, FOR REASONS
THAT ARE HIS OWN WHAT IS REAL
IS THE PIT OF BONES HE COMES
FROM,
       A FISH WITH FROG'S
       EYES,
       CREATION IS PERFECT.
SOMEWHERE A BUDDHA SITS IN
SILENCE AND HOLDS THE
POET AND THE WORLD IN
SEPARATE HANDS AND REALIZES HE
IS BORN TO
DIE.
THE BLOOD OF THE POET
MUST FLOW IN HIS POEM,
SO MUCH SO, THAT OTHERS
DEMAND AN EXPLANATION.
THE POET ANSWERS THAT THE
POEM IS NOT TO BE
EXPLAINED. IT IS WHAT IT
IS, THE REALITY OF THE POEM
CANNOT BE DENIED,
       A FISH WITH FROG'S
       EYES,
       CREATION IS PERFECT.
THE POET IS ALONE WITH OTHERS
LIKE HIMSELF. THE PAIN IS BORN
INTO THE POET. HE MUST LIVE
WITH IT. IT IS HIS SOURCE OF
PURITY, SUFFERING HIS
LEGACY,
THE POET HAS TO BE A
STONE.
       A FISH WITH FROG'S
       EYES,
       CREATION IS PERFECT.
WHEN THE POET PROTESTS THE

DEATH HE SEES AROUND
HIM,
THE DEAD WANT HIM SILENCED.
HE DIES LIKE LORCA DID,
YET LORCA SURVIVES IN HIS
POEM, WOVEN INTO THE DEEPS
OF LIFE. THE POET SHOCKS THOSE
AROUND HIM. HE SPEAKS OPENLY
OF WHAT AUTHORITY HAS DEEMED
UNSPEAKABLE, HE BECOMES THE
ENEMY OF AUTHORITY. WHILE THE
POET LIVES, AUTHORITY
DIES. HIS POEM IS
FOREVER.
WHEN THE POET DIES,
A STONE IS PLACED ON
HIS GRAVE, IT IS HIM,
A PIT OF BONES,
          CREATION IS PERFECT,
IN THE PIT OF BONES
A SKY OF STARS, A HEAVEN OF
SUNS AND MOONS, AND THE GREAT
SUN IN THE CENTER,
          CREATION IS PERFECT.
A MASK CREATED IN THE PIT
IS THE IMAGE OF THE POET.
THE IMAGE OF THE POET
IS A
SECRET.
          A FISH WITH FROG'S
          EYES,
          CREATION IS PERFECT.
I HAVE WALKED IN THIS WORLD
WITH A CLOAK OF DEATH WRAPPED
AROUND ME. I WALKED ALONE, EVERY
KISS WAS A WOUND, EVERY SMILE
A THREAT.
ONE DAY DEATH REMOVED HIS
CAPE FROM AROUND ME,
I UNDERSTOOD WHAT I HAD LIVED
THROUGH. I HAD NO REGRETS,

WHEN THE CLOAK WAS REMOVED,
I WAS IN A PIT OF BONES,
        A FISH WITH FROG'S
        EYES,
        CREATION IS PERFECT.

LONE EAGLE

IT IS SARASWATI AGAIN,
IN THE DANCE OF SHIVA,
THE ONLY DANCE THERE IS,
VINCENT VAN GOGH'S CUT OFF
EAR FLOWING THROUGH THE
IMPRESSIONISTIC SKY, THE BEAUTIFUL
FACE OF RIMBAUD ILLUMINATES
THE FURY MICHELANGELO
HAS RELEASED UPON THE
WORLD. CHARLES LINDBERGH
DREAMS OF THE WATERS HE HAS SEEN.

I AM A CAMERA

THE POET NAILED ON
THE HARD BONE OF THIS WORLD,
HIS SOUL DEDICATED TO SILENCE
IS A FISH WITH FROG'S EYES,
THE BLOOD OF A POET FLOWS
OUT WITH HIS POEMS, BACK
TO THE PYRAMID OF BONES
FROM WHICH HE IS THRUST
HIS DEATH IS A SAVING GRACE.

CREATION IS PERFECT

JANUARY 30, 1976: MESSAGE TO MYSELF

It is the time of illusion and reality,
Russia deliberately creates the illusion of wanting peace,
While preparing feverishly for war.
The slogans used by Communism are based on a desire for peace,
They are illusionary, for they are desiring an atmosphere for war.
The U.N. wants peace, but it must be careful
Not to compromise itself by settling for peace
At any cost. The West cannot rest easy, for Russia is
Anxious for war, while Russia cannot risk a unified Germany.
All the contradictions of the situation heighten the
Dangers of war.

The Ancient Rain is falling. It is falling on the N.A.T.O. meetings,
It is falling in Red Square. Will there be war or peace?
The Ancient Rain knows, but does not say.
I make speculations of my own, but I do not discuss them
Because the Ancient Rain is falling.

The Ancient Rain is falling all over America now.
The music of the Ancient Rain is heard everywhere.

THE ANCIENT RAIN

At the illusion world that has come into existence of world that exists
secretly, as meanwhile the humorous Nazis on television will not be as
laughable, but be replaced by silent and blank TV screens. At this time,
the dead nations of Europe and Asia shall cast up the corpses from the
graveyards they have become. But today the Ancient Rain falls, from
the far sky. It will be white like the rain that fell on the day Abraham
Lincoln died. It shall be red rain like the rain that fell when George
Washington abolished monarchy. It shall be blue rain like the rain that
fell when John Fitzgerald Kennedy died.

They will see the bleached skeletons that they have become. By then, it
shall be too late for them. All the symbols shall return to the realm of
the symbolic and reality become the meaning again. In the meantime,
masks of life continue to cover the landscape. Now on the landscape of

the death earth, the Luftwaffe continues to fly into Volkswagens through the asphalt skies of death.

It shall be black rain like the rain that fell on the day Martin Luther King died. It shall be the Ancient Rain that fell on the day Franklin Delano Roosevelt died. It shall be the Ancient Rain that fell when Nathan Hale died. It shall be the brown rain that fell on the day Crispus Attucks died. It shall be the Ancient Rain that fell on July Fourth, 1776, when America became alive. In America, the Ancient Rain is beginning to fall again. The Ancient Rain falls from a distant secret sky. It shall fall here on America, which alone, remains alive, on this earth of death. The Ancient Rain is supreme and is aware of all things that have ever happened. The Ancient Rain shall be brilliant yellow as it was on the day Custer died. The Ancient Rain is the source of all things, the Ancient Rain knows all secrets, the Ancient Rain illuminates America. The Ancient Rain shall kill genocide.

The Ancient Rain shall bring death to those who love and feel only themselves. The Ancient Rain is all colors, all forms, all shapes, all sizes. The Ancient Rain is a mystery known only to itself. The Ancient Rain filled the seas. The Ancient Rain killed all the dinosaurs and left one dinosaur skeleton to remind the world that the Ancient Rain is falling again.

The Ancient Rain splits nations that have died in the Ancient Rain, nations so that they can see the culture of the living dead they have become, the Ancient Rain is falling on America now. It shall kill D.W. Griffith and the Ku Klux Klan; Hollywood shall die in the Ancient Rain. This nation was born in the Ancient Rain, July 4, 1776. The Ancient Rain shall cause the Continental Congress to be born again.

The Ancient Rain is perfection. The Ancient Rain cured the plague without medicine. The Ancient Rain is vindictive. The Ancient drops are volcanoes and in one moment destroyed Pompeii and brought Caesar down, and now Caesar is fallen. This Roman Empire is no more. The Ancient Rain falls silently and secretly. The Ancient Rain leaves mysteries that remain, and no man can solve. Easter Island is a lonely place.

The Ancient Rain wets people with truth and they expose themselves to the Ancient Rain. Egypt has a silent sphinx and pyramids made of death chambers so that Egypt remembers the day the Ancient Rain drowned it forever. The mummies no longer speak, but they remember the fury of the Ancient Rain. Their tombs have been sawed in pieces and moved to the graveyard to make way for the pool of Ancient Rain that has taken their place.

The Ancient Rain saw Washington standing at Appomattox and it fell on Lee as he laid down his sword. The Ancient Rain fell on the Confederacy and it was no more.

The Ancient Rain is falling again. The Ancient Rain is falling on the waves of immigrants who fled their homelands to come to this home of Ancient Rain to be free of tyranny and hunger and injustice, and who now refuse to go to school with Crispus Attucks, the Ancient Rain knows they were starving in Europe. The Ancient Rain is falling. It is falling on the N.A.T.O. meetings. It is falling in Red Square. Will there be war or peace? The Ancient Rain knows, but does not say. I make speculations of my own, but I do not discuss them, because the Ancient Rain is falling.

The Ancient Rain is falling in the time of a war crisis, people of Europe profess to want peace, as they prepare day and night for war, with the exception of France and England. They are part of the N.A.T.O. alliance. I believe that Russia wants war. Russia supports any Communist nation to war with weapons and political stances on behalf of any Communist political move. This will eventually lead to war—a war that shall make World War Three, the largest war ever.

The Ancient Rain is falling all over America now. The music of the Ancient Rain is heard everywhere. The music is purely American, not European. It is the voice of the American Revolution. It shall play forever. The Ancient Rain is falling in Philadelphia. The bell is tolling. The South cannot hear it. The South hears the Ku Klux Klan, until the bell drowns them out. The Ancient Rain is falling.

The Ancient Rain does what it wants. It does not explain to anyone. The Ancient Rain fell on Hart Crane. He committed suicide in the Gulf of Mexico. Now the Washington Monument is bathed in the celestial lights of the Ancient Rain. The Ancient Rain is falling in America, and all the nations that gather on the East River to try to prevent a star prophecy of 37 million deaths in World War III. They cannot see the Ancient Rain, but live in it, hoping that it does not want war. They would be the victims . . . in Asia, the Orient, Europe, and in South

America. The Ancient Rain will cause them to speak the languages they brought with them. The Ancient Rain did not see them in America when Crispus Attucks was falling before the British guns on the Boston Commons. The Ancient Rain is falling again from the place where the Ancient Rain lives. Alone. The Ancient Rain thinks of Crockett and falls on the Santa Ana Freeway and it becomes a smog source.

The Ancient Rain wets my face and I am freed from hatreds of me that disguise themselves with racist bouquets. The Ancient Rain has moved me to another world, where the people stand still and the streets moved me to destination. I look down on the Earth and see myself wandering in the Ancient Rain, ecstatic, aware that the death I feel around me is in the hands of the Ancient Rain and those who plan death for me and dreams are known to the Ancient Rain . . . silent, humming raindrops of the Ancient Rain.

The Ancient Rain is falling. The Washington
    Monument rumbles.
The Lincoln Memorial is surrounded by stars.
Mount Rushmore stares into every face.
The Continental Congress meets in the home of
    the Ancient Rain.
Nathan Hale stands immaculate at the entrance
    to the Capitol.
Crispus Attucks is taken to school by Thomas
    Jefferson.
Boston is quiet.
The Ancient Rain is falling.

The Ancient Rain is falling everywhere, in Hollywood, only Shirley Temple understands the Ancient Rain and goes to Ghana, Africa, to be ambassador. The Ancient Rain lights up Shirley Temple in the California sky. Meanwhile, in Atlanta, the German U.N. delegation sits comfortably eating in a restaurant that Negro soldiers can't get into, as of some deal between the Germans and the Ku Klux Klan.

The Ancient Rain is falling on the restaurant. The Southern bloc cannot see it.

The Ancient Rain is falling on the intellectuals of America. It illuminates Lorca, the mystery of America shines in the Poet in New York. The

Negroes have gone home with Lorca to the heaven of the lady whose train overflows. Heaven.

The Negroes have gone home to be enclosed by the skirts of their little girl mother. Black angels roam the streets of the earth. Make no mistake, they are angels, each angel is Abraham Lincoln, each angel is guarded by Ulysses S. Grant. They are for the death of the Ku Klux Klan at Appomattox. The sword of Lee is no more.

The Daughters of the Confederacy are having a luncheon at the Beverly Hills Hotel in the Savoy room. They are not Daughters of the American Revolution. They are not the Mothers of Crispus Attucks. They shall have Baked Alaska for dessert. Their lunch is supervised by a Japanese steward, the French caterer has provided them with special gray napkins.

The voice of Robert E. Lee cannot be heard over the rumbles of Grant's tomb. They leave as they came, the Daughters of the Confederacy, each enclosed in her own Appomattox. Back home they go to Cockalo. Crispus Attucks lying dead on the Boston Commons is the burning of Atlanta by the Union Army. John Brown was God's Angry Man. Crispus Attucks is the black angel of America. Crispus Attucks died first for the American Revolution, on the opening day of American glory. Crispus Attucks does not want a white mother. Crispus Attucks is the Blackstone of the American Revolution that is known to God. Crispus Attucks is not the son of the South, not the son of Lee, not the son of Jefferson Davis. The South cannot have Attucks for a son. Crispus Attucks is my son, my father, my brother, I am Black.

Crispus Attucks will never fight for Russia. That cannot be said of the Rosenbergs or Alger Hiss or Whittaker Chambers. Crispus Attucks lives in heaven with Nathan Hale. They go to the same school. They do not live in the South.

I see the death some cannot see, because I am a poet spread-eagled on this bone of the world. A war is coming, in many forms. It shall take place. The South must hear Lincoln at Gettysburg, the South shall be forced to admit that we have endured. The black son of the American Revolution is not the son of the South. Crispus Attucks' death does not make him the Black son of the South. So be it. Let the voice out of the whirlwind speak:

Federico García Lorca wrote:
Black Man, Black Man, Black Man
For the mole and the water jet
Stay out of the cleft.
Seek out the great sun
Of the center.
The great sun gliding
  over dryads.
The sun that undoes
  all the numbers,
Yet never
    crossed over a
    dream.

The great sun gliding over dryads, the sun that undoes all the numbers, yet crossed over a dream. At once I am there at the great sun, feeling the great sun of the center. Hearing the Lorca music in the endless solitude of crackling blueness. I could feel myself a little boy again in crackling blueness, wanting to do what Lorca says in crackling blueness to kiss out my frenzy on bicycle wheels and smash little squares in the flush of a soiled exultation. Federico García Lorca sky, immaculate scoured sky, equaling only itself contained all the distances that Lorca is, that he came from Spain of the Inquisition is no surprise. His poem of solitude walking around Columbia. My first day in crackling blueness, I walked off my ship and rode the subway to Manhattan to visit Grant's tomb and I thought because Lorca said he would let his hair grow long someday crackling blueness would cause my hair to grow long. I decided to move deeper into crackling blueness. When Franco's civil guard killed, from that moment on, I would move deeper in crackling blueness. I kept my secrets. I observed those who read him who were not Negroes and listened to all their misinterpretation of him. I thought of those who had been around him, those that were not Negro and were not in crackling blueness, those that couldn't see his wooden south wind, a tiltin' black slime that tacked down all the boat wrecks, while Saturn delayed all the trains.

I remember the day I went into crackling blueness. His indescribable voice saying Black Man, Black Man, for the mole and the water jet, stay out of the cleft, seek out the great Sun of the Center.

UNCOLLECTED WORKS

TWENTYTHREEJONESCAPE
(for La Martinelli)

Cool shadows blanket dead cities,
falling
      f a l l i n g.
Electric ant hills wherein Love's murdered,
Falling
      f a l l i n g.
Crucified daily on stainless steel crosses,
In gardens relentlessly,
falling
      f a l l i n g.

Free reeds a-drift over fetid landscapes,
the poets,
bearded phoenixes burning themselves forever,
Death's pattern captures eyes,
fixed eye saving sadness,
cast by leafless trees,
Cool key . . . old shadows,
key fall over eggshell plain,
drawn junk, Kung junk,
Old Green river Manchu junk,
Falling
      f a l l i n g
           f a l l i n g.

[*Anagogic & Paideumic Review*, Vol. 1, No. 2, 1959]

LADY

Two
Stones
Beat
Against
Breast
Reflected

Fires
Stop the jazz.
Lady's burning
Her old flame,
Bitch goddess
Of tenderness,
Hardness,
Deepness.
Putting
Us on
To
Sad last
Cues,
Painting
Charred
Remains,
Of all
Old
Flames

[*BEATITUDE*, No. 2, 1959]

ABOMUNISTORICAL ODDITIES

Leonardo da Vinci was really Leonard Grunch of The Bronx, He stumbled into
an abandoned Abomunist time machine taking it with him; The Bronx, that is.

King Edgar IX refused the crown of Luxembourg because he was hung up on a
nun. Crucifixion settled his problem.

Beethoven is reliably reported to have been busted.

Benjamin Franklin was duped by a little boy who couldn't get his kite up.

The mimeograph machine was invented in Tibet in 1789 by Marcel Marceau by
accident as he played with a prayer wheel.

Walt Disney invented Lewis Carroll in 1861 while sliding through a rainspout on a teacup. He fainted, and lost his hat.

—bimgo

[*BEATITUDE*, No. 8, 1959]

FIVE

long forgotten pains, returning, long lost shadows, remembered, breaking bones, drinking blood, thighs kiss

Curious pointless star, rolled, down room stacked, streets, foolishly melting mirrors, o the new christ was too hot for the cool scene, had to fall out behind a square cross, with an addict in the attic. released maddening sad unrehearsed grimaces of morning faces, cooling, exposed bodies, arms, passions, unknown to their owners, givers.

deep is her well, oh so deep, to drink from it is to drown, sink in, washed down canals of her, trapped forever, o naked under descending cloudburst, tears, sperm.

[*BEATITUDE*, No. 9, 1959]

J'ACCUSE

The city is a jealous bitch,
    hardening her sidewalks when she sees us
        walking toward the moon,
            satirically echoing our hesitant steps.

The city is a jealous bitch,
    lighting all the doorways we need,
        to dig into each other's mouth and hair,
            sadistically sowing bus stops in our path.

The city is a jealous bitch,
    purposely growing skyscraping office buildings
        on the vacant lots in which we offered each other
            as one singular tribute, to our personal star.

The city is a jealous bitch,
    lighting the night with morning,
        leaving us writhing with unexploded atoms
            whirling in our loins.

The beautiful city is a jealous bitch.

[*Anagogic & Paideumic Review*, Vol. 1, No. 4, 1960]

ABOMUNIST MANIFESTO (Addendum)

We shall demand drive-in mental hospitals for low
    income groups.
We shall demand that ex-communists be allowed to
    cheer at Army-Navy games.
We shall demand that Mississippi be granted statehood
    in some other country.
We shall demand that all TV screens be painted black
    in memory of General Custer.
We shall demand an autopsy on Davy Crockett and that
    Walt Disney be held without bail.
We shall demand that the Confederate Army be re-
    activated and sent to Cuba at once.
We shall demand company sponsored paternity benefits
    for unwed fathers.
We shall demand that unions be allowed to own govern-
    ments too.
We shall demand that the Beat Generation be granted
    diplomatic immunity.
We shall demand that all Goodyear signs be removed
    from our satellites.
We shall demand that all captured German scientists
    be swapped for Russians.

We shall demand the right to participate in the popu-
lation explosion.
We shall demand that Father's Day be replaced with
group therapy.
We shall demand the unification of West Berlin with
East Los Angeles.
We shall demand that non-residents be allowed to send
Care packages to Alabama.
We shall demand that the government stop cluttering
up our billboards with highways.
We shall demand that the shape of mushrooms be
changed to avoid unpleasant associations.
We shall summon hidden bootleggers waving old 48-star
flags.
We shall get high on small pox serum and use Japanese
kites to skywrite love propaganda.
We shall fly stoned in jet planes and drop poetry on
South Dakota.
We shall dress ourselves in X-rays and crawl into your
automobile radios shouting "Bird" lives.
We shall ride commuter trains in Brooks Brothers space-
suits, dragging Zen blasphemies in our Jetstream.
We shall rendezvous in coffee shops to plot sexy revolu-
tions in South America.
We shall perform Greek tragedies in old folks' homes
on Mother's Day.
We shall wear rotten vegetables in our ears in honor of
dead grocery stores.
We shall burn old jazz records on Sunday mornings in
honor of needy junkies.
We shall seduce middleage virgins in used Plymouths
in honor of togethernesss.
We shall read beat poetry at company picnics to save
baseball for the kids.
We shall sing Bessie Smith's blues at the tomb of the
unknown hustler.
We shall demand that Fargo be declared an open city.
We shall demand that a poet be elected president of
vice, or vice-versa.
We shall demand that the Indians take the country back,
whether they want it or not.

We shall demand that the Constitution be classified top
   secret.
We shall demand that World War III be televised as a
   public service.
We shall demand that TV networks stop interrupting
   the commercials with programs.
We shall demand that science to stop the world from
   spinning as some people want to get off now.
We shall demand the right to live in human dignity. Ha!

[*Nugget*, Vol. 5, No. 6, December 1960]

BLUE THEME

Pale morning light, dying in shadows.
Loving the earth, in midday rays.
Casting blue to the sky, in rings,
Sowing powder trails, across the balcony,
Hung in the evening, to swing gently.
On the shoulders of time, ever growing old.
Swallowing events of a thousand nights,
Blue nights, of dying and loving, all blue.
Gone to that tomb, hidden in whirling air,
Breathing uneven sounds of sorrow,
Rising from the lips of wounded flowers.
Lying in wells of earth, covered with desperate laughter,
Out of cool angles, spread against the night.
Dancing blue images, shades of blue pasts,
All those yesterdays, breaking on pebbled bodies.

Life lying along the sands of blue and coral,
Heaped in mounds, with volcano mouth tops,
Sucking in atoms of air, sprinkling space,
With flecks of brilliance, opaline glistening
In the eyes, fastened on spiraling blue flames.

Blue flames burning, on rusty cliffs, overlooking blue seas.
In blue times, sea birds come to wail, in ice white wind.
And wail in starlight wells, cold pits of evening.

Flinging rounds of flame sheeted balls of jagged bone,
Eaten with remains of torn flowers,
Overwhelming afterthoughts, of binding loves, classic pains.
Casting elongated shadows of early pieces of blue.

Stringing hours together, in some thin melodic line,
Wrapped around the pearl neck of morning,
Beneath the laughter of sad blue seabirds.

[GEMINI, Vol. 3, No. 3, 1960]

HAWK LAWLER: CHORUS

Hawk Lawler was born in Kansas City in a charity ward where his
father was also born, perhaps in the same bed. His early childhood
was that of any Negro child of his town in the nineteen thirties. Reg-
ular—attendance at a seedy rundown school, daily salutes to the flag,
solemn morning pledges of allegiance, and standard Beard Geographies.
A special interest in history led him to build a makeshift log cabin in
his back yard in preparation for the presidency, which his father tore
down for firewood as soon as he discovered what motivated Hawk. His
favorite friends were those with whom he traveled to the relief depot to
collect the family ration of potatoes and dried prunes—these boys he
trusted; others just happened to be boys, too. In school, he was good in
mathematics but hated to do figures on paper. He usually worked out
arithmetic problems in his head long before the rest of the class rested
their pencils.

He attended church each Sunday at the Rising Sun Baptist Church
where he secretly sang hymns in numbers, because he didn't like
hearing the same words all the time, yet could offer no resistance to the
music. His first personal contact with music as an individual act was
when he played triangle in the school band and discovered that when he
pinged his instrument at the wrong times he could feel its tingle separate
and distinct from the other instruments—at which times he would smile
inside his mouth—while apologizing to the leader who was an ex-New
Orleans musician that jazz had passed by, yet secretly enjoyed the hard-
head. He discovered the saxophone while listening to the band tune up
and found that this gilded pipe could play free of the mob; at that in-
stant, he became a saxophone player for life and never touched another

triangle. The only possession of which he was proud was an aging Elgin bicycle he received at Christmas from the Afro-American Doll and Toy Fund sponsored by the local Negro paper and provided for by all good white people of the town. It was given to him during a bleak Roosevelt Christmas for winning the school's annual composition contest. His subject was "Why I want to be President," and he was proudest when the bike was presented to him by a snow-bearded colored Santa Claus, whom he recognized as the Mayor's chauffeur. This cherished trophy he surrendered to Horton, son of the family his mother was washer for, in return for one battered saxophone which he slept with three nights before feeling intimate enough to try it, and when he did finally find sufficient courage to blow it, his die was cast—he and horn were one, world blotted out.

The only two courses available to him outside of regular studies were the Bible and music, and since he preferred playing the saxophone to being God, his choice was preordained. Before long he was being heard in small local clubs with largely blues clientele. Often experiencing that same feeling about words he had once felt in church, he began to blow numbers; he was fired over and over, yet could not stop blowing numbers. He was hired as second-chair man with the Bat Bowles orchestra, with the provision that he refrain from blowing numbers, which he did, until the band's dilapidated bus pulled up in front of the Theresa Hotel on Harlem's busiest corner, in New York City, where without a word, he picked up his horn case and disembarked. For no reason at all, he walked and wondered. He had never seen so many Negroes at one time in his whole life. He wondered if some big dam had burst in Africa and spilled its contents, or laughed at the crazy thought that they were all white and this was some special holiday when they all wore black and brown faces for some religious Mardi Gras. This speculation was soon replaced by sounds smacking into his eardrums which dispelled any notions of masquerade, causing him to finger his case and peer into doorways for that big hidden jazz womb, oozing blues and down warmth, welcome as new shoes but still emptied of his embryonic numbers.

Strange melodic numbers whose sum total was the blues and so personal no Arab would have acknowledged inventing them—his numbers, each one a fragment of a note. In lieu of finding a room, he found a girl, which was easier in a place where there were more girls than rooms, and while he waited for the chance to blow his lover horn again, he blew numbers with his body, which left him sperm-poor and brain-pained, longing to give wind to numbers and breathe life into them. One night his girl-mother-sister-lover-whore had a five-dollar date at one of the better after-hours spots with a leading writer of detective stories, and since this writer was a favorite of his, he went along, taking his horn as always, like some tubular security blanket. Five minutes after he enters the place, God created earth, Christ was born and Gabriel exchanged his trumpet for a saxophone. For there in this headquarters of black revolution sat these long-sought comrades, blowing numbers. Illegal notes floated in air as though they had a right to, floated right into his suddenly blossomed ears, followed him up to the bandstand, crept into his pores as he decased the horn, placed it to his parched lips and sighed, for without willing it they came—numbers, notes, songs, battle cries, laments, jazzy psalms, tribal histories in cubist and surrealist patterns, and an unmistakable call to arms, to jazz, to him, as others put down their horns in silent thanks that he had come, as the drums had promised he would come, come to lead into the unpromised land, littered with pains, odored of death, come to lead, with his pumping, grinning throat. Let us not go into it, we all know he led, though we don't all know how—some of us are more familiar with the intermissions, aware of the passions, privy to the junk, witnesses to the uprising when the handkerchief was cast off; some of us were counters of madhouse excursions, and few of us have withstood the silence, wondering from where it came. Some of us have to know.

[*New Directions* 17, 1961]

THE JESUS SCENE

Jesus Christ, you made it.
Far out Jewish poet
Buggin Roman cats,
Flipping on the nail scene.
You swung on
A tailored cross.
Your mother Mary-O,
Professional virgin,
Your dad,
A square carpenter,
Odd jobber,
Too soon

For the garment district.
He might have made it
Instead of fathering
A
Truth.

[*The Real Bohemia*, Francis J. Rigney and L. Douglas Smith, Basic Books, 1961]

THE LAST TIME I STRUCK A MATCH

THAT PLACE THERE
IN THAT PLACE THERE
AN ECHO IS A SCREAM THERE
A BREATH IS A SOUND THERE
THEY WEAVE THE WINDS THERE
THEY DROP THE RAIN THERE
LAUGHTER SOUNDS ORANGE
NIGHTIME IS GREEN THERE
MYSELF THE ANCIENT CHILD THERE
NURSED AT THE BREAST OF BREATH THERE
WHEN ISIS WAS THE MOURNING HAWK FOR OSIRIS THERE
SLANTED DARKWALKER ON A CURVE OF SKY
PIVOT ON EXISTENCE
STEPPING OFF THE WALL OF EYE INTO MIND WORLDS
CLIMBING THE FENCES OF THE MIND IN BRILLIANT DARKNESS
RUNIC STONE ALONE WEPT AT THE DEATH OF SLEEP
GOLGOTHA IS THE PLACE FOR SKULL AND THOUGHT.
GAUTAMA IS THE HEAVEN ITSELF.

[*UC Berkeley Bancroft Library Archives of City Lights Books 1953–1970*;
Bob Kaufman letter to Lawrence Ferlinghetti, Aug. 1, 1964]

[Addendum to Caryl Chessman section of *Golden Sardine*]

"[the] caravan of sea gulls arrives in america & thousands of ladies who used to throw themselves at chessman when he was a famous mov- ie star in da da abraham lincoln as the classic sand box, basic movie filmed accidentally . . . . & now schools of doctors are jetting about chessman's head & king reappears with handfuls of aeroplanes & clara bow fucking a beatnik & brand new carrots colonies of false teeth cling- ing to their barnacled hulls in storms, & art & now artaud shakes his fist in orozcos as chessman accuses the african saint of sleeping sickness & hundreds of sunday baseball games break out into hip shaking orgies by squads of husky jig-saw puzzling lesbians heroining poems gambled on fixed humming bird races, transfixed by uniqueness & unreality.

chessman is now turning into pornography festivals he is serving jellied shoes to long lines of orozcos in railroad suits & trailed by schools of air mail stamps, chessman makes a sign of the cross & shoots the rowboat dead, sinks to bottom of protective aquaring, bessie smith arrives with orders to burn down mrs beethoven's hairdressing machine, watch fob is now chessman's favorite phrase rocketing himself into great criminal rose bowl day parades, & now orderly parades of british sailors pass in penis formation & chessman flees into an owl, artaud is giving swift lectures on stalled elevators, they take care artaud does not hear himself & drops out of the soap box derby.

& now the women of jerusalem around chessman's display of model gas machines & chessman begins to shout profound things like candy coat all foreign cars at the snow barrier & now chessman is an aircraft carrier sailing in to defend moby dick, we are captured by hostile dragonflys & die of fascination & chessman now screams for sadness and turns into old rusty skate key.

if you take the little road to satori you get fucked,

this is the one fold bullshit Lover of sandwich men &

lady monks waiting to get fucked by mountains.

artaud is in bed with his dead goat writing telephone conversations about laughter & doing the latest dance about krishna, famous hindu movie star chessman has now returned from his first fox hunt, with a hypnotized fox, he stands in the corner & refuses the crown 300 times, offers his hands & turns into big museum before our eyes, we are not astonished & demand opportunity to expose ourselves, chessman offers private showings, we play blind speeches on the open hearth furnaces. ourselves we are blasting from the pits chessman is going to drift to the south pole in his raincoat.

White paper on Buddhist attempt to capture nighttime & now chessman is asking if it is legal to carry concealed cigarette lighters, & chessman waves on total destruction delegations who have to be caucused & chessmanized into china plate souvenir & old anna may wong being followed year in and year out, & finally old ezra tuned in his linguaphone & missed the whole point . . . . . . & now chessman is turned into a fat crosstown subway, his head is filling with total strangers, he waits for someone to say that anxious diplomats have fled their miniature submarines & are feeding chessman & his friends or they would have become aeroplanes long ago.

Now everything is quieter, artaud & chessman are taking turns being felix the cat, chessman complains that felix the cat loves artaud & turns into the united states government, finally chessman blesses terry & the pirates, & artaud walks around the deserted sky, picking up pieces of dr. vincent van gogh."

[*UC Berkeley Bancroft Library Archives of City Lights Books 1953–1970*]

OUT OF IT

My body is a torn mattress,
Disheveled throbbing place
For the comings and goings
Of loveless transients.
The whole of me
Is an unfurnished room
Filled with dank breath
Escaping in gasps to nowhere.
Before completely objective mirrors
I have shot myself with my eyes,

But death refused my advances.
I have walked on my walls each night
Through strange landscapes in my head.
I have brushed my teeth with orange peel,
Iced with cold blood from the dripping faucets.
My face is covered with maps of dead nations;
My hair is littered with drying ragweed.
Bitter raisins drip haphazardly from my nostrils
While schools of glowing minnows swim from my mouth.
The nipples of my breasts are sun-browned cockleburrs;
Long-forgotten Indian tribes fight battles on my chest
Unaware of the sunken ships rotting in my stomach.
My legs are charred remains of burned cypress trees;
My feet are covered with moss from bayous, flowing
  across my floor.
I can't go out anymore.
I shall sit on my ceiling.

[*UMBRA Anthology 1967–68*; this is an early draft of the poem
"Would You Wear My Eyes?"]

GONE FAR ON

Slowing body, hard meat, spiraling cold head
  Soul . . . . . . GONE FAR ON
Picaresque slums Flamencos, Aye; Deny me you.
  Eyes . . . . . GONE FAR ON
O General your fish, venereal children beneath
  Mouth . . . . . . GONE FAR ON
Cast lady of hanging black heeled, ass of glory
  Breast . . . . . . GONE FAR ON
Stick man biter, pricky dancer of fairy such coin
  Arms . . . . . . GONE FAR ON
Faked bitch, hoard of dollar lays in blessing churches
  Legs . . . . . . GONE FAR ON
  Ledges of air and sperm
  Dreams . . . . . . GONE FAR ON

[*UMBRA Anthology 1967–68*]

A BUSY SHIRT DIED LAST NIGHT

The cluttered face of the panhandles, pins our anticipation wings wish-bones die "i just slaughtered my wife & i need five cents to get away, to rosy wineland," we enter chambers of each other lit by phosphorescent black candles, our breaths threaten to extinguish each others flame . . . our scarred towers siphoning oceans. old winds never blow back through time, the wrinkled wings of gone birds folded, old last chance lot, bending the willful bitch onto a bar stool, impaled ontaste drinking unfaithful whiskey as the callous jukebox you aint nothing but a hound dog have they ever heard rock & roll up there in those warmarked ab-beys where latter . . . day sebastians spin the perfect song, the death of desire is branded a rumor of love the shouted talk of winter depravities sounds hollow now & never having killed myself before, i now become new years day mummer no. eighty six millionpoint one, no zero while all the armies knead theirpricks into whistling swords, & death is shin-ingmy black shoes blacker & i imagine that my eyes are disgraced rubies that place a curse on whoever wears them, itry to ignorethem, they hurl giraffes, i submit . . . when theholy man eats onions people began to sun his opinions, he being a glutton punished by onion fever began to doubt himself & became unholy & they stopped his onionsupply & he becamebitter & he stopped loving & died a saint . . . perhaps . . . floyd collins shouts from his cave, be a religiousmystic & diewith your guitar . . . i am smokingmarijuana as fast as i can & calling on carl chessman to save me from despair—was Thomas surprised when the birds told him he died from an insult to the brain? Or did he smile & remember all those ivy fags down at the horse dancing in holy ale dippingtheir scarecrow fingers into the royal whiskey & someones blood . . . i did try to save the world but it kept falling out ofmy pocket, so i stopped . . . maybe when the saints have a union, conditions will change a little, at least the agony. Beethoven is standing in the middle of the ocean & the water is up to his neck, the men from the wax museum yell at him & masturbate behind his back . . . Beethoven with hismarbleears, displays his forehead at the reunion of final agonies, his smoothedrock of sorrow, ecstasies tax on personal ears & audacity cutoffs, that was a lousy joke, camus, that phony California death, admit it, undie soon . . .

[Written in NYC in 1961 and published in *UMBRA Anthology 1967–68*]

ALL THE CATS ARE WRITING POPULAR SONGS, MAN

Under a hanging table sat a stone cat with a painted eyelash
his chiseled eyes and an alchemist's hat on his solid head and a granite
rose in his frightened teeth and a Braille lovesong in his balsam
wood heart . . .

All the cats who sing happy songs
Have metallic tears in their green eyes

All time cats say wail, on some forbidden fence
i, me . . . hang . . . cant . . . pick . . . up
i dig . . . genetic bit . . . cat . . . caught
popping . . . hormones . . .

cool man, try another

vein . . .

that one's

dead

[*Ambit*, No. 39, 1969]

ALABASTER

My cat sleeps in Egypt

I have become accustomed
     to pyramids in the hall
     & sharing my room with the sphinx
     to break the spell of Ra

I offered my cat, a silk nose
& famous copies of fake horoscopes,
He demanded unwritten contracts,
& stipulated regular skin grafts.

[*Ambit*, No. 39, 1969]

FLIGHT

Those crucial times when I have batted .160, my soul
    noticing its helplessness, a time of mental abortion

Those bitter times of taunting my eyes
    demanding visions, while they rested

Those unmarked hours of teasing
    that ghost that calls me you when we speak,

Those lying years of disarming my spirit,
    requesting photographs of bits, felt unseen

Those nighttimes of provoking my brain,
    with non-existent questions of being,

Those nervy moments of begging my mind
    to take me away, aloft, alone.

[*SIXPACK*, No. 1, 1972]

OF MOMENTOUS IMPACT & DRIVERS OF LAST YEAR'S DREAM (FRAGMENT)

of momentous impact & drivers of last year's dream haunting tin littered
launching pads enveloped by crushed hopes of unescaped visionaries
hung from dying rockets in hidden lunatic afternoons of probe & thrust
& naked skies beckoning with ammonia fingers to rootfree wanderers
lost to breast of womanly earth writhing under rabbit couplings of hur-
ried lovers anxiously disappearing into each other seeking the ultimate
bomb shelter deep inside desperate wombs filled with wet butterflies &
shells of deserted silkworms gone forever to weave hirohimo's shroud &
spin flowers into her buried sod dead of shame & fire great gift of kan-
sas orpheus & God was no one's co-pilot but was at washington's cele-
bration a lone mourner at his family's funeral unnoticed with his eyes
of flame amid sheets of swirling vapors of hate & insane embraces blind
animals unaware hot breath puffing through the zoo searing cheeks of
children chewing chocolate bombs & no silverbells evermore in times

of earache commercials vomited from radioactive radios every min-
ute on the minutes sandwiched edgewise between wireless seductions
of charities nurses with vaginas of old gold and silver & no no doctor
appendix can't go to menopause party with you must attend lobotomy
sale with four out of five leading new york maniacs on channel happy
zero & other cathode orgies flowing into wall to wall tombs & save that
poor pregnant wonder horse on five now bite the nipples good I want
to bleed for the camera and for all cold breasts everywhere in captivity
in living rooms dying rooms lonely rooms rooms of hot heads under
chrome in beauty parlors whores rooms in duty parlors good school
girls rooms of friendly masturbations reverberating with father shouts
and anthropology dreams of new guinea bush love plucked from savage
balls & man rooms of leftover sadness scattered on grooved whimpering
asses & board rooms where people are split two for one whenever the
board is bored & rooms of hollowed harts suddenly filling with human
mud rising from bowels of blood

[*Bastard Angel*, Vol. 1, 1972]

CACTUS

Golden Bowl of buttons, gifts of an Indian god,
Brought by an Arizona hipster, blue jeans angel.

Green, dry pulp hearts, pumping color into grey minds,
As imagined desert spreads over the cold, screaming earth

In one large circle, wrapped in staves of rainbows,
Facing each other, allowing not one secret
Of past circles to escape, or enter, or intrude
Upon these imitation moments of plucked laughter.

In point center, wiry dance of ants holds new eyes
Close to naked skies stretched along moving floors.

Orange and lavender insects dance Fandangos,
Giant beetles enemy guitarists, play Mazurkas,
As mating dances of chartreuse ants hold us close.

[*SIXPACK*, 3/4, 1973]

WATER HOLE

heat proof wooden waves within crawling distance,
disguise their cathedral faces with prosaic kitchen tables,
cat eyed aproned incas dispense misleading information,
to natural shouldered successes, seeking words of salvation,
from roman candled offspring of the mushroom culture.
old grey men in old grey coats, ex-people, in an ex-civilization,
exchange small talk with bored parking meters,
unaware of droning vibrations of high tumbling angels,
flying wildly inside each others heads,
as pelvic explosions, ricochet off walls of brain,
breaking into private crucifiction, and crazy fallout.

[*SIXPACK*, 3/4, 1973]

BEYOND SUMMER

Grey, featherless
Birds,
Biting
Savage mouthfuls
Of love
From the
Mutilated corpse
Of an April day.

Seven hawks,
In khaki robes
Saying prayers
Over
The lifeless
Body of
An April night.

Gone, I hope forever,
To drawn summer,
Sent for
Blues flames.

Who else!
Modigliani,
Disturbed poems;
Released demons,
Plunder eyes
Startled fingertips
On unseen glass.

Moist forms
Cruel September
Gathers lives.

[This unpublished poem was located in the Eddie Woods archives
at Stanford University]

A HOUSEBOAT CALLED FULFILLMENT

Homegrown—not to be heard or seated visual blank movie, Houseboat,
by C.B. God.
A haphazard untrue documentary on the hum drummy trackless
existence of beat streetcars living unnoticed among the sad tenement
dwellers, marked only by searing reflections of lowest easternmost side-
ways flat bonfires waiting for the Sholem Cape man Agron Jesuski at
Bodega and Carnicería to open, hoping to successfully break and enter
while the cinnamon rolls toss fitfully on the one cent sale penny counter
wet dreaming jelly empty jelly donuts unaware of the chocolate screams
of unimaginery overeal pre-cooked pre-T.V. Volkswagen dinners, old
Greek-Austro-Hungarian recipe from the bad old days before televi-
sion when people sipped each other's beer and gazed into each other's
screens, when there were no kerosene lamp fanatics, before mushrooms
disappeared into Corsican Pizza Parlors, when tongues were legal and
out in the open, when the deep peeper Players put on double headers
all day and when the famous four ball walk specialist, Saxy Parker, hit
86 homeruns off the famous brainballer Lefcenterighty Al-Swiss Family
Einstein, who broke God's strikeout record in an exhibition game at
Hiroshima and retired to an atheist nunnery for former men at Prince-
ton, New Jersey, where he sent untrue sonatas to Bobby Oppenheimer,
unfamous not spoken to Leftfielder who broke civilization's pledge and
refused to burn down churches, and now manages the Carl Chessman

All Stars, whom no one will play with, and who rides around on Old
No. R.P.M. Jazz records with pictures of Ray Charles not dying in
Brooklyn between the grooves, proud Baby Nothing children, refus-
ing to be either skindivers President or Chess masters at the universal
Death Tournaments where an integrated team of lady novelists play so
unintensely the unmagic people drowning in the tidal subways don't
notice their beards and Norman Rockwell intellectual suits, Dylan
Thomas' campaign ribbons, waving hydrogen cigarette lighters at
Hemarkand Knopot Khorroetc, Precoaxious Heming Toughnik Muscle
Essay of Commentary vous a Journal on Non-Un-American literature,
Non I.L. Peretz Off Broadway Magazine of Jewish opinion by Regional
Gentiles, a guaranteed breakfast of untamed literary conflickes by men
who have all won the Pulitzer Price, the National Book Awards, the Old
Gold and Silver Key for Non-Beatism, neat typing, successful graduat-
ed, know-something intellectuals whose most difficult conflict was to
remember Foreign movies first.

Bob Kaufman
NYC 1961

[*Bastard Angel*, Vol. 2, 1974]

[I AM SITTING IN A PAD . . .]

I am Sitting in a Pad in The Middle of The Step Listening to Jazz on The
Radio & The Soft Female Voice of an Airy Girl Dreaming of Dreams &
Reading Poetry From The Magazine Beatitude, A Paper Book of Cool
Warm Cold and Hot Beatitude From Poets – Whose Voices are Tuned
to Every Inflection of The Life of Man.

Yea

Yea

[*BEATITUDE*, No. 23, 1976]

NO MORE JAZZ AT ALCATRAZ

No more Jazz
At Alcatraz

No trombone for
Al Capone

No piano for
Lucky Luciano

No more cello for
Frank Costello

No more Jazz
At Alcatraz

[Spoken by Bob Kaufman at Specs' Bar in San Francisco,
February 19, 1980; transcribed by Jack Micheline]

SEA POEM

The ship slips from its mooring,
Man and boy, I have
sailed these seas
for thirty years,
The old sailor, walking
between the rows of
sunken ships,
The cruel sea
works its magic.

[BEATITUDE, No. 32, 1982]

sensate organism in blue time of halflife—bearings in the Un-
named Motel where transients to Lake County drive their destination
in hard time—station clearing beyond the channel—rape saxophone of
night where recognizable detonation of walls, chest and drawers in the
abstract pool.

demolition!—nervous system in the Kid's android jungle—he
called you colorless—called you here in this intersection of sensory
reflex—a coincidental time sequence—his metabolism?

"seems to me you answer my veins . . ."

the Blue Consulate was a spot on the map—it was before your
environment—a thousand tongues broadcasting in grey—twitches shot
the entire planet blue—it was an enclosure—seems to be connected to
the word "apomorphine"—like it unfolded the power of silence—answer
the machine and shut it off in 1940 wind of dust and memories—

"the virus cannot be endured for long . . ."

quiver and belch—shreds of a voice—believe it or not its almost
time to say good-bye—listen . . . what transpired was me and him on
the avenue—

insignificant curtains—Washington Park—before blue silence
cast forever into the dust—quivering memories answer the word "apo-
morphine"—it was an environment in grey—where "Points" sharpened
his teeth with fingernails.

The New Riviera Hotel was a cough in time—brown walls and
drawers, radio, lamp—chinese triplicate in the gene code—a three di-
mensional axis goof!—an emulsion across the brain coordinated ancient
tongue—code words through tape—word & image nucleotides insisted
on performance of blood film—

"your grey sky in the happy come of marriage . . ."

measurements and categories—studies by invisible procedure
on the H-Bomb border—modular blood gas conversion—electro-me-
chanical blood—blood stalled on a thousand vascular computers—
brown triplicate—unfolded the machine like one thousand tongues
writing you from the new Riviera—coming forever—radio tracks thru
nylon

" . . . well Kid, you don't have what it takes

—lyrical teeth—Points was standing on the corner of Grant &
Union—under the blue arc a rigid sky forecast in grey—nylon eye be-
hind his mouth—one thousand Washington Park his brain was a direct
blood film—vascular anguish—too much on the corner so he swung his

arm into the fist of time—just like that!—when dust & memories fell
thru his eyes—the enclosure: word "apomorphine."

DUST FOREVER HALFLIFE BEARINGS
transients to Lake County hard time—stations rape abstract saxo-
phone—recognizable drawers in the Kid's metabolism—veins on the
map—it was a thousand tongues broadcasting shot the entire planet ob-
scure—seems to be connected to the power of silence—shreds of a voice
time to say almost good-bye—me an him in machine of 1940 wind—
Washington Park and the new riviera hotel quivering apomorphine into
the dust—anyway only a cough—electric nations in digital circuit—con-
tinuous circus gas, the machine like an H-Bomb conversion—require-
ments you know—Mr. Shadow Mouth was the entire planet like any
man on the street—halflife hardly in the veins—a loud voice—tongues
shredding what transpired in Washington—apomorphine electric—

[CALLALOO, Vol. 25, No. 1., 2002. *Bob Kaufman Ephemera, Givens Collection of
African American Literature, University of Minnesota Libraries*]

A BUDDHIST EXPERIENCE

CANNOT GIVE IT A NAME OR SHAPE,
MIGHT SEEK TO FIND A CONTEXT
TO UNDERSTAND THE LANGUAGE BEING USED,
HISTORICAL, YES,
ALSO SOMETHING ELSE,
HOW PEOPLE EMERGE FROM THE GROUP,
COMPLETE, INDIVIDUAL,
EACH RESPONDING TO SOME HIGHER STONE
OF ORDER UNCHALLENGED
IN THE SEARCH FOR MEANING,
IN REACHING FOR THE PURE RELATION,
TO INTERPRET LIFE AND BY THAT INTERPRETATION
TO LIVE MORE DEEPLY IN ZEN,
ZEN OF THE REAL RED BONE,
LIKE COLTRANE,
WHO IS PLAYING THE SAXOPHONE,
SPEAKING OF LIFE AND DEATH
AND WHAT LIES IN BETWEEN,

THE BALLOONS RISING UP
SEEM TO TAKE THE POET TO THE SKY,
PERHAPS THE SAME SKY AS THE LITTLE FRENCH BOY,
THEY SAILED INTO THE HEAVENS,
NOW THE INYO MOUNTAINS SPEAK THEIR MEANING,
I AM THE SKY ROCK
THE PLUNGING ROCK,
WAITING TO BE SURROUNDED BY CLOUDS,
TO ILLUMINATE THE ANGELS PATROLLING THE EARTH,
THE HEAVENLY BRIGADE MOVING MYSTERIOUSLY
THROUGH EVERYTHING,
SHOULD I SPEAK TO THEM?
I DO.
I ASK THEM FOR A LIFE THAT CAN BE LIVED IN HEAVEN
WHILE BEING LIVED ON THE EARTH,
I ASK THEM TO MAKE THIS POSSIBLE,
THEY SPEAK OF THIS EARTHLY LIFE
AS A TRANSITION TO A DIFFERENT EXPERIENCE,
SOME PLACE ELSE,
PEOPLE SEEM TO HAVE PERSONAL REASONS FOR WHATEVER THEY DO
I MUST FIND MY MOTIVES.

[*Haight Ashbury Literary Journal*, Vol. 1, No. 5, 1984]

PEACE BE WITH YOU

THE GUNS OF WAR ARE SILENCED,
IT IS NOT AS IT WAS
THE CROWD DOES NOT DEMAND BLOOD.
PEACE IS NOT A CASTLE IN SCOTLAND,
IT IS NOT THE FIRST TEXAS BANK,
IT IS NOT THE GETTY EAR.
A CRY FOR PEACE IS HEARD AT BREST-LITOVSK,
THE PAVILION RESPONDS,
WITH THE MUZZLING OF THE CANNON,
IT IS NO LONGER HEROIC
TO WALK INTO THE GUNS,
THE MEN WHO DIED IN PREVIOUS WARS
HAVE BECOME PRESIDENTS & POPES

AND PRINCES OF THE LAND.
NOW THEY WANT A PEACE
THAT CAN BE THE MEANING OF THE CROWN,
IN KOREA AFTER THE KILLING,
THIMINYAYA DEFINED THE PEACE,
PEACE IS THE TRUTH,
THE WORLD MUST EITHER RESPOND TO IT
OR SPONSOR THE BLOODLETTING THAT WAR IS.
I HAVE BEEN IN THE WARS OF THE PAST,
THEY ARE MY MEMORIES OF MY YOUTH,
SICILY, NORTH AFRICA, SOUTH AMERICA,
EGYPT, INDIA, EUROPE,
I KNOW THE KILLING FIRST HAND.
I STAND FOR PEACE
I KNOW WHAT IS HAPPENING AT THE PENTAGON,
WAR CANNOT STOP IT,
NOTHING CAN STOP IT.
I AM A BAGEL SHOP PERSON,
YES I SPEAK FOR PEACE IN THE COUNTRY,
IN THE CITY,
ALL OVER.
SOMETIMES A FAKE CALL FOR PEACE LURES THE WORLD TO WAR,
AS CHAMBERLAIN WITH HIS
"PEACE IN OUR TIME"
SENT THE WORLD REELING INTO WORLD WAR TWO.
BUT THIS IS NOT IT,
THIS IS A MESSAGE
FROM THE CLOUDS,
FROM THE STARS
FROM THE SKY
PEACE.
THIS IS NOT THE END
A THOUSAND MEN LAY DOWN THEIR GUNS,
UNTIL THE PEACE IS AN ORDER
SO MANY DEAD WHO DID NOT SEE
THE VINDICTIVE BUDDHA,
THIS IS THE PLACE THAT WE HAVE TO COME TO,
TO ANSWER FOR ALL THE QUESTIONS WE HAVE ASKED,
THIS IS THE PLACE
AND, THE TIME.

[*Haight Ashbury Literary Journal*, Vol. 2, No. 2, 1986]

THE TRIP, DHARMA TRIP, SANGHA TRIP

IS A DELIBERATE ATTEMPT
TO REBUILD A LIFE,
SEEMS TO BE DEMOLISHED
LIKE AN OLD BUILDING
NOBODY WANTS TO LIVE IN
YET STANDS HOPEFULLY.
SOMETHING MORE THAN MEMORY
IS NEEDED,
WORDS ARE NOT A SOLUTION,
SOMETIMES THEY ARE A PROBLEM,
BUT THE PEAK MUST BE REACHED,

THE ROAD GOES ONLY TO THE TOP OF THE MOUNTAIN,
SEEMS THERE IS NO PLACE ELSE TO GO
LIFE ON A MOUNTAINTOP
WITH SKY ALL AROUND,
A VIEW OF EVERYTHING SPREADING OUT
BEFORE THE EYES,
REPLACING WORDS WITH IMAGES.

[*Haight Ashbury Literary Journal*, Vol. 2, No. 2, 1986]

A CLOSER LOOK

I could die
bent, no teeth,
a smudge of beauty, a cough,
a dip left in the mattress.

I could die alone
laying with the photo
by the clock watching it tick
to the next minute

or in a car wreck, slowly
or quickly, hauled off on a stretcher

under a sheet, yes, look at her there,
undeniably gone.

I could be dying now
thinking of death
as a postponed appointment.
The organs and bones promise

nothing is certain. Not even
you, the life I am constantly living,
root of comfort,
root of despair.

My heart is in fear.
Now it is bursting.
Now it is empty.
Now it disappears.

[Beatitude: Golden Anniversary 1959–2009, 2010]

A FAMILIAR TUNE   *for Lilly May*

I am one who has become,
conceived by thought.
Captivated by desire for recognition
I have positioned various landmarks
mapping a personality.
This daily journey through habits
is a pilgrimage
to worship the god of my creation:
my self, my ideas, my life.

Artist of identity,
I improvised on a common mold
and parade my expressions,
the repetition of all
I have done and known.
These events and their interconnections

are my description,
the form named and labeled
by my habits and motivations.

Inside out I am bone and gut,
meat for hunger,
seed to scatter
as death will destroy and save
some part of what I am
to play later—
like a tune remembered.
I am singing again.
I have sung. I am song.
Stop singing and I am gone.

[*Beatitude: Golden Anniversary 1959–2009*, 2010]

THE STRUGGLE OF MUSCLE

"That 'corpse' you dread so much is living with you right here and now."

—Milarepa

Skin wraps around bone
making the skull lovely,
covering the sockets, the horror
of the empty jaw, rigid teeth,
their hollow white grin. Covering

how the skeleton is no one, how flesh
covers no one, masking the absence
of a person, the world
caught in pockets of thoughts
that feed on believing

the body is home, a haven,
the suggestion of heaven
made by a slip of the tongue
wanting to be God, wanting
to pray away death

though it waits ahead, an abstract
and certain sun burning the horizon,
disappearing each night like a dream,
the dream we sleep in
and wake in each morning—

as the body lives to forget
we are in it, the struggle
of muscle to bend around
the truth, to keep us young,
to keep us quiet.

[*Beatitude: Golden Anniversary 1959–2009*, 2010]

FALLING FORWARD

for Venerable Gyatrul Rinpoche

This cliff is the end of the world
where emptiness becomes the path.
Doubt is the step ahead
not taken, the evasive,
drawn out pause, as if holding
the breath that must be released
in order to truly live.
Even tears leave a blur, like pools
that fill and dissolve, the footprints
that once may have shown
the way back. Landmarks disappear,
the road behind already tangled
with a past reviewed so often
its memory is a corpse.

The sky begins here
and opens with all that is yet
to be fulfilled. No form, no sound,
no thought can be measured—it is clear
the idea of myself cannot be found.
Everywhere, yet unfamiliar,

humming silently with the power
of presence that never falters,
no here, no there, no past or future,
now is. All I know is this stillness
arising as absolute possibility,
a constant readiness to allow being.
This is the movement of becoming.
Why do I hesitate?

[*Beatitude: Golden Anniversary 1959–2009*, 2010]

MINING

Digging beneath
the ideas
no one can truly understand
who I am.
Human. Woman. Aging.
Raging to understand,
wild to love.
Imploding with the world.
Exploding with expression.
Trapped in the fast car
of wanting.
Resisting the pull
of predictable loss.
Strung up by hope,
trampled by fear.
Swollen with desire,
but trying to ignore it
as required.
Twitching without
control, and waiting
to let go. Oh,
Holy Guru,
help let me go.
The pickax ritual of life
is always trying
to climb out

of the mind
that will never rest.
And under the raw earth
and the old bones and fossils,
beneath history and philosophy,
rumor and prophesy,
beyond thought,
what is left?

[*Beatitude: Golden Anniversary 1959–2009*, 2010]

HUMAN BEING

"Just let it be as it naturally is."
　　　　　　　　　　—*Tulku Urgyen Rinpoche*

There is nothing
more relaxing
than the present
moment.
Just right here,
nowhere else.
For once
do not linger
in the past,
do not look
to the future,
do not face
the facts
since they will
make you think.
Leave it.
Let it be.
The mind
becomes
so full
we forget
that it is
open.

Thoughts
will come
and go
if we allow.
Just let them
go about
the business
of illusion
on their own.
If you think
them real,
gently look
at where
they came from.
No one's home.
See?
Now you are free
to be.

[*Beatitude: Golden Anniversary 1959–2009*, 2010]

APPENDIX

POEM

The traveling circus crossed the unicorn
with one silver dollar & pederasty eyes.

if i cant be an ugly rumor i wont be the good time had by all.

A certain terror is more desirable to me than rare—
It's publishing two volumes of my suicide notes.
There are too many lanky basketball players
Newspapering my bathroom floor, and too much
Progress in the burial industry. Let's go back to
Old fashioned funerals, sit around & be sad & forgive
one another, go out side to bury the bottle and borrow stiff
handkerchiefs, and help load the guy in the wagon & flirt with the
widow, & pretend not to see all those people sinking into subways
and going to too many baseball games.

A certain terror is more desirable to me than the thought that I
could die right in the middle of sexual intercourse, & with my new all
purpose transistor blanket, go right on pumping away, with no emotional
let down, if you stop youre dead the jakov syndrome, tell the kids dont
mess around with the light switch, tell them theyll be shocked if they
unplug daddy.

There are too many unfunny things happening to the comedians.
Why dont the monasteries serve hot & cold hero sandwiches & all
kinds of split pea soups & bring the guys to the village once a week
to get laid, & make them stop printing all those fat books, with gods
picture, and all that subway mystery stuff.

A certain desirable is more rare than terror, than that happy shop,
home of free association, where i breakfasted with a suicidal rabbi,
& the worlds champion padlock salesman who wore impeccable seer suckers,
whose only oversight is cannibalism, & who is someday going to eat
himself & get busted if he stays in the flesh game.

All bicycle seats beatified & take on appearance of north poles, other things
Certain is real to me, but what is so rare, as air in a poem.

It's all right, fella, its just God playing dirty jokes again, that was
the old universal gin mill story, with chopin & amelia earhart floating
down the suez canal with dueling pistols in their hair, as the great
symphony of fish play Beethoven's tenth. Bach speaks through the in-
visible glass, breaking the barrier, spinning into the conscious ear of
the belts formed from breathing guesses, down from a . . . blade of night,
steep tongue of sweet disturbance sung from shafts of barely suggested
euphorias among the silver bell chants of the twilight being of
fragmentary existences, thinned gold being that does not exist, the soul . . .
dreadfull in its ages of darkling anonymity, breaking key-lit from the stainglass
windows of our eyes, colored by johann sebastian, perhaps
gods' tic . . . . .

[Note: This version was published in *Ambit*, No. 39, 1969]

ESSAYS

REMEMBERING BOB

excerpt from *Whitman's Wild Children* (1988)

Neeli Cherkovski

In September 1979 Raymond Foye and I planned a benefit poetry read-
ing for *Beatitude*, the poetry magazine founded by Bob Kaufman and
William J. Margolis. For months we edited a selection of poems from
various poets, together with a selection of Kaufman poems never be-
fore published and an essay on his work by Foye. When we finished
editing, we put the work into photo-ready condition and were told we
needed $2,400 for a printing of 1,000 copies. Allen Ginsberg agreed to
participate in the reading, along with Lawrence Ferlinghetti, Joanne Ky-
ger, Harold Norse, Peter Orlovsky—and Bob Kaufman. It was Kaufman's
first major reading in over fifteen years. Foye designed a poster using a
photograph of Kaufman in a striped jacket and a straw hat, standing in
front of the old City Lights publishing offices. The event was not only a
means of raising money but a long overdue tribute to Kaufman as well.

When I told Kaufman that Ginsberg would read, he said, "Allen
Ginsberg is the President of Poetry. He's our Pope. We're going to install
him in Rome. First, we'll have to buy him a cappuccino at the Trieste
and then fly to Rome on a chartered biplane. In Rome, we will all learn
Sanskrit and write a new version of the Mass."

Foye and I were surprised to find a front-page headline in the *San
Francisco Chronicle* on the morning of the reading: "Beat Reunion In
North Beach . . . see page two." Turning the page we found a story on
our reading and background information on the starring poets. "This will
help bring a crowd," I said, as we were worried about meeting expenses.

I'd run into Kaufman earlier in the day and he took me by the collar.
"You'll have to run things when I'm gone," he said. "Bob Kaufman will
disappear someday. Nobody will even notice. You can look for him in the
bayou or in the swamp, but you won't find him."

"Don't forget, Bobby. Tonight. Seven-thirty. We need you there a
half hour before the reading begins."

Two hours before the reading the street in front of the Savoy Café
and Theater looked like the entrance to a major rock concert. We quick-
ly sold out all the seats and then talked to Ginsberg and the other poets
about doing a second performance. Everyone agreed and we sold out a
second show. An hour before the first performance, at 8:00 p.m., a few
hundred disgruntled fans were told that no more tickets were available.

"This is an important event," I told a radio reporter who waylaid me with a microphone on the terrace of the Savoy Tivoli. "Tonight, Bob Kaufman will read *The Abomunist Manifesto*, a major poem of the San Francisco Poetry Renaissance. He has not read together with Ginsberg and Ferlinghetti for twenty years." I went on to say that Kaufman's work had been translated into French and published in two popular editions, but that his work was somehow not appreciated at home.

"Is it true that Governor Jerry Brown will be here tonight?" the reporter asked.

I shrugged my shoulders and went into the theater. Foye and Ginsberg were doing checks on the sound system, and they called me over to coordinate some of the remaining problems.

"Luckily, everyone is here," I said, glancing at my watch. It was twenty minutes before reading time and the Savoy was packed. Then we noticed that Kaufman was missing. Normally this would not be a big worry, but in dealing with the self-proclaimed "abomunist," it would mean he was on a plane to New York or across town at an all-night jazz party.

"I'll run down and see if I can find him," I said. I left the café and looked in on the Coffee Gallery, one of his old hangouts, and then down at the Caffe Trieste. "I saw him a few minutes ago," I was told by one of the poets hanging around. "I think he went up to the reading."

Running back to the café, I was pulled into the theater by Foye. Kaufman was still nowhere in sight. Behind me, Ginsberg, Orlovsky, Ferlinghetti, and the younger poets on the bill sat in anticipation. Foye began the introductions. The glare of the video lights bored in on us. We could barely make out the audience. I had a picture of myself apologizing for Kaufman's absence and reading a selection of his poems. Ginsberg called me over and said I should send somebody out to look for him again. Meanwhile, the reading had begun.

I conjured up images of Kaufman wandering alone by the waterfront docks. Just as I suggested we find a replacement, he came bounding up on stage. Ginsberg launched into *Plutonium Ode*, almost blowing the sound system apart.

"You want me to read *Second April*?" Kaufman leaned over to ask.

"What about the *Abomunist Manifesto*?" I asked.

"Where is it? What have they done to it?" he responded, looking genuinely agitated.

I leafed through *Solitudes Crowded with Loneliness*, his first book, and marked the page where the poem began. Kaufman had brought along a copy of *Golden Sardine*, a collection published by City Lights in 1967. "This is old Beatnik stuff, but I'll read it," he whispered.

It came his time to read. He lifted his thin, dark body from the chair and went toward the dais. Ginsberg smiled at him. The audience seemed to lean forward. There stood diminutive Kaufman with a serape over his flowing white shirt, brown skin radiant as the stage lights hit it. He began to read in a muffled tone that grew clearer as the poem raced toward its conclusion:

ABOMUNISTS JOIN NOTHING BUT THEIR HANDS OR
LEGS, OR OTHER SAME.

ABOMUNISTS SPIT ANTI-POETRY FOR POETIC
REASONS AND FRINK.

ABOMUNISTS DO NOT LOOK AT PICTURES PAINTED
BY PRESIDENTS AND UNEMPLOYED PRIME
MINISTERS.

The Abomunist Manifesto is more of a document than a poem. It has elements of the jazz humorist Lord Buckley, a touch of Edward Lear, and some of the popular philosophy of the time. In a section entitled "Further Notes," Kaufman writes:

Krishnamurti can relax the muscles of your soul,
free your aching jawbone from the chewinggum habit.
Ouspensky can churn your illusions into butter and
give you circles to carry them in, around your head.
Subud can lock you in strange rooms with vocal balms
and make your ignorant clothing understand you.

There is an explicit political meaning to the work, but it is clothed in a language that frees the perceptions from mere journalism. Thinking of the poem, I am reminded of what the poet once said when asked how he felt about being a third-world poet. "There is no third world. There are thousands of worlds. They all exist at the same time, in the same precise moment. I live in all those worlds. That's where a poet lives."

Bob Kaufman strived toward an understanding of the universality necessary for great poetry. He felt that narrow ideological concerns could shut down the "fountain," as he described it to me. He once told me, "I'm black, Jewish, white, green, and yellow with a blue man inside me struggling to come out." Often, he begins a poem with his eyes or his head or some other part of his anatomy, and moves outward into the world. He

213

is not visceral but gracefully attuned to his body as a key to opening "the mysteries" he refers to in his poetry. In "Blues for Hal Waters," he refers to his head as "my secret cranial guitar"; another poem asks, "would you wear my eyes?" Even in the saddest poems he emerges joyous out of ecstatic love for language and its possibilities, reaching out to others:

> My body once covered with beauty
> Is now a museum of betrayal.
> This part remembered because of that one's touch
> This part remembered for that one's kiss—
> Today I bring it back
> And let it live forever.

Believing strongly in the reality his poems created for him, he lived comfortably with them, and that is why he became like a poem, why those who knew him were always treated to gems of language invented spontaneously or brought out of his memory bank of images.

When we first met, at a book party in 1975, he said, "I knew your uncle, Herman Cherry, in Woodstock. . . . Herman Cherry, painted *Fruit Compote* and gave it to me. . . . Herman Cherry flew to the top of the Washington Monument and painted *Fruit Compote*, and then he wrapped it up and gave it to me at the Lincoln Monument. Herman Cherry is an airplane flying over America with *Fruit Compote*, a small painting in a gilded frame that he gave me in Woodstock thirty years ago. . . . I was a labor organizer. . . . Rimbaud is an orange blossom. . . . Cherry is *Fruit Compote* painted for Bob Kaufman, Poet." He then began reciting T.S. Eliot's "The Love Song of J. Alfred Prufrock," gesturing elegantly, moving his wiry body back and forth, his fingers playing an elegant invisible instrument. Three-quarters through "Prufrock" he spliced in lines from Yeats' "Sailing to Byzantium" and "Ode to Walt Whitman" by Federico García Lorca, as well as his own poetry. Through the years I would see a repeat of such performances in cafés, barrooms, and my own apartment, especially in those months Kaufman lived with me after the Dante Hotel burned down.

A week after that first meeting, I was wandering down Adler Alley, a narrow passageway between North Beach and Chinatown, filled with garbage from the nearby Chinese fish markets and flanked on the North Beach end by City Lights Bookstore and Vesuvio's, a bar where Dylan Thomas and Jack Kerouac used to hang out when they were in town. I felt alone and unwanted. Suddenly Kaufman appeared.

"Neeli Cherkovski," he said, looking perfectly serious, "let's find our way to Saturn."

"Bobby, I don't feel good. I'm all alone, I don't have anyone to love me." I looked directly at him, hoping he would provide some words of comfort.

"You're a poet. You can't ever be alone. You have poetry," he insisted, gripping my arm with surprising strength.

He touched me deeply with that exchange, but I never quite figured out how a man who wrote *Solitudes Crowded with Loneliness* would have said what he did.

RAIN UNRAVELED TALES:
EDITING BOB KAUFMAN
Raymond Foye

I first encountered that remarkable face on the cover of a battered paperback in a used bookstore in Lowell, Mass., in 1972: it was *Solitudes Crowded with Loneliness* (New Directions, 1965). If you want to know about Bob Kaufman, just look at the many remarkable photographs of him, as they really tell it all: the power of one man, small in stature, staring into you with dignity and defiance, tenderness and humor. His face is a map: of Africa, of the West Indies and the Caribbean, of his beloved New Orleans and the birth of jazz. It is the face of a holy man on Earth as a hero and a martyr, in the guise of a hipster and flâneur.

From this photograph of Bob Kaufman I first sensed what in the Hindu tradition is referred to as *darshan*: the transformation felt in a master's presence, communicated through the gaze. At any rate, I did judge a book by its cover . . . and quickly purchased it. As I read the first poem, "I Have Folded My Sorrows," I immediately fell under the spell of his gentle yet vivid imagery. His lofty language drew a straight line from Shakespeare to the Harlem Renaissance while his stately cadence, always so rhythmic and dignified, carried me along like the steps of a funeral jazz band following a hearse through the French Quarter. A few months later I found his second book, *Golden Sardine* (City Lights, 1967). Once again the cover photograph of that same wise face gazed at me with understanding. His books were slim, and I essentially memorized them. Intuitively, I understood these poems were oral/aural: they sprang not from the written word but from Orpheus' lyre. I carried these two books with me as I traveled, always placing them on the shelf with his photograph facing out.

Seeking adventure at age nineteen, I arrived in San Francisco on January 1, 1977 and checked into a North Beach hotel nearby City Lights Bookstore. The Tevere Hotel was located in the narrow triangle of land formed by the intersection of Grant and Columbus Avenues and bounded on the north side by Vallejo Street. My room was above the Caffe Trieste and overlooked the Saloon. As I walked down the narrow flight of stairs to the street one morning, a familiar face passed me by. Stunned, I turned to ask, "Are you Bob Kaufman?" Without stopping, and without turning around, he replied, "Sometimes."

In those days Bob Kaufman was more an apparition than someone real. He was an otherworldly but not unnoticed spectre of the bohemian quarter known as North Beach. I have never known anyone whose *presence* was so defined by *absence*. By then he had already retreated into silence and isolation, so for months I watched him from afar as he haunted the streets and alleys like Poe's "Man of the Crowd," never speaking, never stopping, until one evening when he suddenly walked into Specs' Bar and began booming out poetry at the top of his voice: "Let us go then you and I, when the evening is spread out against the sky, like a patient etherized upon a table. . . ." He recited T. S. Eliot's "The Love Song of J. Alfred Prufrock" in its entirety, and then somebody bought him a beer. More poetry followed: Charles Olson's "The Kingfishers," with the line, "What does not change / is the will to change" and Wallace "Stevens' Peter Quince at the Clavier," with the line, "Music is feeling, then, not sound." Soon I learned Bob alternated between silent periods when he did not drink, and boisterous periods when he did. Each period lasted six or eight months. We all waited for those boisterous periods, because otherwise he was entirely unreachable.

Bob was forever walking around with great determination, which always made me wonder just where he was going. One day I spied him through the window of City Lights and decided to follow him, trailing far enough behind that he wouldn't see me. He walked down Columbus to Kearney, then on through South of Market for another dozen blocks until he reached China Basin. This was the docks of old San Francisco Bay which were for Kaufman a kind of home. Pressed up against a chain-link fence for over an hour, he watched the ships come and go, the loading and the unloading. It was then I saw the old merchant sailor in him—the young boy who went to the sea in his teens and stayed on the ships for seven years, traveling around the world and spending his shore leave at exotic ports like Calcutta, where he stayed five weeks. I came to learn a lot about this part of Bob's life from a fellow seaman and veteran of the Spanish Civil War—a rough character named Henry Thomas, who drank 151 proof rum at the Savoy Tivoli bar on Grant Avenue. He was notorious for singing "The Internationale" and other communist anthems when he was drunk. Henry told me Bob was known for taking on the toughest jobs, like climbing the mast during a storm to tie down rigging.[1]

In the North Beach days Bob was living off a paltry check from state assistance. Around the first of the month I would often see him having breakfast, his one meal of the day, at a lunch counter he liked called Curley's on Green and Columbus. By the middle of the month the regular meals ended and he had to get by on what he could bum from friends. One day he came up to me and said, "Hey Raymond, can I have a dollar?" It was very early in our acquaintance and I was surprised that he even knew my name. I remember thinking to myself in astonishment as I handed him the money, "Bob Kaufman just said my name." A week later he approached me and said, "Hey Raymond, can I have five dollars?" And I handed it over. A week later he walked up to me and asked for ten—the following week, twenty. The next time I saw him he casually approached and asked, "Hey Raymond, can I have a hundred dollars?" I laughed, then he did too, and after that the amount he would ask for went back down to five.

In those days I made it my mission to collect as many stray poems of his as I could, from early mimeo zines like *Beatitude*, or from friends of Bob's who had preserved the poems he'd scribbled on napkins and scraps of paper. My mentor in this regard was his wife Eileen Kaufman. She was responsible for preserving most of the poems in *Solitudes*. Bob and Eileen were estranged at the time: she could not control his behavior, and he would not accept control. I preserved these poems in a folio, hoping one day to publish a book that would add to the legacy of *Solitudes* and *Golden Sardine*.

After the Tevere Hotel, I moved into 28 Harwood Alley (since renamed "Bob Kaufman Alley"), to the very same room Bob had briefly occupied, in an apartment I shared with the poet Neeli Cherkovski. That kitchen was the center of social life for the poets of North Beach, and it was crowded from morning till night with the likes of Gregory Corso, Kirby Doyle, Howard Hart, Kaye McDonough, Tisa Walden, Lawrence Ferlinghetti, and dozens of others. Philip Lamantia lived across the alley, and our kitchen windows looked directly into each other's. When Philip was in a social mood he would open his window and say hello. A discussion would ensue and eventually (sometimes after an hour) he would come over for coffee and stay several hours more. Bob was also a regular. I had tacked photographs of him on the kitchen door along with broadsides and fliers for bygone readings. "What am I, the local hero?" he said with a smile one day looking at the photos. On one occasion he even picked up a broadside of his poem *Second April* and gave an impromptu reading. "I feel at home in this neighborhood," he told me one day. "When I'm lost and alone, and Paul Robeson is singing the Soviet national anthem in my head, and I can't sleep, I go out and walk these streets, and I feel at home."

I was in my room listening to a Dizzy Gillespie record when Bob stopped by. He walked in singing scat along with the solo. But he was singing on key and note for note, with absolute precision, as if he had a transcription of the music in his head (which clearly he did). It was then I realized the depth of his involvement with bebop, how this music was at the very core of his work. I never read his work again without hearing those complex rhythms with their streaming melodies and switchback changes: he had stolen their essence with his ears. But the same can be said for many other influences that he absorbed in their totality and then made his own—García Lorca, for instance. There is still so much like this to be unpacked from his poetry.

Sometimes if Bob were in the mood I would visit him at the Dante Hotel. His room was just upstairs from a strip joint called the Condor. We would share a joint and look at art books, of which he had quite a nice collection stacked in piles on the floor. He would buy them from a used bookstore directly downstairs on Broadway. (This was the only extravagance I ever really knew him to indulge in.) He loved Picasso, Miró, Klee, Van Gogh, and the Impressionists. I remember him staring silently for a very long time at Van Gogh's *Night Café*, at last remarking, "Van Gogh is out there, *really* out there," gesturing to the cosmos. "I mean, he's *not* coming back." His favorite books were a multi-volume study, *The Image of the Black in Western Art*, by David Bindman and Henry Louis Gates, Jr. It was a history of the depiction of Blacks in art history, from African masks to the jazz paintings of his friend Bob Thompson. At one point he found a full-page reproduction of a carved wooden mask from Benin that bore a remarkable resemblance to him, a point he silently underscored by holding the book up directly beside his face while staring back at me. After not seeing him for a few months during a silent period, I ran into him and asked if he wanted to hang out in his room. "I threw my marijuana out the window," he replied, and walked away.

Bob had a lot of personal quirks, some of which could be quite annoying. If he turned on the water faucet, he never turned it off: he just walked away and left it running. Once I drove him to a barbecue at his brother George's house in Oakland, and both times when he left the car he didn't close the door behind him. Eventually I just chalked these things up to his "living in the moment." One of the more eventful aspects of encountering Bob was his wardrobe. I never knew anyone with a better sense of style: fabrics, colors, hats. I often wondered how he managed this on his budget. One day he was walking towards me and I noticed he was particularly well dressed in a white dinner jacket and green striped silk scarf.

Suddenly I realized it was my jacket and scarf; he'd just raided my closet on Harwood Alley. He smiled and gave me a big hello and kept moving.

Although Kaufman's personal biography reads quite tragically, full of police beatings, jails, and enforced asylums, he could be lighthearted and a lot of fun to be around. He reminded me of the silent comedians the way his humor came through in his body language—like Buster Keaton or Harold Lloyd, he was small in stature but extremely strong. He had a great sense of physical comedy and a sharp sense of timing full of double takes and mock surprise. Once he entered City Lights just as a car back-fired in the street, and without missing a beat he clutched his heart and staggered through the door exclaiming, "They've shot Bob Kaufman!" His remarks were always terse and often charged with a strong sense of the absurd. I remember him sitting silently at a café table with Allen Ginsberg for nearly an hour when he suddenly looked up and announced with astonishment, "Mars is a red planet!" When I first got to know him I mustered the courage to ask if he was still writing? "Sometimes I want to sing, but I get laryngitis of the soul."

In 1979, Neeli and I edited a special twentieth-anniversary issue of *Beatitude* dedicated to Bob Kaufman, who we both felt was criminally neglected. Bob cofounded the magazine in 1959, but it had languished by 1979. Kaufman's copublisher, Pierre Delattre, referred to the magazine as "a floating crap game," meaning anyone who wanted to edit an issue could. Publishing this anniversary issue was more or less the beginning of a small renaissance of interest in Bob and his work, the point when the next generation picked up on his work and a dozen or more young poets gathered around him. Indeed, a short while after the issue was published and promoted with various readings that Bob participated in, I ran into him in a bar one afternoon. He took me by the arm and presented me to a friend, announcing proudly (and quite uncharacteristically), "This thing we started in the fifties, this Beat Generation, it didn't end back then, it continues. . . ." This was exactly as I had quoted from Ezra Pound in my *Beatitude* essay on Kaufman: "To have gathered a live tradition from the air, or from a fine old eye, the unconquered flame."

Early one morning as I made my way down to the Caffe Trieste, I encountered Bob shuffling around on the sidewalk outside, mumbling something about having survived Dante's Inferno. I assumed it was his usual way of speaking in metaphors. An hour later someone told me that the Dante Hotel where Bob lived had burned. And indeed it had. First I thought of his small room, the art books lost, and so on, and then I wondered about his poems. I had no idea whether he had been writing in those years because he would never say. But the possibility was there.

An instinct told me to make some moves. I waited for the fire crew to depart a few days later, after the building had stopped smouldering, and I crossed the police lines. It was a vast hotel full of cubicles, but fortunately I knew exactly where his room was. It was in the most charred part of the building, and the fire may have actually started in his room. His chest of drawers was reduced to a small pile of charcoal. I dug through the things that didn't burn, the coins and religious medallions. At the bottom of the pile was a thick Moroccan leather binder, soaked with water. I looked inside and glimpsed pages bearing his distinctive handwriting—lettered in both small and large capitals. I took the binder and walked across the street to the City Lights Bookstore, where I'd been working as an editorial assistant for a few months. I carefully peeled off the manuscript pages and laid them out all around the upstairs office. I can still recall Ferlinghetti's look of amazement when he came in to work around 10 a.m. To those few of us for whom Kaufman was a true poetic genius, it was like a door opening into King Tut's tomb. He *had* been writing all those years, and the poems bore the mark of that unmistakable mind and imagination:

I AM A CAMERA

THE POET NAILED ON
THE HARD BONE OF THIS WORLD
HIS SOUL DEDICATED TO SILENCE
IS A FISH WITH FROG'S EYES,
THE BLOOD OF A POET FLOWS
OUT WITH HIS POEMS, BACK
TO THE PYRAMID OF BONES
FROM WHICH HE IS THRUST
HIS DEATH IS A SAVING GRACE

CREATION IS PERFECT

Bob Kaufman

As the poems dried out, I typed them up. Soon I realized that I had enough material to bring out the book I'd been hoping for. These new poems, when added to the ones I'd already collected, formed the second half of what would become his last book, *The Ancient Rain* (New Directions, 1981). But the more difficult part was that first, Bob would need to be convinced they should be published. He steadfastly refused every time I broached the subject. I enlisted his wife Eileen to help out. She had breakfast with Bob and asked him why? "Because I don't think it's going to happen," he replied. I understood he was protecting himself from disappointment, so I sent the manuscript to Fred Martin and Griselda Ohannessian at New Directions; they immediately accepted it. Shortly thereafter, I cornered Bob on the street one morning to show him the galleys and a contract, which to my relief he quickly signed. I also had his burnt manuscripts, which I tried to return. "I don't want them," he said and abruptly walked away. The book came out with Ira Nowinski's magnificent portrait of Bob on the cover, showing him in a Mexican poncho, holding court at the Coffee Gallery.

Having a recent publication made Bob eligible for poetry grants, so I filled out an application for the National Endowment for the Humanities, included the required poems, and got him to sign it. About six months later he came up to me on the street. "Raymond, this check is no good." It was a U.S. Treasury check for twelve thousand five hundred dollars made out to Bob Kaufman. The bank had refused to cash it because he didn't have a bank account. We returned to the bank and I explained it was part of their charter as a bank to cash U.S. Treasury checks, regardless of the payee's relation to the bank. Phone calls were made and Bob became increasingly impatient, insisting that we just leave; it was obvious how much he hated any interaction with authority. Finally, they agreed to cash the check. "How do you want it?" the teller asked. Bob was deaf in one ear and hard of hearing in the other, and it made him shout somewhat when he spoke. "What?" "How do you want it?" "I DON'T CARE!" He yelled. The teller quickly counted out a stack of hundred dollar bills and Bob stuffed them in his pocket and left. For the next several weeks every poet in North Beach was a recipient of his largesse. His wardrobe—never at a loss for stylishness—stepped up a few notches. In a month, he was broke again, but he seemed very happy.

In those days North Beach had a bar on every block, sometimes two or three, each with a different character and clientele. Bob was pretty much a regular at all of them: there was the Saloon on Grant Avenue, a tough biker bar with live blues bands where Bob spent many hours with a girlfriend of the time, the poet Janice Blue;[2] there was the Coffee Gallery, another blues bar where guitarist Michael Bloomfield would occasionally drop by; there was Gino and Carlo's, with a pool table and drug dealers in the backroom; there was the Columbus Café, the San Remo, Specs', and the pricey outdoor Enrico's on Broadway; and there was Vesuvio situated next to City Lights on Columbus, where Bob would often take a morning Irish coffee. But Bob's favorite bars seemed to be those with exotic decor: the Hawaiian-themed bar on the corner of Grant and Green; the Swiss Bar on Broadway, done up like a cozy chalet in the Alps; or the Li Po in Chinatown, a masterpiece of nostalgic chinoiserie named after the Tang dynasty poet, who reputedly drowned while drunkenly trying to embrace the reflection of the full moon in the Yangtze River. The large number of neighborhood bars came in handy for poets like Kaufman or Corso, who could become boisterous after a few drinks and were occasionally 86'd from one establishment or another. In fact, on one visit back to San Francisco from New York, when I bumped into Kaufman on the street and suggested that we have a beer, I had to name three different bars before I hit on one he was allowed in at that moment.

In later years Bob took up with a kind and gentle companion, Lynne Wildey, and his life took on a semblance of domesticity—to the extent that such a thing were possible.[3] The day before he died Kaufman meticulously cleaned his room, dressed all in white, and carefully placed his favorite D. T. Suzuki book on Zen on his bedside table, before he peacefully slipped out of existence.

As a writer Kaufman often relies on seemingly fanciful or extravagant metaphors, however directly behind each of those images lie real life experiences, these often quite dire. As a result of a beating during his days as a labor organizer in the Deep South, Kaufman lost several teeth, lost all hearing in one ear, and suffered tinnitus in the other. These facts are gently masked in a simple seven-line poem:

"MICHELANGELO" THE ELDER

I live alone, like pith in a tree,
My teeth rattle, like musical instruments.
In one ear a spider spins its web of eyes,
In the other a cricket chirps all night.
This is the end,
Which art, that proves my glory has brought me.
I would die for Poetry.

Embedded in other poems you will find references to the attempted suicide of William Margolis, who jumped out a window in Harwood Alley, to the deaths of friends, and to various suicides he'd known. The poem "Rue Miro" is his description of the street by that name that he grew up on in New Orleans. Each stanza in "Unhistorical Events" is about a specific friend or shipmate: Rock Gut Charlie, Cinder Bottom Blue, Riff Raff Rolfe, and Lady Choppy Wine, while the final stanza describes a horrible scene from his childhood when he was chased by a lynch mob and hung by his thumbs in an icehouse in Louisiana, remaining locked inside alone in agony until he was discovered the next day. The reality behind the metaphor is the glue that holds it together; the transformation of that reality is the magic of the poem.

While I enjoy recalling his exuberance and warmth, I have to circle back to his solitude: For most of the years I knew him he was determined to maintain his distance from the social, material world. One *felt* his solitude when one was with him. It was palpable, and almost all his remarks to me down through the years were about this place: "I live in a well of loneliness." "I don't know how you get involved with uninvolvement, but I don't want to be involved." "Wallace Stevens wrote a poem about the motives for metaphor. I want to discover my motives for metaphor." For Bob Kaufman, solitude was not just a metaphor, nor was it a clinical condition. His silence remains a witness to an eternal truth. It was self-imposed isolation, his need for the innermost cave where his sentience might be itself. It is where his poetry came alive without ego or worldly attachment. Fortunately, at times he emerged from that cave to speak to us through his poems.

Notes

1. This might have been the *least* dangerous of Kaufman's tasks, given that he spent virtually the entirety of WWII on the Liberty ships: the U.S. Merchant Marines suffered the highest rate of casualties of any service in World War II, with over fifteen hundred ships sunk. The important story of these ships is still not widely known.

2. Bob and Janice Blue shared writing credit on a book called *Closing Time Till Dawn* (The Bob Kaufman Collective, 1986), transcribed from their spontaneous poetry sessions, although Bob frequently was unhappy when people tried this approach because they didn't understand that when he riffed he was interspersing lines by other poets along with his own—and he didn't want to appear to be plagiarizing. For Bob, all poetry was one.

3. For a touching profile of Kaufman's life during this period see Eric Walker's prose account "The Ancient Rain" in: *Eric Walker: Selected Poems* (New York: Raymond Foye Books, 2019). A brilliant but doomed poet who was found hanging in prison at age twenty-nine, Walker was Kaufman's most direct protégé, and Kaufman even took him in for a time. Also available online at https://brooklynrail.org/2014/12/criticspage/the-ancient-ruin (yes, the last word in the web address is "ruin" not "rain").

INDEX OF TITLES AND FIRST LINES

ny old statues of slant eyed gods and old s
d lost philosophies dropped by alexander
and no conquering of asia today baby greek
salesmen tomorrow more jazz and brand new
rn skies of gray and other subdued colors mix
d rituals and aztec virgins' breasts spouting
s and jazz dear bitch dear bitch dear bitch
here is the robin's nest where is the final sea
es where the sailor sees gulls and other wing
r fear of sea god's wrathful eyes filled with
ou know the score old veteran remover old
angels and ancient dreams of old embryonic
l fields of strange bellies with sandpaper s
other lives cherished from memory of yester
for all time in new year noises of hopes and
lowing through shadow canyons where we sto
ddied toys and bones of phantom friends lost
rms flying in heads of adult children left ove
v that space is the thing of momentous impac
aunting tin littered launching pads envelop
d visionaries hung from dying rockets in h
nd thrust and naked skies beckoning with
ers lost to pursuit of womanly earth writhin
overs anxiously disappearing into each